AF559969

PUNJAB IN PROSPERITY AND VIOLENCE

PUNJAB IN PROSPERITY AND VIOLENCE

Administration, Politics and Social Change, 1947-1997

Edited by

J. S. GREWAL • INDU BANGA

MANOHAR
2024

First published by Manohar Publishers & Distributors 2024

© Institute of Punjab Studies

All rights reserved. No part of this publication may be reproduced or transmitted, in any form or by any means, without prior permission of the editors and the publisher.

ISBN 978-81-19139-66-8

Published by
Ajay Kumar Jain *for*
Manohar Publishers & Distributors
4753/23 Ansari Road, Daryaganj
New Delhi 110 002

Printed and bound in India by Replika Press Pvt. Ltd.

Preface

Founded in 1993, the Institute of Punjab Studies has endeavoured to promote interdisciplinary studies of north-western India (covering the present day states of Punjab, Haryana, Himachal Pradesh in India and Punjab in Pakistan) in broad historical and comparative perspective since the earliest times. The long-term objective of the Institute is to produce and disseminate research-based literature on the life of the people in the geographical region called the Punjab. It has organized seminars on themes like urbanization since the prehistoric times; gender relations through the ages; social transformation in the twentieth century; literature and society; institution of the Khalsa; debates and trends in post-Independence historical studies; Bhagat Singh and his times; Ghadar movement and Freedom Struggle in Punjab; context, significance and legacy of the *Komagata Maru*; and decolonization and socio-economic changes in contemporary Punjab. Scholars from all over India and abroad have participated in these seminars. Some proceedings have been brought out and some are in process.

Punjab in Prosperity and Violence takes a critical look at the Punjab after Partition and Independence. It provides insights into new administrative space, new idiom of regional politics, new demographic scene, new urban centres, emergence of militancy, problem of violence against women, changing position of Dalits in general and agricultural labour in particular, and complexities of village life. Besides civil service and police, the contributors come from the disciplines of history, geography, political science, sociology and English and Punjabi literature. This volume should be of interest to the social scientists, administrators, politicians, journalists and general readers.

The programmes and activities of the Institute of Punjab Studies would not have been possible without the enthusiastic help of the colleagues and researchers from the Panjab University, Chandigarh, active support and cooperation from the scholars in the region, and advice and guidance of the Members of the Society and Governing Body of the Institute.

Chandigarh

J.S. Grewal
Indu Banga

Contents

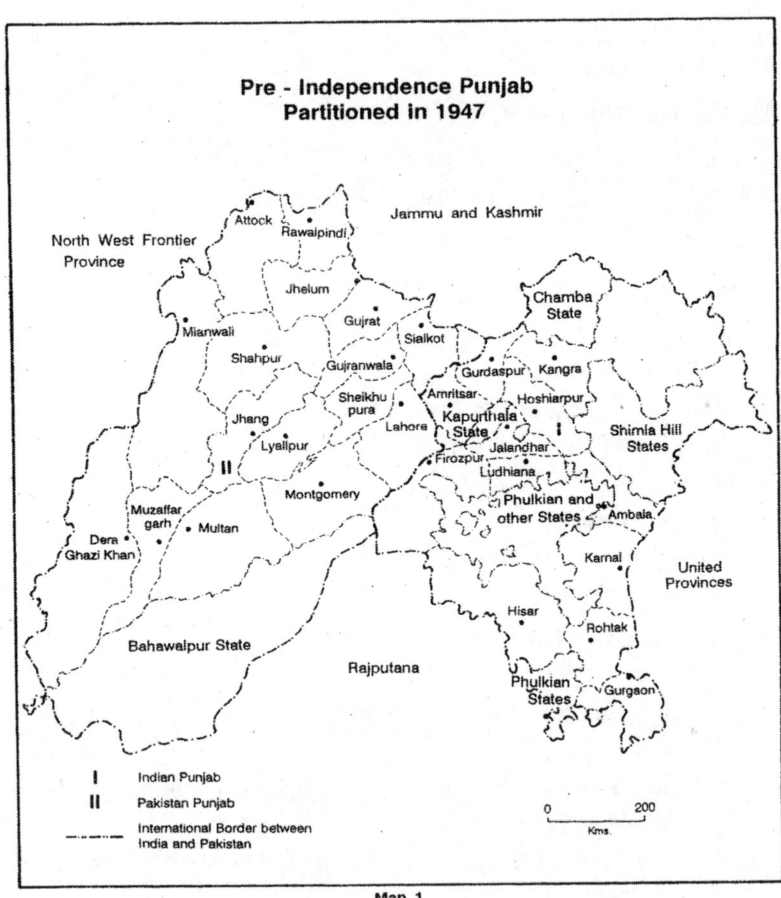
Pre - Independence Punjab
Partitioned in 1947
Jammu and Kashmir
North West Frontier
Province
Attock
Rawalpindi
Jhelum
Gujrat
Sialkot
Mianwali
Shahpur
Gujranwala
Chamba
State
Gurdaspur
Kangra
Sheikhu
pura
Amritsar
Hoshiarpur
Jhang
Lahore
Kapurthala
State
Lyallpur
Jalandhar
Shimla Hill
States
Firozpur
Ludhiana
Montgomery
Phulkian and
other States
Ambala
Muzaffar
garh
Multan
Dera
Ghazi Khan
Karnal
United
Provinces
Hisar
Rohtak
Bahawalpur State
Rajputana
Phulkian
States
Gurgaon
I
II
I Indian Punjab
II Pakistan Punjab
International Border between
India and Pakistan
0
200
Kms.

Map 1

1

Administrative Space

GOPAL KRISHAN and SURYA KANT

Administrative organisation of space refers to the overall arrangement and internal divisions of political areas into an hierarchy of administrative units to manage public affairs. These units form the basis of designing and executing public policy, have a strong bearing on the pattern of supply and utilisation of public services, and are influential in directing and standardising the life of the people (Beaujeu, 1976; Bennett and Chorley, 1978; Garner, 1975).

On the face of it, any administrative organisation of space seems to be a mechanism for a convenient management of large, heterogeneous and disparate units. In spirit, this organisation is deeply rooted in the whole philosophy of government and society in any region. It reflects the basic values, such as efficiency, justice, democracy, and community development (Krishan, 1990). In real life situations, however, the considerations of convenience of management and efficiency outweigh all other factors.

ADMINISTRATIVE AREAS

The most critical factor which distinguishes administrative areas from each other is the degree of 'functional autonomy/ sovereignty' they enjoy. These can, accordingly, be classified into the following four types (Humes and Martin, 1961): (i) supra-sovereign, for example the United Nations and the European Union; (ii) fully-sovereign, such as the United States and India; (iii) quasi-sovereign or the federated state, such as California in the United States and the Punjab in India; and (iv) infra-sovereign or the local authority area, for instance the Orange County in California and Ludhiana district in the Punjab. These four types obviously differ on the spatial scale of their operations.

Another way to classify administrative areas is to categorise them on the basis of their 'function': general purpose adminis-trative areas; special purpose authorities; and regional authorities. The general purpose administrative areas are in the nature of all purpose units, such as the district in India. These provide a multitude of administrative services. The special purpose adminis-trative areas are meant for specific functions, such as school districts in the United States, health units in Botswana, and milk marketing areas in Canada (Massam, 1972). The formation of special purpose authorities is essentially a sectoral division of the general purpose administrative areas. Regional authorities are constituted to manage and provide some higher order service, specific to a particular function or area. Electricity boards, trans-port corporations, and river valley authorities are some such arrangements. These tend to be a hybrid between the general purpose and special purpose administrative areas. Generally these require coordination among a number of general purpose administrative areas (East and Prescott, 1975).

A periodic redrawing of the administrative map is deemed as imperative (Krishan, 1988). This is the practice in almost all countries of the world. In developed countries, such as the United Kingdom, Germany and Sweden, the lowest level administrative units are being consolidated into bigger ones. The latter are rated as economically more efficient. In developing countries, such as India, the process is in the reverse. The existing adminis-trative units are divided into smaller ones. The latter are deemed to be better manageable.

In the United Kingdom, a Royal Commission on Local Government is periodically appointed to advise on the necessary revision of the county and district boundaries. Questions like the optimal area-population size of these administrative units, the desired number of tiers amongst these, and manner of implementation of the recommended changes are examined and debated. All approved reforms of the administrative map come into effect on a single date scheduled for the purpose.

Such an administrative culture is yet to mature in India. Administrative area changes are carried out in an *ad hoc* and piecemeal manner. The concerned reports are treated as strictly confidential, neither subject to the public eye nor open to public debate. Any academic exercise on the matter is grossly constrained by non-availability of authentic material.

COLONIAL ADMINISTRATION LANDSCAPE

The Punjab became a part of British India finally in 1849. An uprising broke out against the British in 1857. It was suppressed and followed by radical changes in administrative policy. Through an Act of British Parliament, the authority to rule India was transferred from the East India Company to the British Crown. In a major administrative reorganisation bid, the former Mughal Province of Delhi, then forming a part of North-West Provinces, was transferred to the Punjab. A number of princely states, such as Patiala, Jind and Kapurthala, were not only allowed to maintain their former status but were also awarded land grants. The Punjab had two segments, the British ruled territory and the princely states.

In 1901, the northwestern part of the Punjab was constituted as a separate province, the North West Frontier Province. In 1912, Delhi was detached to form a separate unit under a chief commissioner. Thereafter, no significant territorial change took place in the boundaries of the British Punjab.

The Punjab of 1901 was divided into 27 districts grouped into five divisions. In 1904, two new districts of Attock and Lyallpur were carved out. Besides, there were 43 native states of varying size and importance, scattered over different parts of the Punjab. The British Punjab accounted for 70 per cent of the total area and the native states for 30 per cent (Table 1).

An average district of the Punjab spread over an area of 3,352 m^2 (8,632 km^2). Districts were divided into tahsils/subcollector- ates. There were 104 tahsils/subtahsils in the Punjab. A tahsil was primarily a revenue administrative unit. It was sub-divided into *kanugo* circles. Each *kanugo* circle had a police *thana*, comprising a group of villages as the lowest unit of police administration. A *patwar* circle functioned as an intermediate tier between a *kanugo* circle and the village for revenue administration.

The British borrowed a number of administrative practices, including terminoloy, from the Mughals. There were some notable departures as well: (i) new tiers of divisions and sub-divisions were introduced for stronger administrative control; (ii) revenue administration was brought down to more local levels of spatial hierarchy; (iii) police administration was also spatially dispersed not only to have a firm grip on law and order but also to make revenue collection more effective (Kant, 1988).

CONTEMPORARY PUNJAB

In 1947, the province was partitioned between India and Pakistan on religious lines. Of its 138,679 m^2 (359,179 km^2), 5 divisions and 29 districts, only 58, 938 m^2 (152,649 km^2), 2 divisions and 13 districts were left with Punjab (East), renamed Punjab (India) on 26 January 1950.

The Punjab native states presented a somewhat different picture. Eight of them, namely Patiala, Kapurthala, Jind, Nabha, Faridkot, Malerkotla, Nalagarh, and Kalsia were constituted into a union, named PEPSU, in 1948. These covered as area of 10, 099 m^2 (26,156 km^2) and were arranged into 8 districts and 25 tahsils.

In another move, the former Punjab hill states were constituted into Himachal Pradesh in the same year. The new unit was a centrally administered territory. It was divided into 4 districts and 23 tahsils. The hill state of Bilaspur, containing the site of Bhakra-Nangal project, was made a part of Himachal Pradesh at a later stage in 1954.

In 1956, PEPSU was merged with the Punjab. Later on, under the Punjab Reorganisation Act, a Punjabi speaking state was carved out of the existing Punjab in 1966. This reorganisation reduced the state to two-fifths the size it had attained after the first reorganisation in 1956. Now it covers an area of only 19,445 m^2 (50,362 km^2). This is just one-seventh of its size before Inde-pendence. Though much reduced, the Punjab was now lin-guistically homogeneous and structurally compact. It was divided into 11 districts, including Ropar, created as a part of the reorganisation.

In the initial phase after Independence, the main thrust was on recasting and re-forming the administrative organisation of space inherited from the British. A notable innovation was the formation of 'the development block' as the basic unit for rural development. It represented a new philosophy in area administration. A message went home that administration was now trying to shift its focus from the maintenance of law and order and collection of land revenue to matters of development. The process of the formation of development blocks in the Punjab was started in 1952, and the entire state was covered by 117 blocks by 1963.

GENERAL PURPOSE ADMINISTRATIVE AREAS

The Punjab at present is organised into 4 divisions, 17 districts, 70 subdivisions/tahsils, 55 subtahsils and 137 development blocks

(Table 2). At the time of its formation in 1966, the state had 2 divisions, 11 districts, 37 subdivisions/tahsils, 13 subtahsils, and 117 development blocks. A tendency toward creation of new administrative units at all levels is unmistakable. The process seems to have gained momentum since the mid-eighties. The number of districts and subdivisions has gone up by one and a half times, that of divisions by two times, and that of subtahsils by four times during the last 30 years. By comparison, the number of divisions as also of districts in the British Punjab had remained constant from 1912 to 1947.

In the chain of general administration, 'the division' represents the first order organisation of the state. Its orgin in India goes back to the British days when in 1829, for the first time, an intermediate authority between the district collector and the provincial government was created in Bengal. In essence, the division emerged through an amalgamation process (grouping of already existing districts) rather than as a partitioning mechanism (of a province). The practice was subsequently followed in other provinces. Every province in India, barring Madras, was organised into divisions.

The division was initially created as a revenue unit. The divisional commissioner not only heard appeals from subordinate revenue authorities but also acted as a supervisory and coordinating authority over collectors and their subordinate revenue officials. Gradually, additional administrative functions and powers were delegated to him. A division got eventually transformed into a general purpose unit.

The advisability of creating an intervening authority between a province and districts was questioned even during the British period. The debate intensified after Independence. It has been argued that the British adopted this system because it helped them to centralize their authority. It could now be changed to a more democratic pattern (Sharma, 1971). Madhya Pradesh, Maharashtra, Rajasthan and Gujarat abolished the divisions in 1948, 1950, 1961 and 1964 respectively. The first three, however have reverted to the old system. The Punjab retained the set up with divisions all through. We are not sure about the advisability of this practice for a small state like the Punjab.

The British had favoured an administrative system that centralized powers and responsibilities in the hands of one person at the district level. As the head of every district was appointed an officer who, in the eyes of most of its inhabitants, was 'the government'

(Simon Commission Report quoted by Shukla, 1976). Independent India continued with the tradition of having the district as the pivot of local apparatus of public administration. The district administration in India is non-elective. An officer from the Indian Administrative Service is placed as its chief. The person is known as Deputy Commissioner in Punjab, District Magistrate in Uttar Pradesh, and Collector in Rajasthan, reflecting the difference in the perceived role of a district head as the custodian of law and order, the dispenser of justice, or the collector of revenue.

There are 17 districts in the Punjab. This gives an area of about 3000 km^2 per district. The comparable figure for India is around 6000 km^2. An average district in Punjab is just one-half of the area of its counterpart in India.

Some parts of a district, depending upon their size or revenue or strategic location, were given the status of a subdivision while the remaining part was divided into tahsils. Some tahsils were further divided into subtahsils. The system continued after Independence under which subdivisions enjoyed higher status than tahsils. In 1985, all the tahsils in Punjab were elevated to the status of subdivisions to confer more powers at this level. Now almost all district-level departments have their field offices at the subdivisional headquarters.

Currently Punjab is divided into 70 subdivisions. This number has grown from 37 in 1966. Of the 33 new additions, 9 came during 1966-85 and the remaining 24 during 1985-96. An average subdivision is now less than 800 km^2 in area. This is a size smaller than what was initially earmarked for a block (1300 km^2).

The block as an administrative tier in district administration was an outcome of the Community Development Programme and the National Extension Service Scheme initiated on 2 October 1952. These were intended as peoples' programmes with government participation and not as government programmes with peoples' participation for rural uplift. Urban areas were kept out of the purview of development blocks. The Punjab now has 137 development blocks. Of the 20 new blocks created during 1966-96, 19 came into existence after 1985; one was added in 1997.

'Special Purpose Authorities' can first be classified on the basis of the spatial scale of their operations into three types: (i) those organised only at the national level, such as railways, tele-communications and defence; (ii) those organised at both the national and state levels, including education, health and civil supplies, known as concurrent subjects; and (iii) those organised only at the state level including police, revenue and rural development, known as state subjects.

Special purpose authorities can be further grouped into six categories on the basis of their specific functions: (i) provision of personal services, such as education, health and communications; (ii) management of environmental services, such as transport, housing and planning; (iii) sectoral administration as that of agriculture, industry and forestry; (iv) conduct of elections; (v) defence; and (vi) data collection, as on weather, population and agriculture.

Sixty-six items are listed as state subjects in the Constitution of India. Important among these are: maintenance of law and order, agriculture, industry, forestry, revenue and cooperation. The state subjects can be taken over by the Central government under special circumstances.

Law and order is a state responsibility and it is assured through police administration. In practically all states, including Punjab, police administration has a six tier hierarchy: police headquarters, range, police district, circle, *thana,* and post. The state is organised in 6 ranges and 22 police districts. By comparison, the number of divisions and districts for general administration is 4 and 17, respectively. The disturbed law and order situation during the eighties dictated a more intense spatial arrangement for police administration.

Agriculture, industry and forestry are among the most important sectors at the state level. Their administration involves policy making and programme implementation. The state government often associates itself with the Central government in executing its schemes relating to these sectors.

Administration of agriculture in the Punjab is three tiered: headquarters, district, and block. In 1972, agriculture administration was reorganised to cover new responsibilities and to remove existing anomalies. Major rationalisation included: (i) enhancement in the powers of the district level officers; (ii) decentralization of agricultural administration to block level; and (iii) greater co-ordination of agriculture administration with that of the other special purpose authorities, such as rural development, *panchayati raj* and co-operation. Certain agricultural regions, such as the border belt, the foothill (*kandi*) zone, and the *bets* (floodplains) were identified and given special attention.

Punjab cannot take pride in its industrial development. Its border location with Pakistan and an almost complete absence of mineral resources partly explain this state of affairs. The state has, however, made commendable progress in agro-based and agro-oriented industries. The administration of industry in the Punjab is three tiered: headquarters, district centre, block office/ industrial estate. Block offices serve rural areas and industrial estates are meant for towns. 'Industrially backward' and 'no industry' districts have been identified at the Central level to receive special assistance.

Although forests cover only 1.5 per cent of the state's total area yet their spatial administration is organised in seven tiers: headquarters, circle, division, range, sub-range, block-round and beat. Special efforts are being made to promote forestry in the foothill districts of Gurdaspur, Hoshiarpur and Rupnagar under the Kandi Watershed and Area Development project assisted by the World Bank. Great importance is being attached to social forestry programme that encourages plantation of trees in village commons. This has made forestry a spatially widespread activity for which additional powers have been delegated to lower levels of the administrative hierarchy.

Historically, land revenue has been the major source of state income in India. Civil administration at local level was virtually synonymous with revenue administration. In the post-Independence era, its importance to state income has greatly declined. Land revenue administration, however, continues to be one of the most elaborately organised systems in seven tiers: headquarters, division, district, tahsil, *kanugo* circle, *patwar* circle and revenue *mauza* (village). It works in close co-operation with the general purpose administration and their spatial organisation largely corresponds to each other. Development blocks are, of course, outside the purview of revenue administration and *kanugo* circles are not general purpose administrative areas.

Among the other special purpose authorities, especially relevant to the rural sector are co-operative societies, rural development, and Panchayati Raj. Co-operative societies are administered through a six tier hierarchy: headquarters, division, district, subdivision, inspectors' circle and sub-inspectors' circle. Rural Development and Panchyati Raj are five tiered: headquarters, division, district, development block, and village.

The environment management in Punjab, as in other states,

remained neglected for long. It was only in 1980 that a separate Ministry of Environment was set up at the Centre. State governments followed suit. The Punjab came to have its Department of Environment in 1981.

The Department of Town and Country Planning, Public Works, Public Health Engineering, Soil Conservation, and Housing and Urban Development were already looking after different aspects of environment but with a very limited success. These authorities arrange their spatial administration in different ways. Public Works Department (PWD) is organised in five tiers; Public Health Engineering, Soil Conservation, Water Supply and Sewerage Board, and Housing and Urban Development in four; Town and Country Planning and Housing Board in three; and Water Pollution Board and Land Use Board have only one tier cash. Their boundaries generally differ from those of general purpose administrative areas.

In terms of spatial organisation, the Department of Regional Planning in the Punjab was earlier divided into three circles: Chandigarh, Amritsar and Hoshiarpur. Each circle tended to enclose highly diverse physio-socio-economic areas. The clubbing of Ludhiana and Hoshiarpur districts in the same circle is one such example. The whole thing was organised on desired lines in 1995. Now, all the 17 districts of the state are divided into 5 circles, each with a considerable internal homogeneity.

Most of the state departments dealing with environmental services are either offshoots of an already existing department or of recent origin. Soil Conservation was earlier a part of the Department of Agriculture, and Public Health Engineering of the Public Works Department. The spatial framework of administration in all such cases was inherited as a legacy. It displays some distortions if looked at purely from the viewpoint of requirement of a particular environmental service today.

'Regional Authorities' are constituted to manage and provide some higher order service specific to a particular function or area. Electricity boards, transport corporations and river valley authorities are some such arrangements. Generally, these require coordination among a number of general purpose authorities (East and Prescott, 1975).

On the basis of the spatial scale of their operations, regional level authorities may be classified into three categories: (i) national level, that treat the Punjab as one of the spatial units of some countrywide arrangement operated by the central government; (ii) state level, that cover whole of the Punjab and are state responsibility; and (iii) substate level, that cover a part of the state and fall under the purview of the central/state government.

National level regional authorities include, among others, Indian Railways, Food Corporation of India, Fertiliser Corporation of India, Oil and Natural Gas Commission, Coal India, Steel Authority of India and Cement Corporation of India. Most of these treat Punjab as a part of their Northern Zone.

State level regional authorities include, among others, Punjab State Electricity Board (PSEB), Punjab Roadways, Punjab State Food and Civil Supplies Corporation (PUNSUP). Punjab State Co-operative Producers' Federation (MILKFED), Punjab State Agriculture Co-operative and Marketing Federation (MARKFED), Punjab State Agro-Industrial Corporation, and Punjab State Small Industries and Export Corporation. Most of these authorities are meant to ensure regularity in the supply and stability of prices of diffe-rent commodities. They are meant also to protect the interests of both producers and consumers.

These authorities organise their spatial administration on different lines, and the number of spatial tiers vary in their case. For example, PSEB organises its activities in six tiers; PUNSUP in four tiers; and MARKFED and MILKFED in three tiers each. The intensity of spatial spread of a service normally determines the number of tiers for its administration. Moreover, spatial organisation, in their case, may not conform to the general purpose administrative areas. It is determined in diverse ways to meet the technical and service requirements of each authority.

Subregional authorities are not function-based but locality based, being specific to a particular area earmarked either for its integrated development or for the solution of an endemic problem. The Punjab government has organised authorities for an integrated development of the state's backward areas, including the border districts of Gurdaspur, Amritsar and Firozpur; the *bet* (flood plain) areas of Ludhiana, Jalandhar and Kapurthala districts; and the *kandi* (foothill) tracts of Rupnagar and Hoshiarpur districts. These authorities are vested with powers essential for coordinating the activities of different general purpose and special purpose authorities. Under the state plans, additional funds are allocated for the development of these backward areas.

CONCLUSION

The spatial organisation of administration in the Punjab since Independence represents both the persistence of the colonial pattern and a process of decolonisation. The basal structure of administrative areas and non-elective nature of the district administration remains practically the same. The change is manifest in creation of the development block as a new tier for rural development, and a rapid increase in the number of special purpose and regional authorities to promote multifarious development. On the whole, a shift in the underlying philosophy of administration from land revenue collection and strict control during the British days to development promotion and populism during the post-Independence era is unmistakable.

We can discern three phases in the process: (i) the phase of administrative area reform during 1947-66 partly as a byproduct of successive reorganisations and partly by way of the formation of development blocks; (ii) the phase of proliferation of special purpose and regional authorities, during 1966-85, with a view to diversifying the development activities and taking care of problem areas; and (iii) the phase of populism, since 1985, which was marked by creation of several new districts, subtahsils, and development blocks in a short span of time.

In the process, the administrative organisation of space in Punjab has been assuming a more complex form over the years. Not only new layers of administrative arrangement were created but also the existing administrative units were subdivided or readjusted in several ways. A simple look at the administrative map of the Punjab as it has taken shape after the formation of five new districts during the nineties shows certain irrationalities. Firozpur district remains unwieldy and Kapurthala fragmented. Boundaries of three districts and seven subdivisions were tampered with to form Fatehgarh Sahib district. Its area is not much bigger than that of an average subdivision in the Punjab, 1144 and 916 km^2 respectively.

A number of issues need to be resolved before we can arrive at the right kind of decisions. The first pertains to the determination of size and shape of the district. There can be three guiding principles for this purpose: maximisation of the access of people to administration; effective supervision by the district administration and minimisation of the cost of the system. A rule of thumb suggests that a district should have a compact shape and its farthest settlement should not be more distant than one hour bus journey from the headquarters. Such a distance could be reasonably placed at about 25 km. Accordingly, a district should cover an area of about 2000 km^2. The Punjab can have 25 districts on this computation.

The second issue relates to the methodology for delimitation of districts. What kind of an area should a district enclose? Should it be marked by a commonality of local historical heritage or identity of people defined in some manner or similarity of physical geography? Should it meet the requirements of delineating meaningful legislative and parliamentary constituencies? Above all, to what extent should the existing administrative boundaries be honoured?

Finally, a vital issue concerns the number of tiers in which the administrative units of different hierarchical order should be organised. Should the Punjab continue with its existing system of divisions, districts, subdivisions, and development blocks or dispense with divisions and subdivisions and retain districts and development blocks only? What is the relevance of a division in a small state like Punjab? Do we need subdivisions when the average number of development blocks in a district is just eight? Multiplicity of tiers in administration is always generative of confusion and delays.

TABLE 1

Punjab: Area, Population, Settlements and Administrative Units, 1901-96

Year	Area (in km^2)	Population (in millions)	Number of rural and urban settlements	Number of administrative units
1901	389,036	26.88	47,256	32 districts 43 Native states
1911	353,095	24.19	44,574	29 districts 15 Punjab states
1921	354,688	24.95	45,409	29 districts 15 Punjab states 28 Simla hill states
1931	354,400	29.13	51,224	29 districts 15 Punjab states 28 Simla hill states
1941	359,179	35.23	52,644	29 districts 16 Punjab states 27 Simla hill states
1951	96,809	12.64	15,277	13 districts
1961	122,005	20.35	22,879	19 districts
1971	50,362	13.55	12,450	11 districts
1981	50,362	16.79	12,450	12 districts
1991	50,362	20.19	12,915	12 districts
1996	50,362	22.29*	12,915	17 districts

Source: Census of India, 1901 to 1991
* Estimated

TABLE 2

The Punjab: General Purpose Administrative Areas, 1966-96

Type	Number in the year 1966	1985	1996
Divisions	2	3	4
Districts	11	12	17
Subdivisions/ tahsils	37	46	70
Development blocks	117	118	137

Figure 1
General Purpose Administrative Areas in India
(A Six Tier Hierarchy)

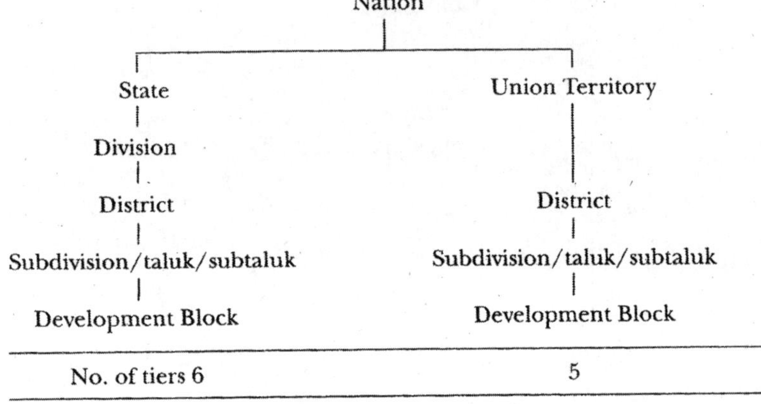

Figure 2
Spatial Organisation of Special Purpose Authorities at the National Level

Postal Services	Justice	Conduct of elections	Census operations	Spatial coverage
Board	Supreme Court	Election Commission Office	Registrar General Office	National and interstate
Circle	—	—	—	State and intrastate
Region	High Court	State Election Office	State Xensus Directorate	
Division	—	—	Census division	
District/Head Post Office	District Court	Election district	Census district	
Post Office	Subdivisional Court	—	Census charge	
Sub-Post Office	—	—	Census circle	
—	—	—	Census block	
Tiers 7	4	3	7	

Figure 3

Spatial Organisation of Administration of Special Purpose Authorities at the National and State Levels in Combine

Spatial coverage	Education						Medical	
Spatial		Ministry of Education					Ministry of Health and Family Welfare	
National and interstate levels								
	University Grants Commission				Indian Council of Medical Research			
		State Ministry of Education					State Ministry of Health and Family Welfare	
	University							
		Directorate	Directorate	Directorate	Directorate	Directorate	Directorate	Directorate
State and interstate levels		College	—	—	—	College	—	
		—	Circle	—	—	—	—	
		—	District	District	District	—	Civil Hospital	District
		—	—	—	—	—	Hospital	
		—	—	Block	Sports Club	—	Primary Health Centre	—
		—	—	—	—	—	Dispensary	Rural dispensary
Number of tiers	2	4	3	3	3	2	7	3

Figure 4
Spatial Organisation of Administration of Special Purpose Authorities at the State Level

Sector	Police	Agriculture	Industry	Forestry	Land Revenue	Rural Development	Soil Conservation
	Headquarters	Directorate	Directorate	Head Office	Head Office	Directorate	Head Office
	Range	—	—	Circle	Division	Division	Circle
	District	District	District centre	Division	District	District	Division
	Circle	—	—	Range	Tahsil	—	Subdivision
	Police Station	Block	Block office/ Industrial estate	Subrange	Kanugo circle	Block	—
	Police post	Focal Point	—	Block/round	Patwar circle	Village	—
	—	—	—	Beat	Village	—	—
No. of tiers	6	4	3	7	7	5	4

PUNJAB
Administrative Divisions
(General Purpose Administrative Areas)
1996
Jammu and Kashmir
Himachal Pradesh
PAKISTAN
Chandigarh
Rajasthan
Haryana
GURDASPUR
Pathankot
Dinanagar
Batala
Dasua
Tanda
Bhunga
AMRITSAR
Ajnala
Majitha
Verka
Tarsikka
Jandiala
Rayya
Baba Bakala
Nadala
Bholath
Bhogpur
HOSHIARPUR
Hoshiarpur -II
Mahilpur
Garhshankar
Anandpur Sahib
Nurpur Bedi
RUPNAGAR
Tarn Taran
Khadur Sahib
Dhilwan
KAPURTHALA
JALANDHAR
Adampur
Jalandhar East
Phagwara
Banga
Saroya
NAWAN SHAHR
Bala chaur
Naushehra Pannuan
Bhikhiwind
Patti
Sultanpur Lodhi
Chohla Sahib
Valtoha
Lohian
Shahkot
Nakodar
Rurka Kalan
Nur Mahal
Phillaur
Aur
Makhu
FIROZPUR
Ghall Khurd
Zira
Dharam Kot
Sidhwan Bet
LUDHIANA
Ludhiana -II
Machhiwara
Chamkaur Sahib
Samrala
Morinda
Majri
Mamdot
Moga -II
MOGA
Jagraon
Sudhar
Pakhowal
Dehlon
Doraha
Khanna
Khamanon
Bassi Pathana
Kharar
Mohali
FARIDKOT
Guru Har Sahai
Begha Purana
Nihal Singh Wala
Raikot
Payal
Amloh
Sirhind
Khera
FATEHGARH SAHIB
Rajpura
Dera Bassi
Jalalabad
MUKTSAR
Kot Kapura
Jaito
Mahal Kalan
Ahmedgarh
Malerkotla
Sehna
Sherpur
Nabha
PATIALA
Ghanaur
Fazilka
Kot Bhai
Gidderbaha
Phul
Dhuri
Barnala
Bhawanigarh
Sanaur
BATHINDA
Nathana
Rampura
SANGRUR
Samana
Bhuner Heri
Abohar
Malout
Khuian Sarwar
Bhikhi
Sunam
Lambi
Sangat
Talwandi Sabo
MANSA
Lehragaga
Patran
Budhlada
Moonak
Jhunir
Andana
Sardulgarh
Administrative area
Boundary
Headquarters
State
Division
District
Subdivision
Development Block
International Boundary
*** Firm Information not available
0
80
Kms.

Map 2

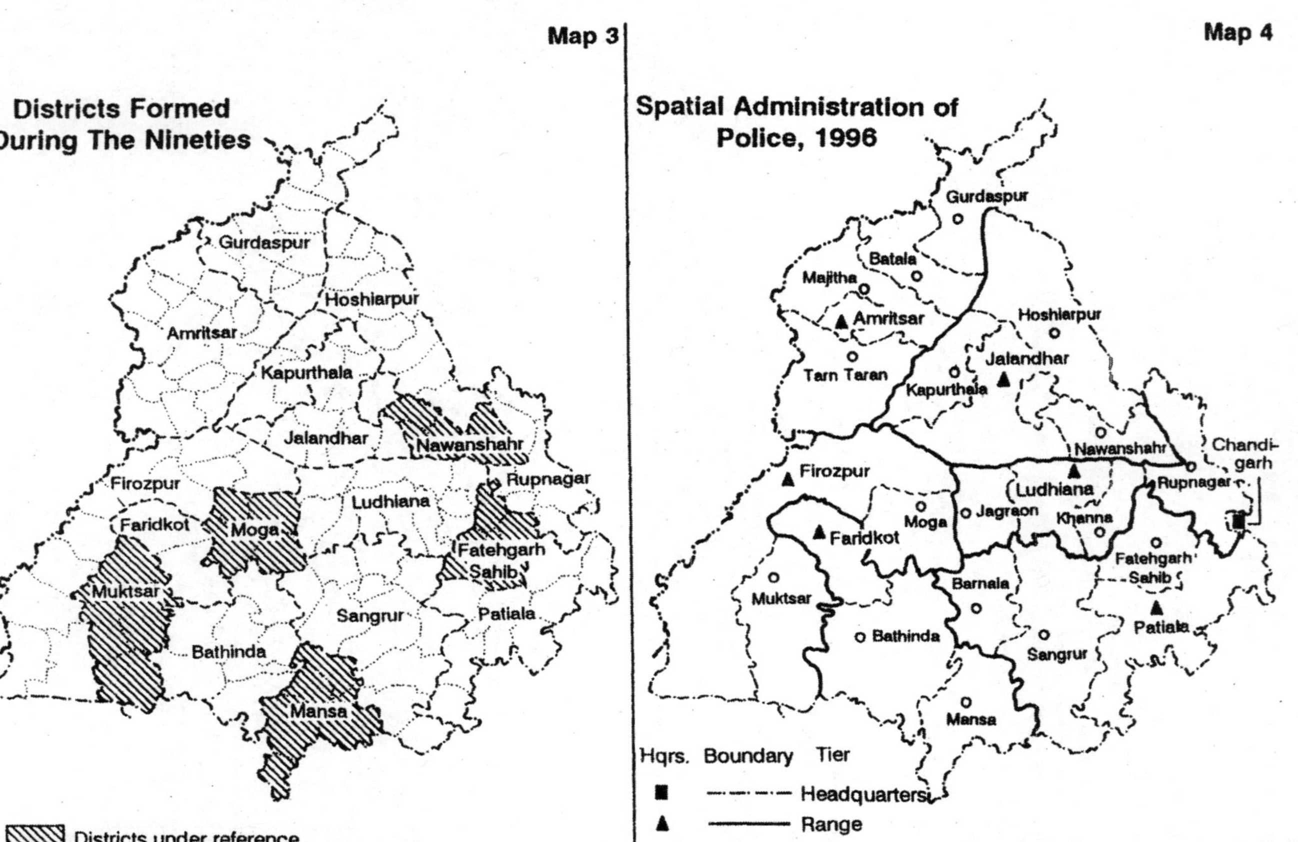
PUNJAB : Spatial Organisations for Administration (i)
Map 3
Districts Formed
During The Nineties
Gurdaspur
Hoshiarpur
Amritsar
Kapurthala
Jalandhar
Nawanshahr
Firozpur
Rupnagar
Ludhiana
Faridkot
Moga
Fatehgarh
Sahib
Muktsar
Sangrur
Patiala
Bathinda
Mansa
Districts under reference
Map 4
Spatial Administration of
Police, 1996
Gurdaspur
Batala
Majitha
Amritsar
Hoshiarpur
Jalandhar
Tarn Taran
Kapurthala
Nawanshahr
Chandi-
garh
Firozpur
Ludhiana
Rupnagar
Jagraon
Moga
Khanna
Faridkot
Fatehgarh
Sahib
Barnala
Muktsar
Patiala
Bathinda
Sangrur
Mansa
Hqrs. Boundary Tier
Headquarters
Range

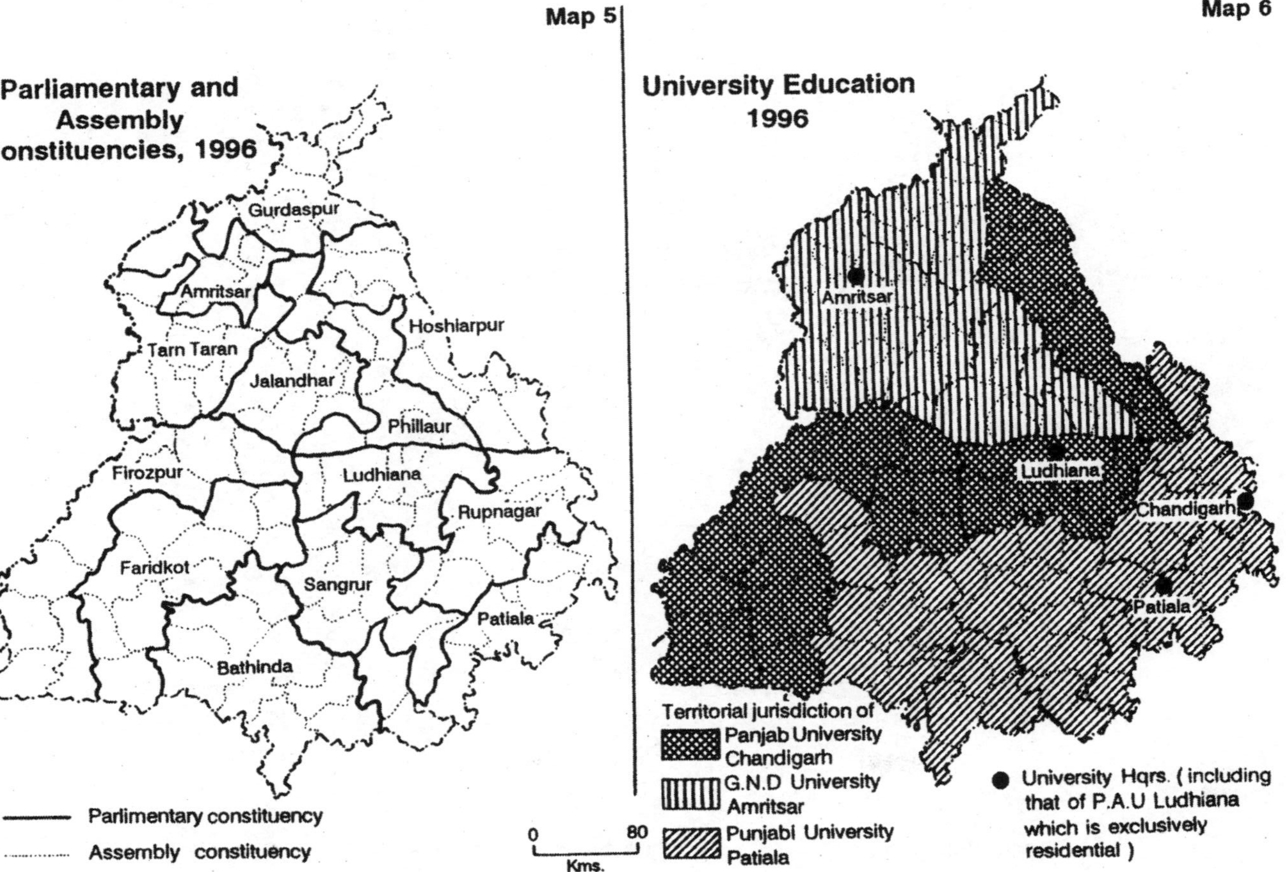
Map 5
Parliamentary and Assembly Constituencies, 1996
Gurdaspur
Amritsar
Tarn Taran
Jalandhar
Hoshiarpur
Phillaur
Ludhiana
Firozpur
Rupnagar
Faridkot
Sangrur
Patiala
Bathinda
Parlimentary constituency
Assembly constituency
0
80
Kms.
Map 6
University Education 1996
Amritsar
Ludhiana
Chandigarh
Patiala
Territorial jurisdiction of
Panjab University Chandigarh
G.N.D University Amritsar
Punjabi University Patiala
University Hqrs. (including that of P.A.U Ludhiana which is exclusively residential)

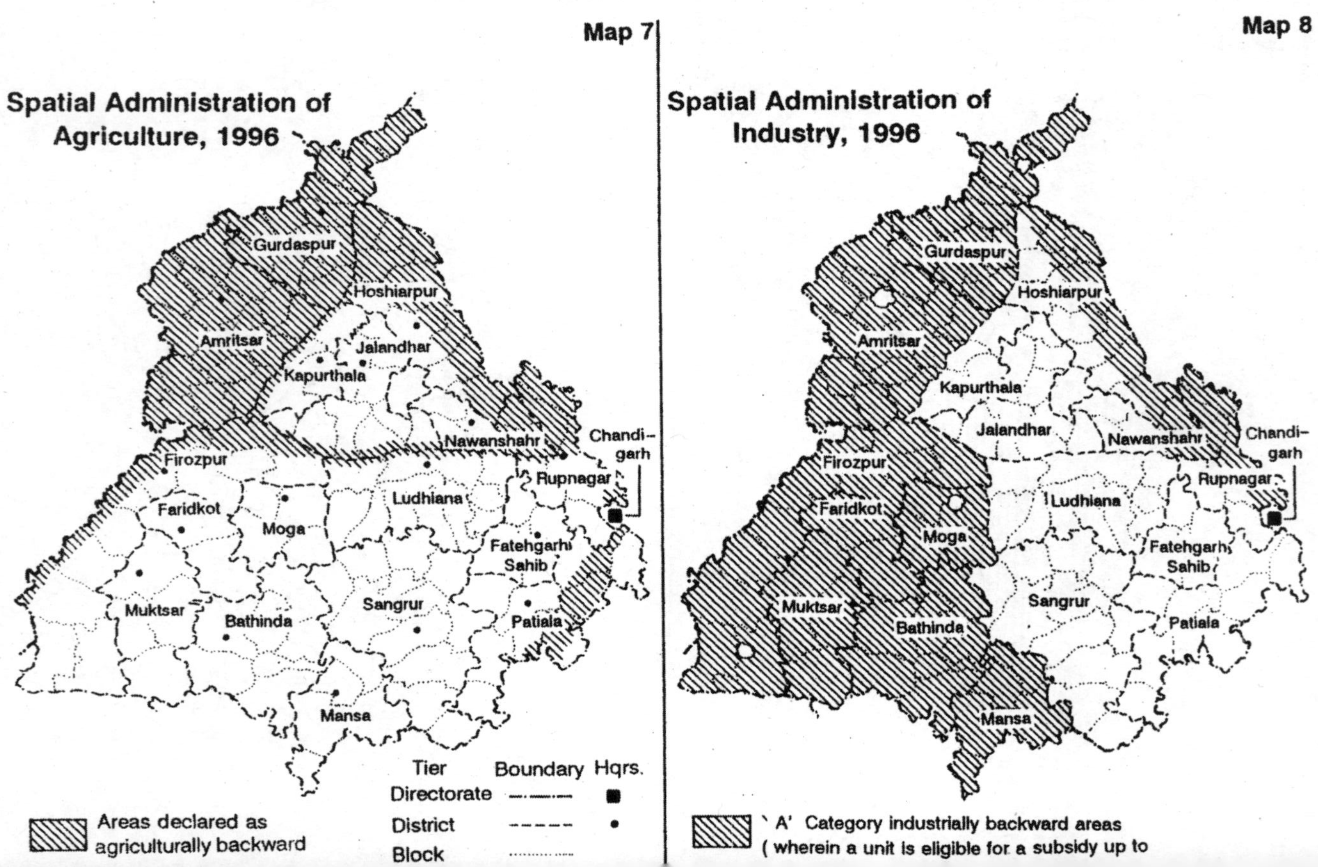
PUNJAB : Spatial Organisations for Administration (ii)
Map 7
Spatial Administration of Agriculture, 1996
Gurdaspur
Hoshiarpur
Amritsar
Jalandhar
Kapurthala
Nawanshahr
Chandi-garh
Firozpur
Rupnagar
Ludhiana
Faridkot
Moga
Fatehgarh Sahib
Muktsar
Bathinda
Sangrur
Patiala
Mansa
Tier
Boundary
Hqrs.
Directorate
District
Block
Areas declared as agriculturally backward
Map 8
Spatial Administration of Industry, 1996
Gurdaspur
Hoshiarpur
Amritsar
Kapurthala
Jalandhar
Nawanshahr
Chandi-garh
Firozpur
Rupnagar
Ludhiana
Faridkot
Moga
Fatehgarh Sahib
Muktsar
Sangrur
Patiala
Bathinda
Mansa
'A' Category industrially backward areas
(wherein a unit is eligible for a subsidy up to

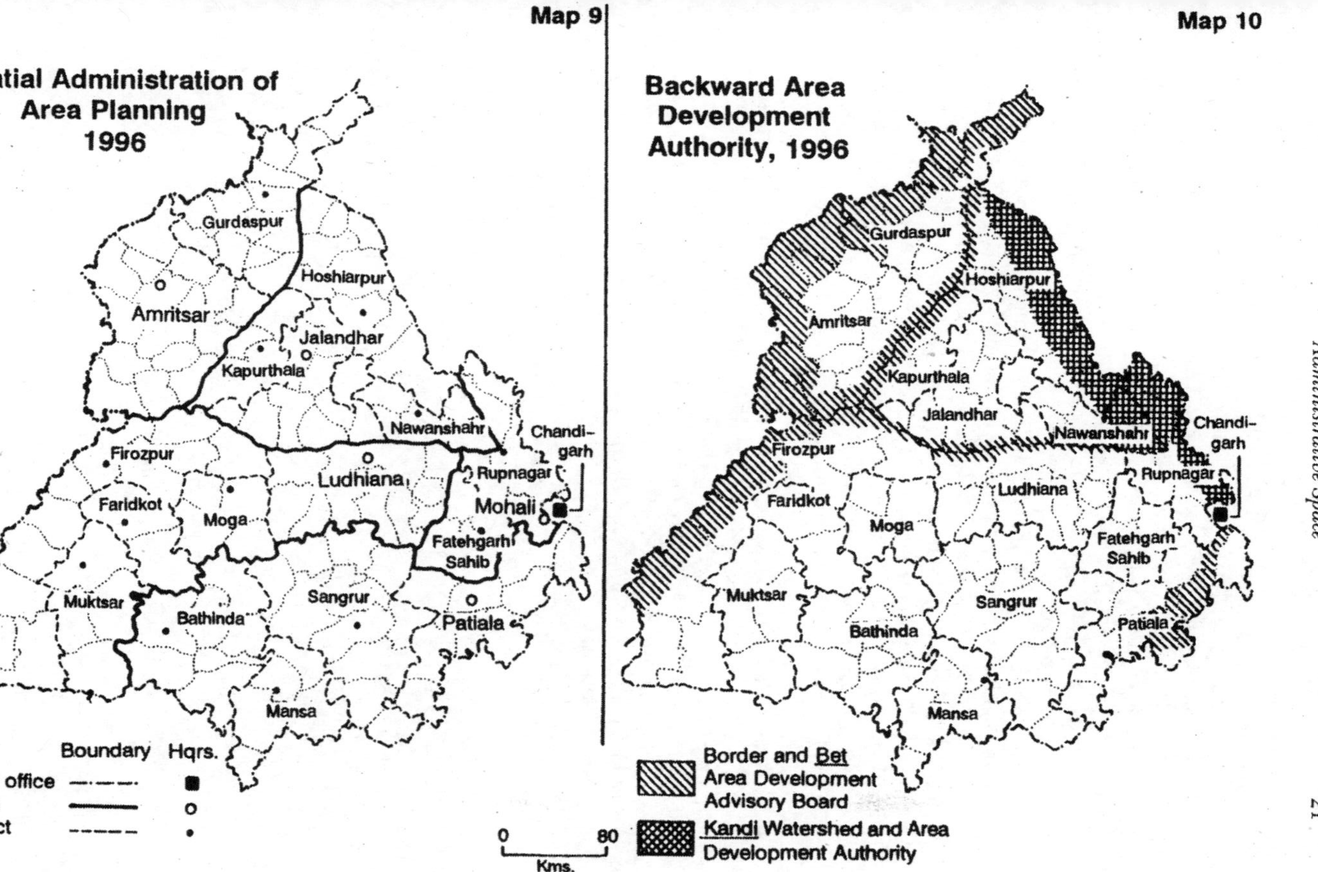
Map 9
Spatial Administration of Area Planning 1996
Gurdaspur
Hoshiarpur
Amritsar
Jalandhar
Kapurthala
Nawanshahr
Chandi-garh
Firozpur
Ludhiana
Rupnagar
Mohali
Faridkot
Moga
Fatehgarh Sahib
Muktsar
Sangrur
Bathinda
Patiala
Mansa
Tier Boundary Hqrs.
Head office
Circle
District
0 80
Kms.
Map 10
Backward Area Development Authority, 1996
Gurdaspur
Hoshiarpur
Amritsar
Kapurthala
Jalandhar
Nawanshahr
Chandi-garh
Firozpur
Rupnagar
Ludhiana
Faridkot
Moga
Fatehgarh Sahib
Muktsar
Sangrur
Bathinda
Patiala
Mansa
Border and Bet Area Development Advisory Board
Kandi Watershed and Area Development Authority

REFERENCES

Beaujeu-Garnier, J. (1976). *Methods and Perspectives in Geography.* London: Longman.

Bennett, R.J. and R.J. Chorley (1978). *Environmental Systems Philosophy, Analysis and Control.* London: Methuen.

East, W.G. and J.R.V. Prescott (1975). *Our Fragmented World.* London: Macmillan.

Garner, B. (1975). 'The effect of local government reform on access to public services: a case study of Denmark'. *Processes in Physical and Human Geography* Eds. R. Peet *et al* London: Heineman.

Humes, S. and E.M. Martin (1961). *The Structure of Local Government Throughout the World.* The Hague: Martinus Nishoff.

Krishan, Gopal (1988). 'The world pattern of administrative area reform'. *Geographical Journal,* 154, 93-99.

Krishan, Gopal (1990). 'Administrative Geography'. *Annals of the Association of Indian Geographers,* 10, 41-51.

Massam, B.H. (1972). 'The spatial structure of administrative systems'. *Association of American Geographers,* Resource Paper No. 12.

Kant, Surya (1988). *Administrative Geography of India.* Jaipur: Rawat.

Sharma, S.K. (1971). *Deputy Commissioner in Punjab.* New Delhi: Indian Institute of Public Administration.

Shukla, J.D. (1976). *State and District Administration in India.* New Delhi: National.

2

Punjab Administration at Work

P. H. VAISHNAV

In 1947 the Punjab bodily inherited the British administrative apparatus minus its European and Muslim cadres. It would, therefore, be appropriate to see what it was like in the colonial period. As elsewhere, it was functioning for an imperial purpose in the Punjab. The priorities of the administration were law and order for the security of the empire and prevention, detection and punishment of crime for the peaceful enjoyment of property of which agricultural lands were much the most important. Land was a source of revenue for the government. Machinery for periodic assessment and collection of revenue, maintenance of land records and agricultural statistics, an hierarchy of revenue courts for adjudicating on disputes and a supervisory hierarchy for overseeing the functioning of revenue officials formed another priority.

On these two priorities was constructed the administrative edifice consisting of the Revenue and Police Departments. Not that the administrative presence in other areas such as public works, education, health, forests etc. was lacking, but the involvement was minimal. Within this range, the quality of the administrative apparatus was very high. Top personnel in all departments were recruited through credible institutions and impersonal procedures and nurtured in an environment of professionalism and integrity. Even the second rung of the services performed with integrity and efficiency. The lowest levels were ill paid, admittedly corrupt and assumed to be the responsibility of the community.

The Punjab was the last to come under British rule. It was a non-regulation province where a strong, authoritarian administration was perceived by the British to be a necessity. The administration functioned in a responsive, even if paternalistic manner. There was a finality about administrative decisions and discipline at all levels was strictly enforced. The immediate supervisory officers were able to intervene promptly and effectively to redress injustice and punish the offender. This minimised uncertainty for the citizen.

Even though the European and Indian parts of the cadres came from universities and an urban background they acquired an intimate knowledge of the rural communities, their economy and culture. Periodic land revenue settlements threw up data that gave valuable insights.

From necessity and tradition, the administration was run on delegated authority, the exercise of which was encouraged. Over the years an agency like the district boards brought about a measure of popular association and decentralisation in the management of the limited rural infrastructure.

A sense of virtual permanence enabled a long term view and firm adherence to priorities. Irrigated agriculture got the highest priority in the Punjab and the administration therefore developed skills and gained experience of construction of canals, practice of irrigated agriculture and water use, agricultural research and extension, development of markets and habitats around them.

Essentially unaccountable to the people, the British administration was conscious of the need for creating its political base among the people in the rural and urban areas. Agricultural expansion and development and the Khalsa and Arya Samaj educational enterprise found scope to flourish under the British.

The Punjab administration acquired a reputation for speed and result-orientation. Later in the thirties the Unionist government provided the elected political executive. Even with its restricted authority, it contributed to satisfying rural concerns and achieved communal harmony right till Jinnah's call for direct action. In the two years of 1946 and 1947, services were inevitably communalised and the British element resigned to the end of the empire, with no will to cope with the carnage of communal violence. There was a crippling uncertainty which told on the administration too.

The partition of the Punjab ended this uncertainty. The categorical underwriting of the administrative set-up and system inherited from the British by Sardar Vallabh Bhai Patel thus meant a continuum (albeit for the new national goals) for the Hindu and Sikh personnel.The political executive too accepted it as a national level decision, while the people of the East Punjab accepted it as a natural set-up after the departure of the British and Muslim personnel.

The political executive served the right purpose of providing the general political will and direction. The value system of the political class was conditioned by the ethics of the freedom struggle. The Chief Ministership alternated between Gopi Chand Bhargava and Bhim Sen Sachar but this did not affect administrative functioning. Both these individuals were moderate in their philosophy and mild in their methods. In such an environment the system-based and result-oriented administration inherited from the British was allowed to play its part effectively and justly.

The major concerns of those years were related to the rehabilitation of a large population uprooted by partition. It was a complex problem but was handled remarkably well, its success owing itself to a happy congruence between the political execu-tive, the administrative leadership, and the public. This was followed by land reforms: ceiling on land holding and security of tenure for the tenants. This meant framing of legislation, and its implementation through the revenue staff and the judicial work concerning litigation arising out of the law. Considering the urgency and complexities of the task, this too was accomplished well. As contrasted with the collusive corruption that characterised the implementation of the 1971 Land Reforms Act, the reforms of the 1950's were a clean affair carried out through a revenue machinery that had retained its name for efficiency. The Bhakra and the Chandigarh capital projects were two outstanding achievements of the Punjab Engineering Services even though technical know-how came from Slocum, an American engineer at Bhakra, and from Corbusier and Jeaneret in the case of Chandigarh.

The other developmental programmes were conceived of by the National Planning Commission along uniform national pattern. There was no design to relate them to local conditions. In the absence of the Panchayati Raj institutions which were not on the national agenda, the village Panchayats and the extension agency of the community projects, later split and multiplied into extension service blocks, consisting of the Block Development Officer and his village level workers, were the sole instruments at the grass-root level. They succeeded in creating a developmental urge and consciousness but could not have gone so far as to develop representative rural institutions beyond the village level.

The Block agency acquired greater importance than the *tahsil* revenue agency which was viewed as regulatory, a British bequest not very relevant in the context of the declining importance of land revenue which was to be abolished altogether in the sixties. The consolidation of holdings, without which productive agriculture and efficient water management would not have been possible, must be regarded as the great achievement of the revenue staff.

With the end of the struggle for freedom, the political class ceased to fear the police. But they had not yet developed ideas on misusing the police for political purposes in the constituency. The police continued to function with autonomy and effectiveness in the matter of prevention of crime, its control and punishment. How justly they performed their duties would not admit of a categorical opinion. Since the Judiciary and the Executive were combined, there was some check. In the regime of Kairon, the magistracy went under in the face of police ascendancy.

The essential point to see is that like the revenue department the police too were viewed as a regulatory bequest of the British. The modernisation and upgradation of the civil police suffered neglect in the same way as the revenue agency. Development had higher priority and greater respectability. There was little realisation that a sound law and order management was a prerequisite of development. This neglect persisted, thereby causing greater dependence at a later stage on the central para military forces. Useful as they are, they cannot serve as a substitute for the civil police.

The overall success of the administration owed itself to the fact that the political executive and the administrative institutions were of a good quality and well aligned mutually. The functioning of both was in congruence with what the society at large expected of the government. Moreover, in the Punjab, more than any where else, government service carried prestige and the authority of the administration commanded respect. Also, the government was regarded by the public as the provider of all things. This also meant the continued absence of non-government organisations and citizen fora. The trend towards centralisation was emerging, resulting in the end of the District Boards without their replacement by Panchayati Raj.

A crack in the social consensus developed during the 1951 census over the language issue. This brought to surface the latent communal consciousness among the people. As an interest group, the services too developed this consciousness. Usually the corrupt and the inefficient in both the communities attributed their suppression, adverse appraisal reports or disciplinary proceedings to communal bias with a view to getting a sympathetic review of their cases. Postings showed a desirable concern for communal balance. On the whole, however, career prospects did not get affected on account of one's community, nor did the collective functioning of the administration. Appraisal reports were as a rule upheld against representations and the fear of disciplinary action kept the personnel in check and politicisation to the minimum.

It was the first reorganisation of 1956 that aggravated the crack caused by the 1951 census into a fracture. Except the erstwhile bilingual Bombay and the Punjab, states were re-organised on the linguistic principle. A wholly uncalled for agitation for the socalled protection of Hindi was launched against the Regional Formula which demarcated the state into Punjabi and Hindi regions. In the Punjabi region Punjabi got the status of the first language and Hindi the second. In the Hindi region Hindi got the first place and Punjabi the second. Punjabi and Hindi did not lose in either region. This was the best alternative to the formation of the Punjabi Suba and Haryana.

The Reorganisation Commission's report in 1955, the non-formation of a Punjabi Suba and the obstinate resistance to the Regional Formula disrupted the social consensus. It was in this environment that the earlier political leadership gave way to Partap Singh Kairon whose impact on the Punjab administration and the state was extraordinary, both for good and ill. He was passionately committed to the idea of a united Punjab and its rapid development. He sincerely felt justified in leaning heavily on the police as the principal instrument for handling the Hindi Raksha Samiti leaders in 1957 and the Akali leaders in 1961. He was conscious of the need for overcoming regional disparities in order to keep the constituent regions of Haryana and the Hills within the composite Punjab and for its rapid development.

Kairon regarded the bureaucracy as a British bequest – slow, procedure bound and not enthused to any dynamic effort unless forced to adopt short cuts. And yet he believed in the bureaucracy as an instrument. He had a dogmatic aversion to the technical services whom he regarded as both corrupt and faction ridden. The severity of his aversion was incredible and inexplicable.

Kairon's priorities were thus clear. The CID, the police and vigilance departments were at the top in the pegging order. He kept this machinery directly under him and except for loyalty to him did not pay attention to its accountability. He made a thorough use of the police for maintaining surveillance on political opponents within and outside the Congress and suppressing agitations with an iron hand. He used the vigilance department for taming other services, especially the engineering services.

Kairon bifurcated the dual charge of the heads of departments as ex-officio secretaries to government in the engineering and the education department. He replaced an educationist with an IAS officer as the Director of Public Instruction. The morale of these services went down as Kairon started leaning more and more on the general services of the IAS and the PCS.

Operational matters got centralised at the secretariat level, largely in his single authority. The ordinary citizen had, therefore, to knock at the doors of the secretariat and eventually at the Chief Minister's door. The intermediate levels were rendered ineffective and irrelevant. Their capacity to respond to public needs diminished. In the absence of a formal power structure at the district level, the extra-constitutional power structure came into play as middlemen. Administration lost its system orientation. This destruction of the system was the greatest disservice of Kairon to the Punjab and its administration. This disservice outweighs his many great achievements. Kairon also installed a model in which there was no inhibition against reliance on the police for political purposes. His successors in the Punjab, and the politicians in other states and at the national level, soon saw the advantage, however short-term, of using the police for political purposes.

Kairon's successors could not have controlled the politicisation and loosening of discipline among the class of employees whose ranks had proliferated into what is called the Inspector Raj. This factor over the years had become an impediment to liberalisation and costly to the community through its growing wage bill and other levies. Another development of the post-Kairon era was the beginning of a tradition of the government ceasing to be a continuum and becoming a succession of regimes. Each successor regime started going into a whole review of the predecessor regime. The services found themselves under a great strain. They were the instruments of action of the predecessor regime and witnesses against them on behalf of the successor regime. The follow-up on the Das Commission set up against Kairon became precisely that. 'Das-Kaironisation' meant reopening all ordres passed not only by Kairon but all other authorities in his time. Such reviews hurt the finality of decision making process, as a change in regime could be used for upsetting previous orders.

This tradition spread to other states in 1967 and to the centre in 1977 where the political process was handed over to the police and judicial commissions. In the Punjab itself there was the Chhangani Commission against Parkash Singh Badal and his colleagues in 1973. Badal reciprocated by setting up the Gurdev Singh Commission against Giani Zail Singh in 1977.

Formation of the Punjabi Suba could not have been resisted indefinitely and the state was reorganised in 1966. Historians may debate endlessly the merits of this decision but the important point to note is that the first ministry in the reorganised Punjab was an Akali-Jan Singh coalition which the Communist Party also joined. Contrary to Hindu fears, the state settled down to normal administration very quickly. The coalition, an alliance of two 'communal' parties, worked remarkably well in terms of freedom from communalism and corruption.

There was no doubt a tendency among a small number of Sikh officers to imagine themselves as the defenders of the Punjab's interests. A small number of Hindu officers showed off their ardour for the yet to be formed state of Haryana. Some politicians were heard commenting on the disproportionate Hindu presence in the government services. This was a valid comment but the disproportion could have been corrected only over time, which it was. On the whole, however, communal relations were unaffected both in the services and at the mass level.

The first cabinet headed by Gurnam Singh, a retired judge and an experienced leader of the opposition, was compact and was imbued with a wish to perform and also concerned about maintaining its image. During his tenure between February and November 1967, the services were allowed considerable freedom of action. The Development Commissioner, the Departments of Agriculture and Cooperation, the District Administration and the Punjab Agricultural University (a great gift of Kairon) were able among themselves to work out the institutionalisation of agricultural development. The Green Revolution was thus launched. The widespread support of the people explains its success.

The contrived fall of the Gurnam Singh Government and the installation of Lachhman Singh Gill's seventeen-member ministry (after defection from the Akali-Jan Sangh coalition) told heavily on the administration. The use of the police in the Kaironite manner went so far as to get them into the House of the Punjab Vidhan Sabha for getting the budget of 1968-69 passed. Gill's tenure saw the climax of politico-administrative deterioration. Earlier, some civil service officers were used to bring about defections from the Akali-Jan Sangh ranks. The Public Service Commission lost its image. On the whole, political and adminis-trative tradition suffered considerably. Such an unprincipled alliance between the Congress and a splinter group of defectors could not have lasted.

After a spell of President's Rule during 1968-69, the Akali-Jan Sangh coalition under the leadership of Gurnam Singh was back but in the two year period, 1969-71, the Chief Ministership changed from Gurnam Singh to Badal as the former defied the will of the Akali High Command. Badal's government did not last long on account of the defections engineered from the Akali fold – this time ironically by Gurnam Singh in alliance with the Congress.

The prompt dissolution of the Assembly by the Governor on Badal's advice led to President's Rule in July 1971. After a spell of six months, the Congress led by Giani Zail Singh came with a clear majority. He was a mild man and let the normal administration function but he did not check the spread of politicisation and was reckless in making discretionary appointments to the Public Service Commission, the Electricity Board etc. Above all, he felt that be could marginalise the Akalis only by outdoing them through encouragement to 'fundamentalism' and to Bhindranwale himself. The Sanjay phenomenon and the Emergency made its own contribution to the decline of Punjab politics and administration.

One feature of the Punjab Administration is its being frequently under President's Rule. Ever since the decision in March 1966 to reorganise the state, the Punjab came under President's Rule from June to November 1966, from August 1968 to February 1969, and from July 1971 to February 1972. In 1977 again it went under President's Rule. The Akali-Janata coalition came to power in the middle of 1977 and lasted upto January 1980 to be followed by President's Rule.

The Badal-Janata coalition came to power as a result of the post-emergency poll. Here too the public consensus gave it strength which it used with relative immunity from corruption and communalism. There was no call for the dismissal of the Badal Government except that the Congress was reciprocating what the Janata did to its governments at the state level.

A short spell of President's Rule in the Punjab was followed by the Congress ministry headed by Darbara Singh, a clean politician but a strong confrontationist in so far as the Akalis were con-cerned. His main problem, however, was Bhindrawale and the emerging 'fundamentalism' backed by terrorism. He received no support from the central leadership and in fact his functioning was made difficult by Giani Zail Singh from the vantage position of the Home Minister. Darbara Singh could not resist the impo-sition of an agreement on the distribution of Ravi-Beas waters. Even so he ran the administration firmly and in a clean manner. His three years were marked by lots of development work, especially power generation. He went out of office in a needless response to the murder of 6 Hindu passengers on a bus by the terrorists.

The President's Rule from 1983 to 1985 was unable to cope with terrorism. The Operation Blue Star of June 1984 was followed by another year of terrorism in the Punjab. The Barnala Government installed in office in September 1985 was purely Akali with a majority of 73 Akalis in the legislative assembly. It could have achieved a lot but its functioning was thwarted both by the central leadership and the Akali dissidents. With the danger of further defection, which had to be prevented, an administrative price was paid by way of appointment of all the remaining legislators either in the cabinet or as chairmen of various public undertakings. For a short period, the ministry was compact and functioned well. The central leadership started talking in terms of 'we' and 'you' rather than treating the Punjab problem as a national problem. Barnala's functioning was thus greatly hampered from all sides. Nevertheless, within the severe constraints imposed by circum-stances outside his control, he functioned in his characteristically calm and balanced manner. His training as a lawyer, his experience as a minister at the state and national level and his moderate temperament relieved greatly the strain of the situation. His great achievement was to pull back the state from the brink where it had reached in the wake of Operation Blue Star of June 1984. Terrorist violence had restarted from the end of 1985 and went on escalating day after day. This brought the Police Department again to the centre stage. Even with the appointment of Ribeiro, an IPS officer of great distinction from Maharashtra, as the Director General of Police with a substantially freehand there was no let up in the violence.

Why the Punjab Police itself could not throw up a leader? The answer lies in the way the police cadre was being managed. It was basically a one man show all along, functioning with no long term view or effort at building leadership. The force and the cadre did not feel the need for community relations nor collaboration with the Executive Magistracy which was marginalised in the name of police autonomy, while the Home Department was in no position to influence police perspectives. But the most important reason for an officer not being available from within the cadre was the fear of a pro-terrorist government coming to power, which frightened the officers of the Punjab cadre. Those coming from outside were relatively free as they could at least go back. At the time of negotiations by the centre with Bhindranwale's nephew in 1988 and later during Chandra Shekhar's Prime Ministership the fear of hostile regimes was great. Even today the police cadres continue to feel insecure from possible revenge or a judicial retrospect on their functioning on a big scale.

The other consequence of dealing with militancy has been that across the force, rapid expansions and promotions have affected their training and capability for normal policing through scientific and methodical investigation within the legal framework for successful prosecution. The most serious result of reliance on police from 1984 to date is that whatever tenuous institutional subordination there was of the police to the government, it has practically ended. The principal problem before the Punjab administration thus is how best to modernise the civil police and to make it function as a service and not a 'force'.

Equally important is the problem of creating leadership in the civil and technical services and giving them functional autonomy so that the Head of Department and the District Officer is made effective in removing public grievances and in planning and implementing development. Today's civil servant and the Head of Department is no more than an extension of the secretariat headed by ministers. The secretary and Head of Department are at best elevated personal secretaries of the minister. The policy function has thus suffered. At the district level, the district officer is a helpless spectator of a suffering public and largely engaged in personal survival and pursuit of his career.

In a comparative view of all state administrations the Punjab Administration still stands out as capable of results. For some inexplicable reason its action orientation survives although its capacity for dismantling the jungle of regulations and the burden of the enforcement machinery on the community level remains severely circumscribed on account of entrenched interests. But given the political will, the higher levels of the administration and the Punjab public could achieve this objective.

The Panchayati Raj which has been introduced recently may hopefully fill the void at the grass-root level though its prospects do not seem promising in the near future.

3

Nehru, Indira Gandhi and the Punjab

TEJWANT S. GILL

A mention of the Punjab in the context of Jawaharlal Nehru's policies and programmes before and after Independence, brings to mind a relationship that was intricate from the very beginning. It becomes evident from the corpus of his writings, speeches, interviews and statements that Nehru began to reflect on the Punjab in the 1920s.[1] His reflections show that the religious composition of the people as much as the political complexion of the province was his primary concern.

Nehru did not feel the urge to ponder over the nature and culture of the Punjab. Acclaiming it as a fertile land inhabited by brave and virile people, he did not reckon with what the *panj-aab* of the Persian chronicles evoked with regard to its natural habitus. This had nothing to do with Nehru's historiography. Its poetic paradigm was nurtured upon male-female or lover-beloved syndrome, which impelled him to write about India as nobility-incarnate with a 'strong and serene face – strong and yet calm and determined, that ancient face which is ever young and vibrant'. The lover-beloved aspect of this syndrome led him to glorify the service of the motherland as 'a unique experience... such an experience as though full of turmoils and hardships is good for a nation'.[2]

Nehru's reflections on the Punjab were occasioned by another paradigm of his historiography. Being ideological, he was impelled to take note of the diversity marking the unity of the country. It was under the burden of this impulse that he sought to relate the problems of the people to the economic, social, political and religious factors of their life. Literacy, planning, industrialisation and socialism were the measures which he suggested for their growth as against communalism, parochialism and linguism which kept them under-developed and backward.

These two paradigms operated in converging parallelism in Nehru's mind. When he reflected upon India as a civilisational unity, it was usually the first paradigm that impelled him to glorify her achievement in the fields of spirituality, literature and culture. Drawn to her poverty at the present historical juncture, he employed the second paradigm to frame policies and programmes for ameliorating the condition of the vast multitude of her people. Impelled to describe the natural beauty of his native land, Kashmir, he invariably took recourse to the poetic means of the first paradigm. Through these means he would evoke the protuberances, curvatures and apertures of this mountainous region as if it were identical with the female body. While reflecting upon the other regions of India, particularly Bengal and the Punjab, which nurtured no feelings of identity and self-identity, he found only the second paradigm relevant for his purpose.

I

Nehru found three religious communities marking the composition of the Punjabi people. They were the Muslims, the Hindus and the Sikhs in order of percentage. Nehru felt that though with the largest percentage, the Muslims were not the addressee to whom as an addressor he could address his message. They were not even the recipients whom as a speaker he could have the disposition to forward his discourse. To all intents and purposes, his address or discourse sought to exclude them as the other. For, without any involvement of the sort, the Muslims could formally be his listeners. The large-scale killing of the Muslims particularly in the erstwhile Patiala state in the aftermath of the partition did trouble him a lot. The expression that he gave to his troubled state of mind was also agonising. However, its significance at that juncture was only gestural or gesticulative.

The exclusion of Muslims as the addressee of his message and the recipients of his discourse was valid because Nehru felt that they aligned themselves politically either with a feudal party, like the Unionist Party under the leadership of Sir Sikandar Hayat Khan, Sir Sundar Singh Majithia and Sir Chhotu Ram, or with a communal organisation like the Muslim League led by the cohorts of

Muhammad Ali Jinnah. This provoked his ire so much that to guarantee their separation from the Hindus and the Sikhs, he started approving of the partition of the country that he had earlier opposed with vehemence. The rationale that he provided was that for the health and survival of the body, it is advisable to amputate the diseased or the paralytic limb. The use of disease imagery that he employed in this regard in his writings, statements, speeches and interviews, included in his *Selected Works* in the second series, is evident enough. 'We agreed because we felt that India's political and social life was being undermined and poisoned by continuous inner conflict and we wanted to put an end to this so that people may consider the questions facing us dispassionately'.[3] That this sought to invert the norms of the paradigm drawing sustenance from the male-female or lover-beloved syndrome, did not visibly exasperate him.

Nehru treated the Hindus of the Punjab as the addressees for whom his address was of significance or the recipients for whom his discourse carried meaning. But they were addressees or recipients of the passive sort. This remained Nehru's position till the time of the partition. His rationale was drawn from the suppression to which they in the course of history had been subjected by the Muslim rulers. Though their invasions made the Hindus aware of the Islamic message of equality and fraternity, they were so caste ridden that it elicited no positive response from them. As recorded in *The Discovery of India,* Islam 'produced powerful psychological reactions among the people and filled them with bitterness'. Nehru felt constrained further to remark: 'There was no objection to a new religion but there was strong objection to anything which forcibly interfered with and upset their way of life'.[4]

The Sikhs at this juncture were the fittest people whom in the active sense of the word Nehru wanted to be the addressee. He was arrested at Jaito in 1923. During his short internment he prepared a statement which he proposed to read in his self-defence in the court at Nabha.

The text of this 'statement' is available in a volume of the first series of *The Selected Works.* It is an eloquent expression of Nehru's admiration for the Sikhs, their indomitable courage and selfless sacrifice. In its concluding paragraph he rejoiced that he was being tried for a cause that 'the Sikhs had made their own'. He marvelled at 'the courage and sacrifice of the Sikhs' and wished for an opportunity to show his 'deep admiration for them by some form of service'. When the opportunity was there, he hoped to prove worthy of 'their high tradition and fine courage'.[5] To impart a proper climax to his enthusiastic admiration, he ended his statement with the traditional salutation of Sat Sri Akal which signifies the Sikh's faith in the invincibility of truth and its praxis.

The event convinced Nehru of the need to bring into the national fold the *morcha* launched by the Sikhs under the leadership of the Akalis. It was at his suggestion that a publicity-cell was set up at Amritsar for this purpose. He recommended the names of A.T. Gidwani and K.M. Pannikar for conducting the affairs of the publicity-cell. Their reports bore testimony to the fact that the basic hindrance in the way of the Sikh espousal of the national cause under the leadership of the Congress Party was the strain that prevailed between the Hindus and the Sikhs.

Nehru's perception of the communal strain revealed to him the negative feature of the Sikh-Hindu relationship. He realised that the Sikhs were obdurate and had no generous word or gesture for the people of the other community. This perception of their obduracy was fair enough but the historical reasons for the Sikhs adopting such an attitude are not articulated anywhere in his writings. He did not take adequate note of the fact that in the eighteenth and nineteenth centuries the Sikhs had waged relentless struggle both against the Mughal governors and the Afghan invaders. This struggle bore fruit in the form of sovereign Sikh rule in late eighteenth century and under Maharaja Ranjit Singh. It was for the first time that the Punjab felt itself as a sovereign entity. This sovereignty also laid claim to the fact that the Muslims and the Hindus comprising 90 per cent of the population accepted the political hegemony of the Sikhs. Likewise the Sikhs had no compunction in consenting to their cultural supremacy.

In his *Glimpses of World History,* Nehru had words of praise for Maharaja Ranjit Singh. To his engaged mind, Ranjit Singh's kingdom was 'a great Sikh state' that 'weakened and began to break up soon after his death'. Ruefully recollecting that it was not possible even for the later Mughals to suppress the Sikhs when they were a hunted minority group, he commented that it illustrated the old maxim: 'one rises in adversity and falls after a success is attained'.[6] 'By the time he came to write *The Discovery of India* his mind had got reflective enough. In this new state of mind he found Ranjit Singh's kingdom 'a marginal state' that could not succeed in the real struggle for supremacy against the British.[7] Both these observations are profound but they do not encompass the whole problematics of the Sikh kingdom and the traumatic impact of its end on the Sikh psyche. Rather than dialectical and historical, these observations entailed a positivistic perception.

For all the defining and redefining involved, Nehru did not articulate how this traumatic impact resulted in a sort of disorientation for the Sikhs. Howsoever vague, he had an inkling of this disorientation. That is why he felt that Sikh nationalism that arose from the end of the nineteenth century was only a 'sectional nationalism' working for a more distinct and separate existence. At the same time its negative aspect was offset by what he viewed as positive, that is, 'an amazing exhibition of courage and endurance'.[8] Thus an element of criticism, albeit a mild one, was added to his enthusiastic admiration for the Sikhs. As compared to this criticism, it was condemnation, though compas-sionate, that he reserved for the Hindus at this historical juncture. In the second volume of the series, he recorded the bitterness that the Hindus had invariably nurtured for the Muslims and the Sikhs. Characterising it as an essential feature of the Hindu psyche, he found that 'this bitterness of the Hindu against the Sikh and the Muslim' was chiefly due to 'the realisation of his utter weakness and humiliation'. The irony of the situation was that this bitterness, instead of urging him to better himself or make himself stronger, turned to 'hatred and curses'.

That his criticism did not get the better of Nehru's admiration for the Sikhs was proved by the deep regard that he had for their organising capacity. As compared to the Hindus and Muslims the Sikhs formed a minority, marginal in number to the multitude of the two majorities. All the same he found them invulnerable not because the Hindus and the Muslims were considerate but because the Sikhs were well-organised and even ready 'to defend themselves from unrighteous attacks'. He felt that the fissure in the Hindu-Sikh relations had deprived the Congress 'of much of the good of the Akali civil disobedience'. Since the Akali civil disobedience was something to be emulated, he wanted this fissure to end. He found that both the communities wanted this undesirable divide to go but nothing could be done because 'each was afraid of lowering its prestige by taking the first step'.[9]

The organising capacity of the Sikhs, he thought, could be useful both at the national and the international level. The national purpose could be served by bringing the *morcha* launched by the Sikhs under the hegemony of the Akalis into the broad framework of the satyagraha espoused and initiated by the Congress Party. To serve the international purpose, however, it was desirable to associate the Sikhs with the movement against imperialism.

In the third volume there is a letter by Nehru to an organiser of the Sikh League, presumably Mangal Singh Gill, suggesting 'it will suit the Sikh League better to become an associate body...of the league against Imperialism'. He conveyed this information to V. Chattopadhyaya who was then the most important Indian working for the Congress. At the same time, Nehru expressed the fear that the leaders concerned were 'hardly likely to pay much attention' to the matter because they seemed 'to have developed a very strong communal outlook'.[10]

For all his scepticism, Nehru cherished the hope that the Sikhs would advocate the cause of anti-fascism at the international level. That he had no such hope from the Hindus and Muslims is evident from the double spectre of fascism that he found lurking over India on the eve of the partition. In the first volume of *The Selected Works* in the second series, he confirmed the growth of fascist tendencies amongst the Hindus and the Muslims. It was his conviction that 'the two-pronged Indian fascism threatened to wipe out the proud culture and civilisation' of the country.

Regarding them as two opposing forces, he believed that the components of India's two-pronged fascism, mutually contributed to the growth of each other. Equi-distant in theoretical perspective, they did not provoke him in an equal measure. It was the Muslim fascism under the leadership of the Muslim League that in the first instance he was led to oppose after the formation of the Interim Government. He believed that 'the best manner in which the existing situation' could be improved was 'by educating the Muslim peasantry against the poisonous communal propaganda of the league'.

However, Nehru failed to embark on this ideological programme on account of communal riots in several parts of the country. He felt that any compromise with the Muslim League was impossible because its leaders had 'intellectual and mental affinity with senior Government officials like Governors'. In the event, 'mass slaughter, arson, burning of human beings, rapes, abduction on a large scale, forcible conversions and all manner of other things' exasperated him extremely. At the most he could hold out a general threat that if anybody has mistaken my silence, he does not know, or give a sermon in appreciation of 'courage and strength' along with the advice that they had to be directed to proper channels and not frittered away in outbursts of communal frenzy.[11]

The deteriorating situation in the country made Nehru so helpless that he felt like putting the whole blame on Hindu fascism. It seemed to him that 'the responsibility for the disturbances lies on the Hindus as they are in a majority'. He remained fraught with doubt, disillusion and agony. Caught in a predicament, he either condemned such psychic factors as animality, fear and 'anarchy of the mind' or involved self-sacrifice almost as a metaphysical panacea. Urging the students to do relief work, he solemnly remarked, 'I will congratulate the students if a few of them have to die in their endeavour to restore confidence'.[12]

That Nehru did not apprehend the growth of fascist tendency among the Sikhs is a factor of which the members of this community can be proud even at the present historical juncture. It is also a tribute to his secular outlook that is extremely difficult, if not impossible, to maintain in India even now. More so, it was difficult to maintain such a secular outlook before Independence when political activity was disposed to derive vital impulse from communal and religious considerations.

II

After Independence when Pakistan became a separate country and the Muslims claimed to have realised their destiny, Nehru's perception changed with regard to the Sikhs as well. Either his priorities changed or a deep disillusionment set in his mind about their intentions. From now onwards, he began to address the Hindus as his addressees of the active sort, with the Sikhs feeling themselves rendered passive recipients of his discourse. It was Nehru's perception perhaps that in the emergent situation, the Sikhs were no longer imperative for countering the Muslim communalism as they had been earlier. Feeling themselves thus reduced in significance, the Sikhs became self-centred and in this self-centredness Nehru decoded their disposition to imitate the Muslims. This decoding he magnified to the extent of feeling that the Sikhs posed a danger to the edifice of secularism that he sought to build so assiduously in the country.

No wonder, in Nehru's perception every claim put forth by the Sikhs became suspect. Even their genuine claims of which the one for the linguistic reorganisation of the Punjab was incontrovertible, became controversial. So much so that he got sceptical about the linguistic veracity of even the Punjabi language. In the thirteenth volume of the second series, he pointed out to Bhim Sen Sachar, the then Chief Minister of the Punjab, that 'Gurmukhi was not advanced to be a medium of instruction after the matriculation'. Here the substitution of Gurmukhi, the name of the script, for the Punjabi language, was rather strange. Then in a letter to C.M. Trivedi, the then Governor of the Punjab, he passed an inexcusable stricture on Punjabi literature itself. Without entertaining any doubt about his misinformation, verging on disinformation, he wrote: 'There is hardly any literature in Gurmukhi, so far as I know except some sacred literature'.[13] How one wishes that he had avoided the subterfuge of an immodest assertion through a modest claim. In his speech in the Lok Sabha delivered on 30 August 1961, he gave expression to his scepticism in a circumlocutory way. Reiterating that Punjabi was the language of Punjab, he referred to the usage of Persian script. He forgot that the Persian script was common with the Muslim writers whereas the non-Muslim writers had invariably employed the Gurmukhi script. Then he claimed that Punjabi was 'a home language'.[14] It was an ambiguous way of calling it a dialect. He forgot that Dogri, a dialect to which his Government awarded the status of language, was actually a spoken form of Punjabi. In fact, Punjabi under its ambience had several other dialects in the eastern and the western parts of the Punjab.

Nehru ardently championed Punjab's claim to literacy and progress. Perhaps he visualised some sort of a common culture to grow in the Punjab. May be, the Regional Formula was a measure in the same direction. The Regional Formula identified a Punjabi and a Hindi region. In the former region Punjabi was to be the primary language with Hindi as the secondary one. Likewise, in the latter region Hindi was to be the primary language and Punjabi as the secondary one. Both the regions were to be administered by two regional committees, claiming substantial powers. Nehru believed that with the implementation of the Regional Formula no further question would be left out from the language point of view. This was rather a wishful thinking because in recalcitrance he had to confess that what to speak of problems relating to power politics between the Hindus and the Sikhs, it did not even solve the language question. Symptomatic of it was the census of 1961 in which the Hindus settled in the Punjabi region were instigated to declare Hindi as their mother-tongue. In all candidness Nehru felt that 'it was not a truthful statement and it did a lot of harm'.

Holding the Akali Dal and certain Hindu organisations as equally guilty for causing this strain, the Congress had recourse to the policy of deferral. Smacking of manipulation in the vulgar sense of the word, this policy provided the Congress with political space for rule in the Punjab. The damage this rule caused to the social and cultural fabric was tremendous. Nehru, with all his subtlety and sobriety, failed to award hegemonic meaning to his own value-based strategy as distinct from the opportunistic policy of his party. As a result his vision of the Hindus and the Sikhs as 'interwoven like the warp and woof of a fabric' proved to be an illusion. No less illusory was the commitment he candidly articulated in the following words:

> What troubles me is that if we separate them applying the principle of division, we shall be tearing a finely woven tapestry into two bits and spoil it. Such a tearing process will have aweful consequences. Tearing up an integrated community into two is a terrible thing. With all my desire to be flexible, I find it impossible to adapt myself to the idea.[15]

Rather than grow into a resilient strategy to resolve the issue, this sort of thinking resulted in a diffident policy, meant to complicate it further. No wonder the Akalis got extremely desperate, launched one *morcha* after the other. They even talked in a vein sounding secessionist to chauvinistic ears. So the issue lingered on till Mrs Indira Gandhi made it explosive on the one hand by granting a truncated Punjabi Suba and on the other hand by dispossessing it of its resources.

III

Recapitulation of events after Nehru's death in 1964 shows that the policy to resolve this highly convoluted problem has been one step forward and two steps back. Nehru's diffidence was replaced by 'doubleness' that became more and more the hallmark of Indira Gandhi's policy. As one step forward, she accepted the demand for linguistic reorganisation of the Punjab. When the Punjabi state was actually reorganised it became evident that two steps had been taken backwards. Happy with the thought that their long cherished demand was accepted, the Sikhs felt nonetheless exasperated to find that the reorganised state was a truncated state. The exclusion of Chandigarh and other Punjabi speaking areas which were in the parent state under the Regional Formula, and the central control over water, disconcerted them so much that they felt cheated if not betrayed by the whole exercise.

To cover up the raw deal meted out to the reorganised state, Indira Gandhi had recourse to a subterfuge. To please the Sikhs, she played to the gallery by identifying her lineage with a cherished event in their history in utter disregard of historical veracity. In a speech on the occasion of the tri-centenary celebrations of the martyrdom of Guru Tegh Bahadur, known to have laid down his life for the religious cause of the Kashmiri Pandits, sought to underline her identification with the Sikh community. The Hindus of Kashmir had approached Guru Tegh Bahadur with the complaint that they were being forced to change their religion: 'That was the time when many families including mine were compelled to leave Kashmir and settle elsewhere so that they did not have to give up their religion'

The second sentence implied that her family too was beholden to the Guru for his martyrdom. It also owed a special gratitude to the savant who 'stood up not merely for his co-religionists but for followers of other religions also'.[16] Her observation was nothing less than a concoction. Jawaharlal Nehru has given an altogether different version of his ancestor's migration from his native land. It was several decades after the Guru's martydom that his ancestor 'came down from that mountain valley to seek fame and fortune in the rich plains below'.[17] Not religious oppression but search for fame and fortune was the motive for migration from Kashmir.

Indira Gandhi's speech gave no consolation to the Sikhs in their exasperation. Short of the inclusion of Chandigarh and the Punjabi-speaking areas into the reorganised state and the settlement of the river-waters dispute in accordance with the riparian principle, nothing could pacify and conciliate them. For Indira Gandhi this was an impossible proposition. So, in the Sikh psyche, the impression got ingrained that she was biased against the Punjabi Suba. The territorial issue and the water-dispute substantiate the charge. Rather than resolve Rajasthan's demand for water at the national level, she regarded it solely as a responsibility devolving upon the Punjab. In lieu of Chandigarh she insisted upon Punjabi area to be transferred to Haryana though the Regional Formula had specified it for the parent state.

As a diversionary tactic, Indira Gandhi encouraged the Akali leaders to raise in the first instance the so-called religious demands. They would readily succumb to this temptation, dictated partly by their political naivety and partly by their vested interests. Hypothetical as those religious demands were, she had no hesitation in accepting them. She would have no compunction then in using this acceptance as a gloss to cover her duplicity in respect of the substantial demands of the reorganised state. Thus on 4 July 1984, when replying to discussion on the White Paper on the Punjab she was in a tight corner, the acceptance of the so-called religious demands came to her rescue almost as a reprieve. As certified by her, they pertained to (a) banning of intoxicants in Amritsar, (b) relaying of *kirtan* on All India Radio from the Golden Temple, (c) permission for Sikh passengers to carry *kirpan* on domestic flights, and (d) an All-India Gurdwara Bill for awarding control to the SGPC of all historical *gurdwaras* situated in India.

It is doubtful whether orders to the effect have been carried out though over twelve years have gone by since their acceptance was announced. Whether any advantage would have accrued to Sikhism and the Sikh community from their acceptance is a matter of even more doubtful conjecture. Only the All India Gurdwara Bill might have made a difference and for that reason perhaps absolutely nothing has happened on that score. Indira Gandhi did of course get the opportunity to forward a claim of this sort: 'I was specially pleased that my relationship with the Sikh community was a close one and a very friendly one. And I cannot imagine that any Sikh should think that I would do anything, that I would be responsible for anything that could hurt their feelings'.[18]

Supposing a grain of truth to be there in what she pleaded, the point to know is as to who gave the hurt and that too to the extent of destroying the Akal Takht, burning the Sikh Museum and the Reference Library, and destroying so many valuable gifts and rare manuscripts. Since all this destruction could not be wished away at will, so she had to explain it and that she did by a characteristic ambiguity which actually explains nothing:

I do not want to go into the details of who built up whom because no body built up any person. It is the situation and the circumstances which built up a person and that person took advantage of it; whether he really was in control of the situation himself, I am not in a position to say. If I did not take any names it was because of this. Otherwise also I rarely take names. But I feel there were certain forces behind these happenings, some may be within the country, some be outside.[19]

In this paragraph, a demonic person, presumably Sant Jarnail Singh Bhindranwale, was being valorised and rendered anonymous. The motive to valorise him and render him anonymous was not stated but her innocent denial was substantiating it as if through textual subversion. So the problem before her was retrospectively to obliterate his links with the Congress Party. What better method could there be for that than portray herself as a 'damsel-in-distress'.

Adept in this tactic, she portrayed herself as a person who had suffered so much abuse:

I have said before in this House and I say it again that I have heard abuse since I was a small child. I have had falsehood flung against my family and those were the days when I used to lose my temper. But long ago, I had decided that it was not worth my while losing my temper with such people.

As if the domestic and social context was not enough, she related to it the international context as well: 'How is it that all these forces are directed against me? Against India also, but more especially against me'.

This scenario, more appropriate for a damsel-in- distress in a film, was not suited to the world of politics in which violent forces unleashed by her were intent upon her elimination. She was eliminated by her own security-guards. She left her mantle to a young man whose sole qualification rested in being a prince-charming. He tried to solve a political problem by state terror. After his cruel death, this policy has been implemented further with devilish skill. So the Punjab is back to normal as it is claimed by all and sundry. If now there is nothing wrong with this long suffering land, it is perhaps in the sense in which Bertolt Brecht wrote of Germany by invoking her through an addressor who had nothing wrong with him/her:

For nothing
Can be wrong with me if I myself
Am nothing.[20]

NOTES

1. Jawahar Lal Nehru's corpus comprises *Glimpses of World History, An Autobiography, The Discovery of India, A Bunch of Old Letters, Jawaharlal Nehru's Speeches* (4 Vols), *Selected Works of Jawaharlal Nehru* (10 Vols) first series, *Selected Works of Jawaharlal Nehru* second series, of which 14 volumes have so far appeared. Meticulously edited by the distinguished historian S. Gopal, they will hopefully be more than 50 in number. The writer of this paper has published 20 review articles in *The Tribune* on these volumes and other writings published on Jawaharlal Nehru during the last ten years.

2. *Jawaharlal Nehru's Speeches* (1957-63). New Delhi: Publications Division, 1964, IV, 20.

3. *Selected Works of Jawaharlal Nehru* (second series). New Delhi: Jawaharlal Nehru Memorial Fund, 1986, IV, 269.

4. *The Discovery of India.* Calcutta: Signet Press, 248.

5. *Selected Works of Jawaharlal Nehru* (first series). New Delhi: Orient and Longman, 1976 (reprint), I, 375.

6. *Glimpses of World History.* Bombay: Asia Publishing House, 1967 (reprint), 424.

7. *The Discovery of India,* 290.

8. *Glimpses of World History,* 747.

9. *Selected Works* (first series), II, 138, 151.

10. Ibid, III, 137, 148.

11. *Selected Works* (second series), I, 26, 51, 53.

12. Ibid, 57, 87.

13. Ibid, XIII.

14. *Speeches,* 15.

15. Ibid, 17, 18, 19.

16. *Selected Speeches and Writings of Indira Gandhi 1971-1977.* New Delhi: Publications Division, Ministry of Information and Broadcasting, 1984, 832.

17. *An Autobiography.* London: The Badley Head, 1936, 1.

18. *Selected Speeches and Writings* (January 1982- October 1984). New Delhi, 1986, V, 79.

19. Ibid, 86.

20. Bertolt Brecht, *Poems.* Ed. John Willet. London: Eyre Methuen, 1976, 452.

4

The Punjab Congress

P. S. VERMA

It may be pointed out at the outset that the Congress Party in Punjab before partition did not command much influence among Muslims, Hindus or Sikhs. Not until the 1946 general elections, when the Muslim community united behind the Muslim League, did the Hindu community and a large part, but not a majority, of the Sikh community vote for the Congress Party. Prior to this, the Unionist Party had monopolised the Muslim support. The Akalis were a force among the Sikhs and certain communal groups wielded considerable influence among the Hindus, particularly in the urban areas. The Congress Party has been able to make some advance in mobilising support of the people only after 1947.

The Congress Party won around 60 per cent assembly seats in the first three general elections in 1952,1957 and 1962. Even the Akali Dal's 'warlike' campaign over the issue of Punjabi Suba in 1962 failed to win more than 19 seats with only 11.7 per cent votes in the entire state. This was, comparatively, lower than the Akali Dal's performance of 33 seats with 14.7 per cent votes in the 1952 assembly elections. The divisions within the Akali Dal and its merger in the Congress in 1956 by the efforts of Partap Singh Kairon, the then Chief Minister of Punjab, might have basically contributed to the decline of the Akalis in 1962. However, certain pro-Akali stances of Partap Singh Kairon had created a strong resentment among the Hindus, particularly in the Haryana belt, as a result of which the number of Congress seats also declined from 122 in 1952 to 90 in 1962. Interestingly enough, this gave a big boost to the Jana Sangh Party whose tally increased from 2 in 1952 to 9 seats in 1962. However, the Congress continued to maintain its hold in Punjab till the reorganisation of the state in 1966. Since 1966, the Congress Party has won three out of seven assembly elections but it has lost considerable support. Its all-Punjab character became doubtful over the years. The present paper examines the electoral performance of the Congress Party and the social profile of its legislators elected to seven consecutive assemblies since 1 November 1966.

I

The support structure of the party in the state has considerably weakened and the alternative is provided by the Akalis. Till the sixth assembly elections of September 1985 the alternative could emerge only in the form of an alliance or coalition, consisting of diverse groups such as the Akali Dal, Jana Sangh, Janata Party and the Communist Parties.These coalitions were, however, always led by the Akali Dal. In the 1985 elections, the Akali Dal on its own achieved a spectacular victory and emerged triumphant, capturing as many as 73 out of 115 seats. The Dal contested only 100 seats and polled 38.5 per cent of the total votes cast during the September elections. The Congress Party could win only 32 seats – almost half its strength of 63 in the previous assembly elections held in June 1980. The fall of the Congress vote from 45.2 per cent in 1980 to 37.9 per cent in 1985 could be seen as a big jolt to the party in the state. The Akali Dal, though it contested 15 seats less than the Congress, had an edge over the Congress and managed to secure 0.7 per cent more valid votes than the Congress (I). Interestingly, while calculating the percentage of valid votes polled by the Akali Dal in the 100 seats that it contested, it was found that the Dal had secured as much as 44.03 per cent of the valid votes polled in these constituencies. There was an impression that in 1985 the Congress wanted to hand over power to the Akalis so that they would tackle the problem of terrorism on their own. It may be true. But the ground reality in the state was such that any amount of seriousness on the part of the Congress would have hardly mattered.

Before the 1985 elections, the Congress Party had always secured a higher percentage of popular votes than the others in all the state assembly elections: 37.5 per cent of the total valid votes cast in 1967, 39.2 per cent in 1969, and 42.1 per cent in 1972. This, as a matter of fact, was considerably higher than the score of the other contending parties, including the Akali Dal, the major rival of the Congress Party in the state. Even in the 1977 state assembly elections, when the number of Congress MLAs was reduced to 17 and the party was nowhere near the 58 seats won by the Akalis, its poll percentage of 33.6 was still higher than that of the Akali Dal's 31.4 per cent. It may be mentioned here that the Congress Party in 1977 had contested only 96 seats whereas in 1985 it contested all the 115 seats for which the elections were held.

In the February 1992 elections, the Congress claimed a landslide victory but the major Akali groups had boycotted these elections. It was, of course, a blunder that they committed. Besides the boycott, the poll was held in an extremely adverse condition which obviously affected the polling, particularly in the countryside, in a big way. The polling was as low as 24.2 per cent for the state assembly and 22.9 per cent for the Parliamentary seats. Only 10.2 per cent, i.e. 13,16,062 votes were cast in favour of the Congress out of a total of 1,29,18,558, votes in the state. However, the Congress won as many as 74.4 per cent of the state assembly seats and 92.3 per cent of the Lok Sabha seats. Although a turning point, these polls fell far short of gaining popular support of the people as most of them, particularly in the countryside, stayed indoors and did not participate in the voting process. On account of meagre polling, some critics called the state assembly 'an apology' for a representative democratic body. Subsequently, the late Beant Singh left no stone unturned for gaining support of Punjab peasantry and made definite inroads into the countryside during the Panchayat elections and assembly and Parliamentary by-polls but a clear picture could emerge only in the next general elections.

From Table 1 given at the end it is clear that the electoral performance of the Congress Party during the two assembly elections, i.e. 1972 and 1980, has been the most significant and satisfactory since the formation of the present state of Punjab. The political parties such as the Akali Dal and Jana Sangh/BJP which usually derive their maximum electoral support on the basis of religio-lingual, regional and other primordial considerations, failed to mobilize enough support in their favour during these two elections. The major factor in their failure to muster sufficient support during both these elections was, probably, their own failure in providing a better and stable government to the people when they had been in power in 1967-71 and 1977-80. This enabled the Congress to regain people's support and woo them in its favour during the 1972 and 1980 assembly elections. The convenient and populistic slogans – 'stability' and 'Garibi Hatao' in 1972 and 'elect the government that works' in 1980 – made it easier for the Congress to win as many as 63.5 per cent of the assembly seats in 1972, and 53.8 per cent in 1980.

On the contrary, the Akali Dal, which had won 43 seats in 1969 and 58 in 1977, got 24 seats in 1972 and 37 in 1980. Moreover, compared with the previous poll percentage, it lost 1.8 per cent of the valid votes in 1972 and 4.5 per cent in 1980. Similarly, the Jana Sangh which had won 9 seats with 9.8 per cent of the valid votes in 1967 and 8 seats with 9.0 per cent in 1969 failed to win even a single seat out of 33 it contested during 1972 assembly elections. Its poll percentage was also reduced to 4.9 in 1972. The Janata Party, which in the case of Punjab basically represented the erstwhile Jana Sangh Party, had obtained 25 assembly seats with 14.93 per cent valid votes in 1977. However, it lost its credibility among the voters and got split into groups. Thus the BJP, which contested 41 assembly constituencies in 1980, could win only one seat and failed to secure more than 6.43 per cent of the valid votes polled in the state. The performance of the Jana Sangh/ BJP in 1972 and 1980 stood at the lowest ever in the post-reorganised state of Punjab. It went even lower than its performance in the pre-reorganised Punjab wherein it had won 4 seats with 7.7 per cent of the total valid votes cast in the Punjabi speaking region in 1962.

However, the Akali Dal, though it faced frequent splits and divisions and also failed to provide a stable government whenever it came to power, did not suffer to the extent the Jana Sangh did during the two elections. The Akali Dal has never been reduced to its position of 1962 when it won only 19 seats with 19.9 per cent valid votes cast in the composite state of Punjab. The Congress Party, though it achieved a spectacular victory in 1972 by winning 66 seats (including one uncontested seat) out of 104 in the House, and also helped its election ally (the CPI) in winning as many as 10 seats (highest ever for the CPI in Punjab), could not significantly affect the Akali Dal's base in the countryside. The Akalis still secured 24 seats with 27.6 per cent of valid votes cast in 1972. These seats mostly represented the Sikh peasantry from the Malwa region.

The Akalis contested only 72 seats out of the total 104 in the House in 1972. It will be relevant to mention here that the Akali Dal did not contest the elections as a united force in 1972. It was rather split into three groups out of which two – the Akali Dal (Sant) and the Akali Dal (Gurnam Singh) – entered the election fray. Gurnam Singh had headed the Akali-led coalition ministry in Punjab between

March 1967 and November 1967 and from February 1969 to March 1970. The Gurnam Singh faction unsuccessfully contested only four seats in 1972 but factional manifestations in the Dal during the elections certainly affected its position among the electorate.

Most interestingly, 91.7 per cent seats out of the total seats that the Akali Dal had won in 1972 were from the Malwa region. Some parts of this region have greatly prospered and the landed Sikh aristocracy has acquired a dominant position in the Akali Dal in particular and the Panthic politics in general. Owing to the increasing hold of the Akalis in the countryside, the base of the Congress Party, barring the Hindu dominated areas of the Malwa region, started facing an erosion. As a matter of fact, during a majority of the assembly elections in the post-reorganisation period, the Akali Dal has been able to win over half of the seats from this region. Moreover, out of the total seats which the Akalis have won in the various state assemblies, 76.9 per cent in 1967, 65.1 per cent in 1969, 91.7 per cent in 1972, 62.1 in 1977, 59.5 per cent in 1980 and 65.7 per cent in 1985 belonged to the Malwa region. This points to two broad features of Akali politics: (a) an emerging role of the organised landed class, and (b) the strong and stable regional base of a religion-based party in the present state of Punjab. The big landowners in Punjab, whatever their number, are largely concentrated in some districts of the Malwa region. This region, in fact, has bacome the hub of Akali politics in the post-reorganisation period. Some large landowners belong to the Congress Party also but their influence over the Sikh peasantry seems to be less significant. They can put up a challenge to the Akalis only with the support of Hindu voters. However, the Akalis do not wield such a significant influence over the Sikh peasantry in the Majha and the Doaba regions where the landholdings are also relatively much smaller. The 1985 elections were an exception for an obvious reason.

The gains of the Congress in the 1972 elections were relatively more strident and significant in the areas dominated by the Hindus. Almost all the urban and semi-urban constituencies in the state have preponderant Hindu population. In addition, some of the districts such as Jalandhar and Hoshiarpur are Hindu majority districts. The Hindus also form a sizable group in certain other districts. For example, according to the 1981 census, Hindus comprise 48.1 per cent of the total population in the Gurdaspur district, 44.3 per cent in Firozpur, 42.3 per cent in Patiala and 41.8 per cent in Ropar. In electoral performance the Akali Dal in these areas in most of the elections has lagged behind the Congress. The Jana Sangh had considerable following among the Hindu voters in certain urban areas such as Jalandhar, Amritsar, Pathankot and Ludhiana. But it was completely routed in the 1972 general elections. To a certain degree, its coming closer to the Akali Dal and its dismal performance while in power with the Akalis, has, more than any other factor, alienated the Punjabi Hindus from it. Moreover, in the Sikh majority state of Punjab the Jana Sangh, which exclusively depended on the Hindu trading community, could not have helped to become a powerful rival of the Akali Dal. Therefore, the support of most of the Punjabi Hindus to the Congress Party in 1977 has by and large continued.

However, with the increasing hold of the Akali Dal over the Sikh peasantry, the representative character of the Congress Party has been considerably undermined. Gradually, its base, to a considerable extent, has shifted to and got concentrated and stabilised in the areas dominated by the Hindus and Harijans. In brief, it would not be an exaggeration to say that the electoral base of the Congress Party has steadily become Hinduised and got concentrated in certain districts where the Hindus and Harijans form the major chunck of the population. A large number of the seats won by the Congress Party in each assembly in the post-reorganisation period have been from districts such as Hoshiarpur, Gurdaspur, Firozpur, Ropar and Patiala. Factually speaking, 64.5 per cent of the Congress seats in 1967, 60.5 per cent in 1969, 63.6 in 1972, 82.4 in 1877, 58.7 in 1980 and 56.3 per cent in 1985 came from these districts.

Interestingly, if we focus our analysis on the major towns which fall in the categories of class I and II, it would be found that the Congress has been able to win most of the assembly seats representing these areas. The 1977 elections, during which the Congress was reduced to a skeleton, were, of course, an exception to this. In the 1980 assembly elections the Congress won 23 (92 per cent) out of the total 25 seats belonging to these 16 major towns of the state. Similarly, it won 15 (60 per cent) of them in the elections held in 1985. The percentage of these urban seats out of the total seats won by the Congress Party during these two elections became as high as 36.5 in 1980 and 46.9 in 1985. It may be mentioned here that total assembly seats in these towns do not exceed 21.4 per cent of the 117 seats in the House. Thus the Congress Party's score in the bigger towns dominated by Hindus has become crucial and decisive. Since these constituencies have mainly Hindu electorate, the Akali Dal generally does not put up candidates for most of them. In 1985, however, the Akalis won 5 seats out of these 25 constituencies, but these were won by Hindu candidates who were not formal members of the Akali Dal .

Besides the bigger towns in the state, we have also calculated the voting percentage of the Congress Party on the basis of its performance in other Hindu dominated areas, though only for the 1980 and 1985 assembly elections. These elections represented two trends: in 1980 the Congress romped home with a clear majority but in 1985 it got badly mauled by the Akalis. In the Hindu dominated areas the performance of the Congress during both these elections has been significant. A close look at the figures in terms of rural-urban voting pattern reveals that the Congress Party in elections would have been left only with a few seats had there been no adequate support for it in the urban and other Hindu dominated areas. As many as 26 seats out of 32, won by the Congress in the 1985 elections, were won from areas preponderantly dominated by the Hindu and Harijan voters.

However, a section of Harijans has drifted away from the Congress and extended support to the newly formed Dalit Soshit Sangharsh Samaj Samiti which has emerged as the BSP. In the Doaba region where the proportion of scheduled castes in the total population comes to over 33 per cent, this group has challenged the Congress (I). Strikingly, the proportion of the scheduled castes in the Jalandhar district happens to be 36.3 per cent. In 1985 the Dalit candidates did not win any seat but in the Doaba region they polled more than one lakh votes, which otherwise would have gone to the Congress candidates. This drift of the scheduled caste voters away from the Congress in the recent elections gave maximum benefit to the Akalis in the rural constituencies. The Akali Dal had captured 6 assembly seats out of the total of 12 in the Jalandhar district which in itself appeared to be a record in the electoral history of the state. The Congress lost at least four assembly seats in the Jalandhar district. The Dalit candidates got 6190 votes in Nakodar,11,006 in Banga, 13,573 in Nurmahal and 5738 in Phillaur. All these four seats were snatched by the Akali Dal by low margins. For example, in Nakodar the Congress candidate lost by 2016 votes, in Banga by only 728, in Nurmahal by 2166 and Phillaur by 2469 votes. In the 1992 assembly polls the BSP won as many as six seats from the Doaba region. This shows that the constituency of scheduled castes may no longer stay with the Congress in the state.

II

In the context of this analysis, systematic study of the Congress legislative elite in the Punjab also becomes relevant. We may examine the socio-economic background of the Congress legislators elected to the state assemblies since the formation of the present state of Punjab. The variables of analysis include: age, religion, caste, sex, rural/urban background, occupation, past legislative experience and education of the Congress MLAs. Much of what follows is based on information available in the Who's Who of the legislative assemblies and the data collected through personal interviews with some individuals, supplemented by information gathered from various sources such as newspapers, periodicals, the Congress office (Chandigarh) and other knowledgeable persons.

AGE

With regard to age, the legislators under study have been distributed into three broad groups: (a) 25-40 years, (b) 41-55 years; and (c) 56 years and above. In each case the age has been counted on the basis of the date a legislator was elected to the state assembly. As regards the numerical proportion of the aforesaid age group, Table 4 reveals that the middle age group of 41-55 years has been preponderant among the Congress legislators. While the lowest ever for this age group was 40.6 per cent in 1985, the highest was in 1969 when as many as 81.1 per cent of the Congress legislators represented the middle age category. Incidentally, any rise or fall in the strength of this age group has been in inverse proportion to the fall or rise in the strength of the younger and older age group MLAs. The lowest ever for these two age groups was in the 1969 state assembly when only 10.8 per cent MLAs belonged to the younger age group and 8.1 per cent to the older age category. Likewise, the highest happened to be in 1985 when 28.1 per cent of the Congress MLAs represented the younger age group and 31.3 per cent of the older age category.

BACKGROUND OF THE YOUNGER AGE GROUP

In terms of their socio-economic and political background most of the younger age group MLAs in the state assembly have come from the relatively prestigious and privileged sections having considerable standing in the state and local level politics. Factually speaking many of the youngsters represent the well-known state or local level political families, being blood-relations of ex-MLAs and ministers. Economically, most of them represent relatively better-off families. Even the scheduled caste members of this age group represent the relatively better-off families of old Congress ministers, class I officers etc.

RELIGION

Prior to the 1980 assembly the majority of the Congress MLAs were recruited from the Sikh community. So much so that the percentage of the Sikh Congress MLAs in the 1967 state assembly was as high as 68.7. But since then there has been a constant rise in the proportion of the Hindus among the Congress MLAs. Out of the total Congress MLAs there were only 29.2 per cent Hindus in 1967, but their strength increased to 59.4 per cent in the 1985 state assembly.

CASTE

While looking into the caste background of the Congress legislators, it was found that during the 1960s and 70s the Jat-Sikhs formed the single largest caste group in the state assembly. In the case of the 1967 assembly, almost half (i.e. 47.9 per cent) of the total Congress MLAs were Jat-Sikhs. Their proportion continued to remain over 42 per cent upto the 1972 state assembly. But in 1977 it decreased to 35.3 per cent and further fell sharply in the 1980 and 1985 elections. On the contrary, the proportion of the urban caste groups such as Brahman, Bania, Khatri and Arora which was only 16.7 per cent in 1967 became double in 1980. In the 1985 assembly, it went up to 43.8 per cent.

URBAN/RURAL BACKGROUND

There has been a consistent rise in the strength of the urban group among the Congress MLAs. This somehow indicates that the influence of the Congress Party in the urban Hindu dominated constituencies has been steadily growing whereas its base in the rural areas is shrinking. In the assemblies of 1967 and 1969 the proportion of the Congress MLAs from the rural constituencies was as high as 66.7 and 64.9 per cent, respectively. But this trend during the 1970s began to face an erosion and further fell sharply in the 1980s. Interestingly, the percentage of Congress MLAs from the urban constituencies became as high as 50.8 in 1980 and 62.5 in 1985. Such an erosion of the Congress base in the countryside may be mainly attributed to the growing alienation of the Sikh peasantry from the Congress organisation. It will be interesting to mention here that out of the total 12 rural constituencies which were won by the Congress in the September 1985 elections, five were preponderantly dominated by the Hindu and Harijan voters. Of the remaining, three were reserved seats and one was won by a prominent Jat-Sikh Congress leader whose family, barring only a few occasions, has been representing the area from the first general elections onwards. The rest of the three rural constituencies (Nawan Shahar, Majitha and Beas) won by the Congress in 1985, incidentally, fall in the Doaba and Majha regions which were traditionally considered to be the strongholds of the Congress Party.

OCCUPATION

The Congress legislators under study encompass a wide variety of occupational groupings. However, in many cases it has been found that the legislators instead of representing a pure occupational category practice multiple professions. As an example, those who fall in the category of agriculturists have also taken up other occupations such as legal practice and multifarious business activities involving transport, poultry, dairy, horse-breeding, cinema houses, petrol pumps, liquor contracts, rice-shellers, cold storages, cooperative sugar mills etc. In such cases we have categorised them on the basis of their main sources of income. According to this, 43.7 per cent of the Congress MLAs in 1985 represented the business category. Next to them, 31.3 per cent fell in the category of professionals such as legal and medical practitioners, journalists, civil engineers, school and college teachers. The proportion of agriculturists came to only 21.9 per cent in the 1985 assembly. Interestingly, among those who represent the business category some happened to be among the leading industrialists, transporters and contractors. Similarly, among the agriculturists a few were among the leading landlords in the state. The leading landowners, however, are not confined to the traditional agricultural activities and have diversified into other occupations such as horse-breeding, poultry, transport and the like.

In the case of the 1980 assembly also the number of business class MLAs was relatively larger than that of the other occupational categories, including the agriculturists. But prior to this, the proportion of agriculturists among the Congress MLAs had been higher than the other groups. So that in the 1969 state assembly, half of the Congress legislators were recruited from the class of agriculturists. This indicates that the group of agriculturists among the Congress legislators remained dominant and stable during the sixties and seventies but in the 1980s it has faced a sharp decline. This resulted in the preponderance of MLAs following urban occupations such as business and professions. It was also reflected in the religious and caste composition of the Congress MLAs as the proportion of Hindus and non-Jat-Sikhs among them in the assembly had become decisive. This may be attributed to the factor of Akalis' increasing hold over the Jat-Sikh peasantry of Punjab in particular and over the other caste groups of Sikhs in general.

EDUCATION

Barring only a few state assemblies (as in 1969 and 1972) there has been a constant rise in the proportion of MLAs who obtained college and university education. In the 1967 assembly the percentage of Congress legislators representing the category of graduates and above was 41.7. In the 1977, 1980, 1985 and 1992 assemblies their representation rose to 47.1, 46.6, 62.5 and 60.92 respectively.

Postscript

In the Parliamentary polls of November 1989, the Congress was trounced by the Akali Dal associated with Simranjit Singh Mann. The two other Akali Dals, 'Badal' and 'Longowal', failed to win any seat. The Akali Dal Mann, which contested eight seats out of thirteen, captured six seats with 29.2 per cent valid votes. The Congress contested all the thirteen seats but won only two, with 26.5 per cent votes. The valid votes polled by the Akali Dal (B) and Akali Dal (L) were as low as 5.3 and 1.3 per cent, respectively. The BJP lost all the three seats it contested and got no more than 4.2 per cent valid votes. The results, on the whole, were seen as reflecting the pressure of militancy in the state.

Militancy was receding by February 1992 when fresh elections were held. The Congress won a 'landslide' victory because the Akalis in general boycotted the polls. The Congress felt jittery about the under-represented character of its government. The total turnout was as low as 24.2 per cent for the state assembly and 22.9 per cent for the Parliamentary seats. Only 10.2 per cent votes were cast in favour of the ruling Congress out of the total 1,29,18,558 voters in the state, though the Congress got 74.4 per cent of the votes polled for the state assembly and 92.3 per cent for the Lok Sabha. The critics looked upon the state assembly as 'an apology for a representative democratic body'. To remove this stigma, the Congress went for the Municipal elections in September 1992 in which 70 per cent urban voters cast their votes. Thereafter the Congress Chief Minister, Beant Singh, mounted an all out offensive against the militants and the Akalis of all hues. In January 1993, elections to the village Panchayats were held. The turnout of voters was as high as 82 per cent. The Akalis also participated in the Panchayat polls. With these elections, the militant violence lost ground and virtually disappeared. The people accorded full recognition to Beant Singh and his close associates. Beant Singh could claim that 72 per cent of the elected Panches and Sarpanches were Congressites. The Akalis failed to pose any serious challenge to the ruling Congress in the Parliamentary by-poll in Jalandhar in May 1993. The Akali Dal (B) candidate was trounced by the large margin of 1,15,984 votes.

However, the peace-card failed to sustain the tempo in favour of the Congress for long. The growing state of corruption, nepotism, infighting, police atrocities, credibility gap, and knocks from the judiciary started spoiling the gains obtained from the restoration of peace and normalcy. In the three subsequent by-elections of May 1994 and June 1995, the Congress succeeded only at Nakodar with a margin of merely 10,314 votes. In the other two by-polls, that is Ajnala and Giddarbaha, the Congress was defeated by the Akali Dal (B) by a margin of 10,314 and 2,115 votes, respectively. Among other things, these victories heralded the revival of moderate Akalis and put the Congress on the defensive. Badal adopted extremely moderate postures focused on peace, Hindu-Sikh unity, Punjabiat and nationalist-secularist idiom. He rejected the controversial 'Amritsar declaration' and discarded the traditional Akali appeals to emotive issues. He asserted that the rejection of the Congress in Ajnala and Giddarbaha by-polls was not only a verdict against Beant Singh's government but also 'an eye-opener to his Akali friends who were misusing religion for their own vested interests'. Badal's moderate line not only restored his hold over the Sikh peasantry but also threatened the Congress in its Hindu strongholds. The assassination of Beant Singh on 31 August 1995 made the Congress virtually leaderless in the state. The Congress was totally disarrayed and acutely factionalised.

In the Parliamentary polls of April 1996, the Congress won only two seats (Gurdaspur and Amritsar), with 35.1 per cent of valid votes. In the remaining 11 seats it was defeated by the Akali Dal (B) - BSP alliance. This new alliance between the landowning peasantry and the landless lower classes in the state was first formed in the wake of the Giddarbaha by-poll in June 1995. It took away the traditional Scheduled Caste voters from the Congress in its strongholds, particularly in the Doaba region. The Akalis won 8 and BSP 3 seats, with 38.1 per cent votes. Erosion in the support base of the Congress (I) in the other states also had an impact on its electoral prospects in Punjab. The displacement of the party from power at the Centre in 1996 further damaged its electoral performance. This was clearly revealed in the polls of February 1997. There were three broad alliances in the elections : the SAD (B) and BJP, the Congress (I) and CPI, and the SAD (Mann) and BSP. The last alliance was formed when much of political ground was captured by the other two combinations. The SAD (M) - BSP alliance was aimed at cutting into the vote-banks of the other two major alliances. This strategy worked more against the Congress because the BSP snatched away more than 13 per cent votes in 67 seats that it contested. These votes could have gone otherwise to the Congress nominees. Had the BSP aligned with the Congress, both of them would have retained a couple of more seats in their respective strongholds. As the SAD (B) - BJP alliance started gaining ground, the Hindu voter of the Congress also became indifferent to its claim to have restored normalcy and revived democracy in the strife-torn state. Most voters perceived in fact that the SAD (B) - BJP alliance would perform better in the peace-building process through Hindu-Sikh amity. Furthermore, the image of the Congress among the voters in respect of development activities, administrative matters and job avenues was quite low. The party experienced the worst-ever electoral performance in the state in 1997. It secured only 14 seats with 26.6 per cent valid votes, which was worse than its performance in 1977 when the party had secured 17 seats with 33.4 per cent valid votes.

By contrast, the SAD (B) and BJP saw the best-ever performance, securing 75 and 18 Assembly seats, respectively. The Congress was routed in its strongholds of the Doaba and Majha regions. The bulk of Hindu and Scheduled Caste voters shifted their loyalty to the BJP and the BSP. At its low ebb, the Congress failed to put up a candidate in the Qila Raipur Assembly by-election held in June 1997.

TABLE 1

Electoral Performance of Political Parties in the Assembly Elections in Punjab (1967-1992)

Year	Congress		Akali Dal		JS/ BJP		CPI-CPM		Janata Party	
	Seats	VV*	Seats	VV	Seats	VV	Seats	VV	Seats	VV
1967	48	37.5	26	24.7	9	9.8	8	8.4	–	–
1969	38	39.2	43	29.4	8	9.0	6	7.9	–	–
1972	65	42.1	24	27.6	–	4.9	11	9.8	–	–
1977	17	33.6	58	31.4	–	–	15	10.1	25	14.9
1980	63	45.2	37	26.9	1	6.4	14	10.8	–	3.2
1985	32	37.9	73	38.5	6	4.4	1	6.4	1	1.0
1992	87									

* Stands for the percentage of valid votes.

TABLE 2

Congress Party's Electoral Performance in the Sikh and Hindu majority areas (1980 and 1985)

Nature of Constituencies	Total valid votes polled		Valid votes polled by the Congress Party	
	1980	1985	1980	1985
Rural constituencies where the Sikhs have edge over others	38,14,331 (43.6)	41,49,840 (35.3)	16,63,587	14,68,008
Urban/Towns constituencies where the Hindus have edge over Sikhs	24,37,695 (47.8)	26,74,518 (41.7)	11,64,120	11,15,542
Total	62,52,026	68,24,358	28,27,707 (45.2)	25,83,550 (37.9)

TABLE 3

Region-wise Performance of the Congress Party in the Assembly Elections (1980 and 1985)

Region	Total valid votes polled		Valid votes polled by Congress Party	
	1980	1985	1980	1985
Majha	13,83,850	14,37,983	6,38,307 (46.1)	5,64,186 (39.2)
Doaba	13,04,043	13,56,056	5,87,772 (45.1)	5,62,946 (41.5)
Malwa	35,64,133	40,30,319	16,01,628 (44.9)	14,56,418 (36.1)
Total	62,52,026	68,24,358	28,27,707 (45.2)	25,83,550 (37.8)

TABLE 4

Age-wise Distribution of the Congress MLAs (in percentage)

Age	1967	1969	1972	1977	1980	1985	1992
25-40 years	27.1	10.8	16.7	11.8	25.4	28.1	17.24
41-55 years	52.1	81.1	60.6	70.6	44.4	40.6	55.17
56 & above	20.8	8.1	22.7	17.6	30.2	31.3	27.59
Seats	48	37	66	17	63	32	87

TABLE 5

Religious Composition of Congress MLAs (in percentage)

Religion	1967	1969	1972	1977	1980	1985	1992
Hindus	29.2	31.6	37.9	47.1	50.8	59.4	33.3
Sikhs	68.7	65.8	60.6	52.9	47.6	40.6	66.7
Muslims	2.1	—	1.5	—	1.6	—	—

TABLE 6

Caste- Composition of Congress MLAs
(in percentage)

Caste	1967	1969	1972	1977	1980	1985	1992
Brahman, Bania, Khatri Arora etc.	16.7	18.4	24.2	23.5	31.7	43.8	24.14
Jat Sikhs,	47.9	42.1	43.9	35.3	28.6	18.8	44.83
Hindu Jats, Kamboj, Ramgarhia etc.	14.6	13.2	12.1	23.5	19.1	6.2	9.19
Scheduled Castes	20.8	23.7	19.7	17.7	20.6	31.2	21.84
Seats	48	38	66	17	63	32	87

TABLE 7

Urban/Rural Composition of Congress MLAs
(in percentage)

Background	1967	1969	1972	1977	1980	1985
Urban	33.3	34.2	50.0	47.1	50.8	62.5
Rural	66.7	63.2	50.0	52.9	49.2	37.5
NR	—	2.6	—	—	—	—
Total	48	38	66	17	63	32

TABLE 8

Occupational Composition of Congress MLAs
(in percentage)

Occupation	1967	1969	1972	1977	1980	1985	1992
Business	22.7	23.7	33.3	41.2	44.4	43.7	24.14
Agriculture	45.8	50.0	42.4	47.0	38.1	21.9	56.32
Profession	20.8	21.0	19.7	11.8	14.3	31.3	19.54
Others	10.5	5.3	5.3	–	3.2	3.1	–
Seats	48	38	66	17	63	32	87

TABLE 9
Educational Status of Congress MLAs
(in percentage)

Education	1967	1969	1972	1977	1980	1985	1992
Literate	14.6	31.6	13.6	5.8	14.3	6.3	5.75
Matric/Inter	35.4	52.6	47.0	47.1	39.7	31.2	32.18
B.A. & above	41.7	13.2	39.4	47.1	46.0	62.5	60.92
Seats	48	38	66	17	63	32	87

5

Sikh Identity, the Akalis and Khalistan

J. S. GREWAL

'Sikh politics' after Independence may be defined as politcs based professedly on Sikh identity. In the world of politics and scholarship, the term used generally for 'Sikh politics' is 'communal' or 'fundamentalist'. It is more to the point that the constitutional movement for greater autonomy for the states in India and the militant movement for a sovereign state outside the Indian Union, both get related to conscious-ness of a distinct Sikh identity. Therefore, we may discuss Sikh identity as well as the movements for autonomy and 'Khalistan' for a proper understanding of Sikh politics after Independence.

I

The term 'Khalistan' was used by a medical doctor, V.S. Bhatti of Ludhiana, as the title of a pamphlet in 1940, published soon after the Lahore Resolution of the All India Muslim League, popularly known as the 'Pakistan Resolution'.[1] Dr Bhatti's *Khalistan* was meant to be a counterblast to the idea of Pakistan supposed to be embodied in the Lahore Resolution. Covering much of the area between the Chenab and the Jamna, the Khalistan of Dr Bhatti was meant to serve as a buffer state between India and Pakistan. With the Maharaja of Patiala as its head, Khalistan was to be a 'theocratic' state, consisting of several federating units. A corridor was to link it with the Arabian Sea. Master Tara Singh, who was President of the Shiromani Akali Dal at this time, denounced the pamphlet for confounding the confusion already created by the Muslim League. Two conferences were organized by Baba Gurdit Singh of *Komagatamaru*, a known supporter of the Indian National Congress, to popularize the idea of Khalistan. However, Maulana Abul Kalam Azad expressed his disapproval of Khalistan by stating that some Akalis were using the Congress platform to propagate the idea of Sikh Raj for scuttling the idea of Pakistan.

The term Khalistan was never appropriated by the Akalis but in their opposition to the idea of Pakistan in the 1940s they did come out with counter proposals. With the prospect of freedom coming closer, their concern for the future became greater. In March-April 1942 Stafford Cripps conceded in principle that it was not obligatory for a province to join the Indian federation. This concession appeared to carry the implication that the Punjab could become an autonomous political unit outside the Indian state. The Akali leaders did not like to be subordinated permanently to Muslim majority. The Sikh All-Parties Committee submitted to Cripps the proposal of a province with different boundaries and different proportions of the three major communities of the Punjab. The name given to the province of their conception was 'Azad Punjab'. This gave the impression as if it was meant to be an independent state. Keen to sell the idea to Hindus and Sikhs, the Akali leaders explained subsequently that this province was meant to be a part of the Indian federation. The term *azad* was meant to suggest that each community of this province would be free of the fear of domination by another community.[2] The Muslims and Hindus of this province would account for the bulk of its population: 40 per cent each. The Sikhs would form the remaining 20 per cent. Rooted in a genuine fear of creation of Pakistan which would place the Sikhs under the domination of a hostile community for ever, the *azad* Punjab scheme was essentially a defensive strategy adopted in response to the recognition of the idea of Pakistan by the British Government through the Cripps proposals and by the Congress through its resolution of 2 April 1942. In their opposition to the idea of Pakistan, the Sikh leaders did not hesitate to share platforms with the leaders of the Hindu Mahasabha who stood for India as a single political unit. Unlike Khalistan, the Azad Punjab was to be a part of India; it was also to have a democratic constitution. All that the Sikhs could hope to gain was possibly an effective collaborative role in the affairs of the Azad Punjab.

The Azad Punjab remained on the political agenda of the Akali leaders for about two years. After the 'C.R. Formula' and the Gandhi-Jinnah talks on that basis, the Azad Punjab scheme was theoretically modified in two ways. Its name was dropped to bring in the idea of a Sikh state; and this state was meant to be sovereign. However, in terms of the religious composition of the people in this state there was no change. Furthermore, its creation was conditional upon the creation of Pakistan. During the second half of 1944 the idea of this conditional sovereign Sikh state was advocated not only by the Akalis but also by many other Sikh leaders. This viewpoint was spelt out in a memorandum submitted to the Sapru Reconciliation Committee early in 1945 by Sikh leaders who represented nearly the entire community. The memorandum underlined the fact that, accounting for four million persons in British India, the Sikhs were numerically next only to Hindus and Muslims. Their political, economic and historical importance was much greater than their numbers. Their contribution to the defence and economy of the country was unique.The Punjab was their 'holy' land as well as their homeland. Nonetheless, the constitutional reforms of 1935 had reduced them to 'a state of political subjugation'. The Hindus as well as Muslims had disowned their mother-tongue in favour of Hindi and Urdu. Discrimination against the Sikhs was exercised even in matters of religion. The Sikhs were opposed to 'any partition of India on a communal basis'. However, if the Pakistan scheme was accepted they would 'insist on the creation of separate Sikh State'. The basic demand of the memorandum was a strong, united India, and weightage for the Sikhs in a reorganized Punjab.

The Sikh leaders in general and the Akali leaders in particular tried to promote their idea of a Sikh state in 1945. At the time of the Shimla Conference in June-July, Master Tara Singh met Lord Wavell and emphasized that the Sikhs were strongly opposed to the creation of Pakistan. At the same time he expressed the view that if Pakistan was to be created then Jinnah should agree to the creation of a separate state for the Sikhs. The Akalis fought the elections of 1945-46 in cooperation with but independently of the Congress. Opposition to Pakistan and not a Sikh state was the foremost item on their agenda. The landslide in favour of the Muslim League more than neutralized their own unprecedented success in the elections. From a mere possibility, Pakistan advanced now to the stage of probability. Two days before the arrival of the Cabinet Mission in March 1946, the Shiromani Akali Dal passed a resolution in favour of 'the creation of a Sikh State'. When Master Tara Singh met the Cabinet Mission he underlined that the Sikhs were opposed to any division of India, but if a division was decided upon, a separate state should be created for the Sikhs with the right to federate with Hindustan or Pakistan. Giani Kartar Singh was more categorical and asked for a separate Sikh state irrespective of whether or not Pakistan was created. The pleas and arguments of the Sikh leaders cut no ice with the Cabinet Mission. Its recommendations went not only in favour of the idea of Pakistan but also against any reorgani-zation of the Punjab. The idea of a Sikh state was thus wholly set aside. In theory, the Akalis had the option to seek concessions from Jinnah as the condition of their consent to opt for Pakistan. In practice, they favoured the idea of getting the Punjab divided with the support of the Congress. During the last year of colonial rule, the Akalis worked in close cooperation with the Congress, and no Sikh leader talked of a Sikh state.

Understandably, the most elaborate argument in support of a sovereign Sikh state was published before the recommendations of the Cabinet Mission were made public. In April 1946, Gurbachan Singh of Sikh National College, Lahore, and Lal Singh Gyani of Sikh Missionary College, Amritsar, published their *Idea of the Sikh State* on the premise that the Congress would not resist the demand for Pakistan and India would be divided in the near future into Hindustan and Pakistan as two independent countries. Freedom for Hindus and Muslims would mean 'slavery' for the Sikhs who too constituted a 'nation'.[3] As a nation, the Sikhs had the right to 'self-determination', admitted to be the 'right of nations all over the world'. As stated in the then recent resolution of the Shiromani Akali Dal, no constitutional safeguards and weightage were adequate for ensuring the growth of the Sikhs as 'a nationality with a distinct reli-gious, ideological, cultural and political character'. An autonomous Sikh state, therefore, was 'the unconditional, absolute and minimum demand and political objective of the Sikh Panth as a whole'. This proposed state was to be 'democratic in constitution': it was to have 'a socialistic economic structure'; and it was to give 'full protection' to the minorities.

Gurbachan Singh and Lal Singh go into the background of the demand for an autonomous Sikh state. Its origins could be traced indeed to the 'historical traditions' of the Sikhs, their 'inner urges' and their 'political ideals'. So long as there was no discussion of 'any political future' there was no occasion for giving expression to the concerns of the Sikh Panth. With the Simon Commission, however, the situation began to change. The Muslims of the Punjab began to clamour for a permanent majority in the province and the Sikhs responded by suggesting to Mahatma Gandhi in 1930 that a new province should be carved out of the existing Punjab. In 1931 they made the same suggestion to the Viceroys, Lord Irwin and Lord Willingdon. This demand was presented at the second Round Table Conference by Sampuran Singh and Ujjal Singh.

However, the Sikh demands went unheeded, and the Communal Award was given. The Provincial Autonomy established on its basis caused terrible hardships to the Sikhs. Their religious rights were sought to be thwarted and their national language, Punjabi, was sought to be suppressed. In 1940 came the Pakistan Resolution of the All India Muslim League. The Indian National Congress sought to appease the Muslims at the cost of the Sikhs. This disillusioned the Sikhs: 'in this situation emerged a further step in the old Sikh demand for splitting up the Punjab, called the Azad Punjab Scheme'. Its purpose was to ensure that the Sikhs held 'the balance of power' in the new province. They were canvassing support for this idea when 'Gandhi-Raja Formula' was floated. Its acceptance would have divided the Sikhs into two parts in two different states. Therefore, the Sikhs asked for a separate Sikh state. This was the only way in which they could survive 'in the midst of aggressive communalism'.

In the present-day world of total organization and mobilization of peoples no 'minority' could survive without 'political strength'. The aggressive communalism of Muslim and Hindu majorities presented a grave threat to the Sikhs and their identity. They needed a state in which they were free from aggression and in which they could make laws for themselves. 'The Sikhs do not seek to dominate anyone. They want to establish a secular democratic state, *in which the bulk of the Sikh population may be concentrated.* The economic basis of life in such a state is bound to be socialistic, in accordance with the traditions of the Sikh society, and the inner urge of the hardy, self respecting Sikh peasantry'.

Sikh nationhood was essentially the product of Sikh history. Organized as 'the Khalsa', the Sikhs acted as a distinct and separate nation in the days of the *misls* and Ranjit Singh (late eighteenth and early nineteenth century). They established a theocratic political organization first, and then a monarchical system. They were now organizing their national life on the democratic principle. The Gurdwara Reform Movement was a decisive landmark in the revival of the Khalsa. They began to run 'a kind of parallel Government' in the form of the Shiromani Gurdwara Prabandhak Committee which 'issued commands and ordinances, organized jathas, fought the bureaucracy and through its actions galvanized the entire Sikh people with a powerful feeling of their aroused nationhood'. With the emergence of the concept of the 'Indian Nation', Hindus, Muslims and Sikhs came to be treated as 'communities', with the result that these 'nations' were sought to be subordinated to the Indian Nation. The Sikhs had come out of this illusion 'fostered by the lust for domination by Hindu majority'. Having formed a true conception of their status, they demanded 'a National State for themselves'. No Sikh entertained any doubt about his nationality being different from that of the Hindus. The latent nationhood of the Sikhs had reasserted itself.

Gurbachan Singh and Lal Singh give a whole chapter to the views of a number of political thinkers and leaders to prove their point that the Khalsa constituted a distinct 'nation'. They go on to argue that modern 'political theory has recognized in practice the principle of providing national states to the various nationalities'. More than forty new nation-states had emerged in Europe. The Jews had been promised a national home in Palestine, 'their sacred land'. The Sikhs were demanding nothing more than establishing them-selves as 'a governing group, along with other groups in a democratic system'. The areas asked for the Sikh state were the areas covered by the Sikh homeland, 'a broad compact area of which the Central Punjab is the nucleus'. More specifically, this 'Sikh Zone' covered the Lahore and Jullundur Divisions, parts of the Ambala and Multan Divisions, the Sikh princely states and the state of Malerkotla, and certain hill areas in the North and North-East. 'It is in this land, which by virtue of proprietorship, development, historic-associations and religious sanctity already belongs to the Sikhs, where the Sikhs wish to find a safe home, free from interference'. More than eighty per cent of the Sikhs lived in this zone and owned more than a quarter of its land.

Gurbachan Singh and Lal Singh do not mention the percentage of Sikhs in the total population. Nevertheless, they refer to 'minorities' within the Sikh state to whom a free, prosperous, happy and contented life is promised. But if the Sikhs were to be politically dominant in the Sikh state, it could not have a democratic constitution, because the Sikhs could not form a majority in the area of the Sikh state. Or, was it simply assumed that there would be no absolute 'majority' in the Sikh state? If so, the Sikh state differed from the Azad Punjab only in being sovereign. In no sense could it be called 'a Sikh State'.

For a quarter of a century after the publication of *The Idea of the Sikh State,* there was no talk of Sikh state or Khalistan among the Sikh leaders. In October 1971, the idea of Khalistan was advertised by Dr Jagjit Singh Chauhan in the *New York Times.* Four years earlier he had enjoyed a short spell of power as a minister in the Cabinet of Lachhman Singh Gill who remained, at the mercy of the Congress, Chief Minister of the Punjab for nine months in 1967-68. Living now in England, Chauhan had no following in the Punjab. Whenever he visited India he was treated well by some eminent leaders of the Congress. His idea of Khalistan was treated as a hoax but it could embarrass the Akalis and tickle their opponents in politics. About a decade later, in June 1980, Balbir Singh Sandhu announced the formation of Khalistan, claiming himself to be the Secretary of the National Council of Khalistan with Jagjit Singh Chauhan as its President. This organization existed only on paper. In March 1981, a U.S. citizen, Ganga Singh Dhillon, who was known to Chauhan, addressed the annual session of the Sikh Education Conference organized by the Chief Khalsa Diwan, and put forth the view that the Sikhs formed a 'nation'. The implication was that any demand for independence could be justified on that basis. Soon afterwards, however, the Chief Khalsa Diwan dissociated itself from Dhillon's statement and reiterated its complete loyalty to the Indian State.

Besides the National Council of Khalistan, the White Paper on the Punjab published by the Government of India mentions another significant group which operated from overseas, the Dal Khalsa. It had been formed at Chandigarh in April 1978. Its President was a stenographer of the Panjab University who had published a pamphlet on Khalistan. The term Dal Khalsa served as a reminder of the 'national army' of the Sikhs which had succeeded in establishing sovereign Sikh rule during the late eighteenth century. Actually, however, the Dal was opposed to the Sant Nirankaris. In 1979 it contested elections for the Shiromani Gurdwara Prabandhak Committee, but without any success. In 1982 the responsibility for throwing the head of a cow in a Hindu temple was reported to have been claimed by the Dal Khalsa. The Dal was generally associated with Sant Jarnail Singh Bhindranwale but he never acknowledged that it had anything to do with him. Indeed, the founding of the Dal Khalsa is attributed to Giani Zail Singh who paid the bill for its first meeting at the Aroma Hotel at Chandigarh and who used to ask journalists to give prominence to its activities. From the viewpoint of a movement for Khalistan, the activities of the Dal in the Punjab were hardly of any account.

The Khalistan movement has been associated with Sant Jarnail Singh Bhindranwale more than with anyone else.What has been published on his life and of his speeches enables us to notice some of the relevant aspects of his activities and attitudes. He was initially a protagonist of religious reform. At the age of thirty, he assumed the headship of the Damdami Taksal in 1877 on the death of his predecessor, Sant Kartar Singh Bhindranwale. An open conflict with the Sant Nirankaris, who were looked upon as heretical by Sant Kartar Singh Bhindranwale, was a legacy inherited by Sant Jarnail Singh. What happend on the Baisakhi day of 1978 at Amritsar was an extension of this legacy, underlining the religious dimension of Sant Jarnail Singh's outlook and attitude. Till his death in June 1984 he continued to declare that religion was his sole concern. For him, the *Adi Granth* was the only sacred scripture of the Sikhs; Guruship was vested in this Granth, giving it the status of Guru Granth Sahib. The Khalsa code of conduct provided the only valid mode of life for the Sikhs. He believed in fact that the antidote to external and internal threats to Sikhism was strict conformity to the Khalsa way of life. Insistence on the maintenance of the external form and hostility to drugs and alcohol appear to flow from his religious outlook. That this concern distinguished him in his own eyes from the other Sikh leaders comes out clearly in a statement he made in 1984: 'I am only responsible for the cause of Sikhism. Preaching the symbols of the faith. My responsibility is to see that your beards remain intact, your hair is uncut, and that you do not go after the evil things in life, like alcohol and drugs'.

However, there was another dimension of his religious outlook. To bear arms was a religious duty of the Sikhs. The choice of arms was not confined to the sword (*kirpan*) as one of the five obligatory Ks. The choice was extended to modern weapons, which also carried the implication that they were meant to be actually used. The use of physical force was for him a legitimate part of religion. The encouragement and the form which he gave to violence has to be seen in this context. If anything, his insistence on the use of arms went on increasing. Quite explicitly he told his audience on the roof of the Langar when he was virtually confined to the Golden Temple complex: 'For every village you should keep one motorcycle, three young baptised Sikhs and three revolvers. These are not meant for killing innocent people. For a Sikh to have arms and kill an innocent person is a serious sin. But, Khalsaji, to have arms and not to get your legitimate rights is even a bigger sin. It is for you to decide how to use these arms. If you want to remove the shackles of your slavery you must have a plan'. In other words, you had to be up in arms against the enemies of the faith. In his mind, hostility towards the government was easily transferred to 'Hindus': 'If you do not have the five "ks", if you are not armed with a rifle and a spear, you will be given the beating of your lives by the Hindus'. The reference here is to the killing of Sikhs but even otherwise Sant Jarnail Singh could bracket 'Hindus' with the government. 'I only finish those', he said on another occasion, 'who are enemies of the Sikh faith like policemen, government officials and Hindus'.

The language used by Sant Jarnail Singh Bhindranwale has been generally interpreted in support of the view that he was leading an armed struggle for Khalistan. Naturally, his movement is looked upon as 'secessionist' as well as militant. The White Paper issued by the Government of India refers to secessionist and anti-national activities which had the objective of establishing an independent state for the Sikhs with external support. The activities of Sant Jarnail Singh are included in this view of the situation. However, when he was asked by a journalist in 1983 whether or not he supported the demand for Khalistan, his reply was not unambiguous: 'I am neither in favour of it nor against it. If they give it to us, we won't reject it'. He repeated this in March 1984. In one of his morning *darbars* on the roof of the Langar he asked the audience if they wanted the Anandpur Sahib Resolution implemented in full. Hands were raised by the congregation and Sant Jarnail Singh was satisfied: 'You need not say any-thing more'. He warned the Akali leaders that if they accepted anything less than all the demands in the Anandpur Sahib Resolution he would expose them before the Sikhs. On the eve of the Operation Blue Star, when the Akali lealders were in favour of a settlement with the government, he refused to agree to anything less than the Anandpur Sahib Resolution. Thus, whereas his activities and his informal responses to questions on Sikh independence may seem to point towards Khalistan, his formal stand did not go beyond autonomy for the Punjab as a part of the Indian Union.[4]

Articulation in favour of Khalistan became more pronounced after the death of Sant Jarnail Singh Bhindranwale. For this development, it is possible to see the relevance of the Operation Blue Star and the anti-Sikh riots in Delhi in the wake of Indira Gandhi's assassination. Even more important was the failure of Rajiv-Longowal Accord. In any case the number of militant groups and the number of young men who joined them during seven years after the death of Sant Jarnail Singh appears to have been far larger than their number during the seven years of his own activity from 1977 to 1984. Many of the Sikhs living in Great Britain, Canada and the United States were vocal in favour of Khalistan. many of the militants working in the Punjab too made no secret of their political objective. Continuity was provided by two important organizations: the All India Sikh Students Federation (which had been closely associated with Sant Jarnail Singh under the leadership of Bhai Amrik Singh, the eldest son of Sant Kartar Singh Bhaindranwale), and the Damdami Taksal. On their initiative, a meeting of the Sarbat Khalsa (in theory, the entire body of the Sikhs) was held at the Golden Temple on 26 January 1986. A flag of Khalistan was hoisted and the Akal Takht re-built by the government was demolished. Khalistan was proclaimed a few months later. In August 1987, at a convention called by the Acting Jathedar of the Akal Takht, Professor Darshan Singh, it was declared that the goal of the Sikh Panth was to have a political set-up in a given area in which the Sikhs can experience a glow of freedom (presumably within the Indian State). This did not satisfy the militants. They continued their activity for at least five years more.

II

Turning to the Akalis and their politics, we may recall that in the last year of colonial rule they had cooperated with the Congress to get the province partitioned. This freed them from what they called 'Muslim domination'. But in itself the partition could not solve their problems. They had to pursue their old concerns in the Indian Union. These were essentially three: adequate share in political power, promotion of Punjabi language in Gurmukhi script, and protection of their religious identity. All these concerns were actually three aspects of a single concern – the position of the Sikh Panth in free India.

The partition brought about an important demographic change in the East Punjab. The Hindus formed more than sixty per cent of the total population of the state. Their leaders were anxious to retain this majority status. The Sikhs formed about 35 per cent of the total population, a much higher per-centage than what they had in the British Punjab. Further-more, they were concentrated in six districts in which their population was actually more than half: Amritsar, Gudaspur, Jalandhar, Hoshiarpur, Ludhiana and Firozpur. Then there were the princely states in which the Sikhs had a majority on the margin. This demographic change eventually came to have an important bearing on their politics. Used to weightage in the British Punjab, the Akali leaders thought of weightage first in free India as well. However the idea of weightage to religious minorities was categorically discarded by the Constituent Assembly. The Akalis demanded proportionate representation on the basis of joint electorates, with the right to contest the general unreserved seats. This too was rejected by the Constituent Assembly. The Akali members of the Assembly were so resentful that they refused to sign the Constitution to be adopted on 26 January 1950.

The Akali members of the Punjab Legislative Assembly had joined the Congress Assembly Party in March 1948 and three months later Giani Kartar Singh was included in the Cabinet in place of the Congress Sikh member Ishar Singh Majhail. Within a year Gopi Chand Bhargava was replaced by Bhim Sen Sachar as the Chief Minister of the Punjab. In consultation with Giani Kartar Singh, Sachar evolved in 1949 a language formula which is known as the Sachar Formula. A Punjabi zone was created by his scheme by adding the Ropar and Kharar Tehsils of the Ambala District to the six districts of Sikh majority. Punjabi was to be the medium of education at the primary level in all the schools of this zone. Hindi was to be introduced in the last year of primary education. In the Hindi zone, the position of Punjabi was to be reversed. The Akalis had some reservations about detail but they welcomed the formula as a reasonable solution of the language problem. Unfortunately, this scheme was not acceptable to the Arya Samaj leaders of the Punjabi zone. They refused to implement it. In fact the reaction among the 'Hindu' leaders was so strong that Sachar lost his Chief Ministership and Bhargava was back in office by October 1949. The Akali members felt ineffective in the new ministry. Before long, the Working Committee of the Akali Dal decided to revoke the merger of the

Akalis with the Congress on the grounds that the Congress leaders had belied all their hopes of constructive sympathy and support.

In 1952 the Akalis fought the elections on a new issue: the Punjabi-speaking state. The idea of reorganization on the basis of language was not new. It had been an important item on the agenda of the Congress. After 1947, however, the Congress leaders were no longer enthusiastic about linguistic states. In 1948 the Dar Commission recommended that no linguistic state should be created without the consent of a substantial minority included in its area. Its report was accepted by a committee consisting of Nehru, Patel and Sitarammaya who made a recommendation of their own that in North India no provincial boundaries should be changed irrespective of the merit of any such proposal. In the British Punjab, reorganization had been suggested from time to time to accommodate the interests of religious communities. But languages and scripts too had come to be associated with them: Urdu and Persian script with Muslims, Hindi and Devnagri script with Hindus, and Punjabi and Gurmukhi script with Sikhs. Therefore, the question of language appeared to carry political implications as well. In 1950 Hukam Singh tried to clarify that the demand for a Punjabi-speaking state was democratic and secular.The Working Committee of the Akali Dal passed a resolution in favour of a state on the basis of Punjabi language and culture. Some of the Hindu leaders of the Punjab reacted to the demand by telling their followers to return Hindi as their mother-tongue for the census of 1951. They had canvassed for Hindi before 1947 also, but now their idea was to thwart the forma-tion of a Punjabi-speaking state by demonstrating that there was a substantial Hindi-speaking population in the proposed Punjabi-speaking state. The movement for a Punjabi-speaking state continued for more than a decade and a large number of Punjabi-speaking Hindus returned their mother-tongue as Hindi in the census of 1961 as well.

With their defeat in the elections of 1952, the Akali aspiration to be 'free and equal partners in the destiny of the country' became stronger. Before the year ended, Potti Srira-mula died on fast for the creation of Andhra Pradesh, and the Prime Minister announced the separation of Andhra from Madras as a Telugu-speaking state. As the movement for linguistic states gained momentum, the formation of States Reorganization Commission was announced before the end of 1953. The Akali leaders prepared their case on the basis of pre-1947 data. According to them there was an area of

35,000 square miles in which nearly 12 million persons spoke Punjabi. The Sikhs formed much less than a half of the total population of this area. Nevertheless, the proposal was countered by the protagonists of Maha Punjab who advocated the merger of Himachal Pradesh and a few districts of Uttar Pradesh as well as PEPSU with the East Punjab. Without going into any detail of either the mounting tension between the two parties or the arguments which they used, we may note that the Commission came to the conclusion that the majority of the people were opposed to the creation of a Punjabi-speaking state, and recommended merger of Himachal Pradesh as well as Pepsu with the East Punjab. The Akalis rejected the Commission's report on the day following its release on 9 October 1955.

Hukam Singh evolved a formula which met the essential demands of the Akalis without the creation of a Punjabi-speaking state. It came to be known as the Regional Formula. PEPSU alone was to be merged with the East Punjab, and the whole area was to be divided into two 'regions'. One of these was to be the Punjabi region in which the medium of school education was to be Punjabi. The other region was to give the same status to Hindi. Both the regions were to have regional committees for legislation on fourteen important subjects. The Regional Formula came closest to accommodating the political and cultural interests of the Akalis. They accepted the scheme. The Working Committee of the Akali Dal decided to have no political programme of its own and to concentrate on the religious, educational, cultural, social and economic interests of the Sikh Panth.

The reorganized Punjab state was inaugurated on 1 November 1956 when Partap Singh Kairon was the Chief Minister. The Akali legislators joined the Congress Party. The Hindi Raksha Samiti agitated against the scheme and Kairon remained reluctant to allow the regional committees to legislate. In fact he tried to keep the former Akali leaders out of the Legislative Assembly and to dislodge the Akalis from the SPGC. Given Kairon's attitude and outlook the Regional Formula had little chance of success. Within a few years, the Akalis felt obliged to revive the movement for a Punjabi-speaking state.

The agitation launched by Master Tara Singh in 1960 proved to be a failure. By 1962 his place was taken by Sant Fateh Singh who presented the demand as clearly a linguistic demand. Both the leaders demonstrated their patriotism during India's war with China. During the war with Pakistan in 1965 Sant Fateh Singh demonstrated his loyalty to the Indian State even more conspicuously. Nehru had died in 1964 and Kairon had been assassinated in February 1965. There were new actors on the scene. Soon after the cease-fire in September 1965 the Union Home Minister announced that the issue of the Punjabi speaking state would be examined all afresh. Lal Bahadur Shastri appointed a Parliamentary Committee under the Chairman-ship of Hukam Singh, who was now the Speaker of the Lok Sabha. To advise the Parliamentary Committee, a Cabinet Sub-committee was also constituted. It consisted of Indira Gandhi. Y.B. Chavan and Mahavir Tyagi. Indira Gandhi became the Prime Minister in January 1966 after the death of Lal Bahadur Shastri. On 1 November 1966 was inaugurated the Punjabi-speaking state.

However, the Akali agitation did not end with the reorganization of the Punjab in 1966. In fact, Sant Fateh Singh went on fast unto death within seven weeks of the inauguration of the new state. It is important to know why. Contrary to the general impression, the new state was not created in accordance with the recommendations of the Parliamentary Committee constituted by Lal Bahadur Shastri. Indira Gandhi was unhappy with this committee, especially because of the views of its Chairman. In her *My Truth* she makes it abundantly clear why she was not in favour of creating a Punjabi-speaking state: she did not wish to deviate from a well considered policy of the Congress, and she did not wish to let down the 'Hindu supporters' of the Congress in the Punjab. Both these concerns arose from electoral considera-tions. She did not wait for the recommendations of the Parliamentary Committee. A resolution of the Congress in march 1966 accepted the principle of reorganization of the Punjab. A commissioon was appointed, known as the Shah Commission. The terms of reference given to the Commission stipulated use of the census of 1961 for data on language, and to treat the *tahsil* as a unit. Consequently, genuinely Punjabi-speaking villages and Chandigarh were left out of the Punjab. Furthermore, the Union Government took over the power and irrigation projects and became the arbiter of river waters in case the two new states failed to come to an agreement. Sant Fateh Singh protested against all these decisions even before the new state was inaugurated. In December 1966 he went on fast on the issue of Chandigarh. The issue is still unresolved, like the issues of river waters and Punjabi-speaking territories.

To these issues was added another : the relations of the state with the Centre. The idea of autonomy had begun to be aired before the rcorganization of thc Punjab in 1966. In May 1965 'Justice' Gurnam Singh, leader of the opposition in the Punjab Assembly, moved a resolution at a conference in Ludhiana in favour of a self-determined status for Sikhs within the Indian Union. It was interpreted by the language press in the Punjab as a demand for a sovereign Sikh state. In July 1965 Master Tara Singh, who was no longer influen-tial, gave an elaborate argument in support of the idea of 'a Sikh Homeland', an autonomous state within the Indian Union. Opposing the Punjab Reorganization Bill in the Parliament Kapur Singh referred to Nehru's statement of July 1946: 'I see no wrong in an area and a set-up in the North wherein the Sikhs can also experience a glow of freedom'. Kapur Singh argued in favour of a Sikh Homeland with a special internal constitution and a special relationship with the Centre irrespective of the number of Sikhs in this homeland. With this background, the experience of the Akalis as the ruling party in the new Punjab between March 1967 and June 1971 convinced them that they could not exercise power adequately, or for long, under the given constitution which placed the states at a great political and economic disadvantage in relation to the ruling party at the Centre. Within three years the Punjab was twice placed under the President's rule, a euphemism for the rule of the ruling party. The Akalis lost the elections in 1972. A year later came the Anandpur Sahib Resolution. Its basic thrust was on a genuinely federal system with only defence, foreign affairs, communications, and currency as the prerogatives of the Centre. Couched partly in the language of the supporters of a Sikh Homeland , it was interpreted by the opponents of the Akalis as 'secessionist'. The Akalis returned to power in 1977 and in a crowded conference held at Ludhiana in 1978, they reiterated their stand without any ambiguity in favour of a truly federal system.

The most important issues for the Akalis had, thus, emerged on the reorganization of the Punjab in 1966 and before their return to power in 1977: Chandigarh and other Punjabi-speaking territories, Centre-State relations, and river waters. On two of these, Indira Gandhi had already taken decisions.. On the issue of Chandigarh Sant Fateh Singh had announced his decision to go on fast on 26 January 1970 and to immolate himself on 1 February if Chandigarh was not given to the Punjab. Indira Gandhi awarded Chandigarh to the Punjab. The award was meant to be implemented five years later, in 1975. At the same time she awarded part of Fazilka *tahsil* to Haryana with a corridor on the Punjab border with Rajasthan to link the awarded territory with the state of Haryana.

Indira Gandhi's decision on river waters came in 1976, after the Akalis had put up probably the strongest opposition in the country to the Emergency imposed by her in 1975. The non-riparian Rajasthan was given 8.00 maf of water. Of the remaining 7.20 maf, she gave 0.20 to Delhi and divided the rest in two equal shares for Haryana and the Punjab. Thus, the Punjab was to get 3.5 maf of water, which was less than what the state was actually using. The Akalis took up this matter with Morarji Desai as the Prime Minister. He could tell the Rajasthani leaders that their state was not a part of the Indus rivers basin but he was not prepared to change the award. However, he had no objection to the Punjab going to the Supreme Court for adjudication. The matter was lying with the Supreme Court when the Akalis lost the elections in 1980.

In July 1981 Sant Harchand Singh Longowal, who had conducted successful agitation against the Emergency as the President of the Akali Dal, presided over a World Sikh Conference which directed the Akali Dal to plan *dharmyudh* for pursuing the Anandpur Sahib Resolution. Agitation was launched in September and memoranda of demands were sent to Indira Gandhi. She met the Akali leaders on 16 October 1981 primarily to identify issues which could then be taken up by the Foreign Minister P.V. Narasimha Rao. A meeting with him later appeared to be 'a waste of time' to the Akali leaders. They met the Prime Minister again on 26 November. The suit of the Punjab regarding the river waters was pending in the Supreme Court. Indira Gandhi was not in favour of revising her earlier decision but she gave assurances of much larger supplies of water and energy to the Punjab in the future on the basis of more scientific exploi-tation of resources. Within five weeks, however, she gave a unilateral decision, adding 0.72 maf of water to the Punjab's share from the estimated surplus of 1.32 maf. Significantly, she gave 0.60 maf out of this surplus to Rajasthan, making it clear to the Akalis that their talk of Rajasthan not being a riparian state was a contemptible non-sense. What is more, all the three Chief Ministers concerned accepted this decision, and the Chief Minister of the Punjab was obliged to withdraw its case from the Supreme Court. It was also decided to complete the Satlej-Yamuna Link (SYL) canal for Haryana in two years. On their third and last meeting with the Prime Minister on 5 April 1982 the Akali leaders got the impression that she had already made up her mind to let the issues wait. But they were wrong. She was keen on the construction of the SYL canal.

The *nahar roko* (stop the canal) *morcha* of the Akalis against the construction of the SYL canal failed to evoke much response. Another call a month later failed to mobilize the peasantry. The Akalis decided at last to launch a *dharmyudh morcha* on 4 August to get all their demands accepted. Soon afterwards, Sant Jarnail Singh Bhindranwale was allowed to join the *dharmyudh morcha*. The *morcha* picked up. It became increasingly difficult for the government to find room for the agitating volunteers in the existing jails. By the middle of October Indira Gandhi decided to release the Akali volunteers on the Diwali day. Swaran Singh hammered out a mutually acceptable formula on the important issues of Chandigarh, river waters and the Centre-State relations. A cabinet sub-committee consisting of Pranab Mukherjee, R. Vankataraman, P.V. Narasimha Rao and P.C. Sethi accepted the formula and Swaran Singh told the Akali leaders that the government had approved of it. But the statement placed before the Parliament turned out to be materially different from what had been agreed upon. The Prime Minister had changed her mind. The Akalis decided to hold a demonstration in Delhi at the time of the Asiad. Amrinder Singh negotiated another mutually acceptable agreement. It was sabotaged by Bhajan Lal, Chief Minister of Haryana, with the assurance that he would not let the Akalis pass through his state. He proved to be truer than his word. No Sikh was allowed to pass through Haryana without being humiliated. Many of them lost not merely metaphorically their honour but also literally their turbans.

Not to have gained anything through negotiations was a setback for the Akalis, and it appeared to justify the idea of militancy propagated by Sant Jarnail Singh. In any case, his popularity increased in 1982-83. And so did militancy. He appeared to be running a parallel government. The Akalis pursued their *morcha* against all odds as a political necessity. Sant Harchand Singh Longowal asked the Akali legislators to resign their seats with effect from 21 February 1983. He gave a call to exservice men for a meeting at Amritsar. Nearly 5,000 responded. In April 1983 the Akalis organized their *rasta roko* (blocck the roads) campaign. Twenty-six persons were killed in the violence that erupted in spite of their peaceful intention. In June, they organized their *rail roko* (stop the trains) campaign and the government decided not to run any trains. Yet there was some violence. The *kam roko* (stop work) campaign of August 1983 proved to be a great success. And so was the *bandh* they organized in February 1984 to demonstrate their strength and their trust in non-violent agitation. Within a week, a meeting of five Akali leaders, five cabinet ministers, five secretaries and fifteen leaders of the opposition parties was held at Delhi. It came close to a successful settlement but anti-Sikh violence was orchestrated in Haryana, and the Akali leaders returned to the Punjab. Before the end of the month, the Akalis burnt the pages of the Constitution containing Article 25 (2) (b) at Delhi and Chandigarh. They were arrested, but the government also announced its willingness to amend the article. Early in March, Indira Gandhi unilaterally appointed the Sarkaria Commission to go into Centre-State relations. It did not help the Akalis to withdraw the *morcha.* They were prepared to work out a reasonable settlement in the last week of May but nothing short of the demands of the Anandpur Sahib Resolution was acceptable to Sant Jarnail Singh who had moved into the Akal Takht in December 1983.

At the time of the Operation Blue Star Lt General Sunderji was told by the government that there were two groups in the Golden Temple complex, one that of Sant Jarnail Singh Bhindranwale and the other that of Sant Harchand Singh Longowal. He was also instructed to ensure that there was no fighting between the two groups. The 'extremists' were to be flushed out without any damage to the Golden Temple and the least possible damage to the Akal Takht. These instructions indicate that Sant Longowal and his followers were not to be treated as 'extremists'. Some writers have wondered that they 'surrendered', or they did not resist. Quite simply, they were neither rebels nor up in arms against the state. The government knew this better than anyone else. They were arrested and detained. When they were released from detention, they strongly condemned the action of the government. Nevertheless, Sant Longowal signed an accord with the Prime Minister, picking up the old threads of Chandigarh, river waters and Centre-State relations, and adding some new issues. He was assassinated before the elections were held. The Akalis fought the elections, won, and formed the government. The Accord failed and so did the Akalis in containing militancy. They did not contest the general elections of 1992 but they fought by-elections with considerable success against all sorts of disadvantages. In the Parliamentary elections of May 1996 they won eight out of thirteen seats, under the leadership of Parkash Singh Badal who is known for his moderate views and an open attitude towards non-Sikhs. Advocacy of militancy, or independence, on the part of an Akali leader is looked upon as deviation and not as the norm. The political objective of the Akalis has been greater autonomy for the Punjab, and for other states. Their approach has been either constitutional or agitational, but not militant. They are quite distinct from the militants who stood for secession, and they have enjoyed much greater support. They have won the general elections of 1997.

Nevertheless, there has been a general tendency to look upon them as secessionist. This may be due partly to sheer ignorance and partly to deliberate intention to malign them as political opponents. This may also be due to the distant background of the 1940s when the Akalis, conditionally or unconditionally, put forward the idea of a Sikh state. The concentration of the majority of the Sikhs in a contiguous area lends much greater plausibility to aspiration of sovereignty. Their compromising gestures towards the militants in the recent past may be yet another reason for bracketing them with the secessionists. Many of the Akali leaders have shown willingness or even keenness to participate in the mortuary rites (*bhogs*) of some known or alleged militants. More important perhaps were their dealings with Sant Jarnail Singh Bhindranwale. One of the Akali demands, for instance, was his release in 1981. In 1982 he was allowed to merge his *morcha* with the Akali *dharmyudh*. No one could stop him from staying in one of the 'hostels' of the SGPC, where the government also could reach him if it wanted to, but towards the end of 1983 he was allowed to stay in the Akal Takht, which could not be done without the tacit consent of the SGPC. But this tacit consent sprang from helplessness more than anything else. Sant Jarnail Singh on his part did not care much for Sant Longowal who demonstrated his opposition to the methods of Sant Bhindranwale even before he had moved into the Akal Takht. In 1984 there was an open hostility between them.

Why the Akalis did not always keep a politically respectable distance from Sant Jarnail Singh Bindranwale is a relevant question. According to Mark Tully and Satish Jacob, Giani Zail Singh enabled Sanjay Gandhi to discover Sant Jarnail Singh for breaking the Akali

Dal after its electoral success in 1977. They also looked for a cause which could be both religious and political. For this they identified the Nirankaris. The Dal Khalsa, floated by them some time later, was also anti-Nirankari. After the death of twelve Sikhs at the hands of the Nirankaris on the Baisakhi day of 1978 at Amritsar, anti-Nirankari agitations were encouraged not by the Akalis but by the local committee in charge of *gurdwaras* in Delhi controlled by the Congress party. The Dal Khalsa as well as Sant Jarnail Singh contested elections for the SGPC in 1979 against the Akali candidates. In 1980 Sant Jarnail Singh campaigned for Congress candidates, including R.L. Bhatia. He is believed to have shared a platform with Indira Gandhi. In any case, she admitted that he had supported a Congress candidate. After the murder of Baba Gurbachan Singh, the Nirankari Guru, in April 1980, Giani Zail Singh told the Parliament that Sant Jarnail Singh had nothing to do with the murder. After the murder of Lala Jagat Narain in September 1981, the Chief Minister of the Punjab wanted to get Sant Jarnail Singh arrested as a suspect. He was in a Haryana village at that time. Giani Zail Singh rang up Bhajan Lal to tell him not to let the Sant be arrested. When the Punjab government did arrest him in October, Giani Zail Singh told the Parliament that there was no evidence of his involvement in the murder. He was released. 'The government has done more for me in one week', he remarked, 'than I could have achieved in years'. After the murder of Santokh Singh at Delhi in December 1981, his memorial service was attended by Sant Jarnail Singh as well as Giani Zail Singh and Rajiv Gandhi. The Akalis may not have known all this, but they knew that Sant Jarnail Singh was being supported and protected by the Congress to undermine the Akalis. They, in turn, were tempted to use Sant Jarnail Singh against the Congress if and when they could.

When the Akali leaders met Indira Gandhi in October 1981 for the first time, they told her that Sant Jarnail Singh was being backed by the Congress. If some of the Akali leaders maintained their contact with him till the end, so did some of the Congress leaders. The Sant had fallen out with the Congress by the end of 1981 but the Congress did not fall out with him. Indira Gandhi continued to consult Giani Zail Singh when he became the President of India. It was possibly due to his influence that Sant Jarnail Singh was not arrested after the murder of the D.I.G. Atwal in April 1983. When the government of Darbara Singh was suspended and the President's rule was imposed in the Punjab after the cold-blooded murder of some Hindu passengers in the first week of October 1983, a senior colleague of Darbara Singh claimed that President Zail Singh was in daily contact with Sant Jarnail Singh. The implication was that Darbara Singh's downfall had been brought about through the Sant's instrumentality. Indira Gandhi maintained contact with Sant Jarnail Singh through R.L. Bhatia who remained in regular contact with Bhai Amrik Singh till April 1984. Even if the idea of the President and the Prime Minister of India was to use Sant Jarnail Singh for their purposes, the knowledge of his connection with them added much to his prestige and influence. The Akalis had to contend with him, his prestige, and his influence.

III

Both the Akalis and the protagonists of Khalistan invoke Sikh identity as essentially relevant for their political programmes. It figures prominently in their political discourses and praxis.[6] What they share is primarily the Khalsa or Singh identity. This identity is visible in their external appearance. They wear *kesh* and turban, keep a flowing beard and uncut hair, carry a *kirpan*, and wear *kara* and *kachh*. These four symbols begin with the letter 'k'. The fifth 'k' is *kangha* or the comb tucked in the *kesh* for keeping the hair clean and orderly. These five Ks form the most important items in the Khalsa code of conduct (*rahit*). The strictest prohibition is on the use of tobacco in any form. The Damdami Taksal was more strict about these symbols than the contemporary Akalis. But strict insistence on the five Ks is a legacy of the Akali Movement. Sant Jarnail Singh favoured the idea of bearing modern weapons in addition to a long sword. For prohibition, he added drugs and alcohol to tobacco. On the first point, he was closer to the Khalsa of the eighteenth century. On the second point he was more in conformity with the *Adi Granth*. Whereas the followers of Sant Jarnail Singh insist on *amritdhari* identity, involving the observance of the five Ks after baptism of the double-edged sword (*pahul* or *amrit*), the Akalis prefer this identity but do not seriously object to what may be called the Singh identity as less exacting than the *amritdhari* identity. Besides carrying the epithet 'Singh' in one's name, by far the most important items of this identity are keeping the hair uncut, wearing turban, and refraining from the use of tobacco. Ordinarily, the Singhs of this description would also wear *kara* and less frequently also *kacch.* Theoretical preference for *amritdhari* identity is thus common to both the Akalis and the Dam-dami Taksal, but they differ in actual practice. Since the *keshdharis* have been far larger than the *amritdharis,* the Akalis have worked with a much broader base.

Apart from external appearance, the Akalis and the Damdami Taksal observe distinct rites of passage – ceremonies connected with birth, marriage and death. On these, as on several other occasions, the *Adi Granth* is of crucial importance. No such ceremony can be performed without the *Adi Granth.* This is because the *Adi Granth* is not only the exclusive scripture of the Sikhs in the eyes of the Akalis and the followers of Sant Jarnail Singh but also the embodiment of the Guru. Therefore, Guru Granth Sahib is its proper title. This title and this attitude spring from the doctrine of the continuity of Guruship. Guru Nanak, the founder of the Sikh faith and the Sikh Panth, was followed by nine successors. Just as he chose Angad to be the Guru, and Guru Angad chose Amar Das, and so on, Guru Gobind Singh chose the *Adi Granth* to be the Guru. What ended with the death of Guru Gobind Singh was personal Guruship and not Guruship itself. The reverence and regard which the Sikhs of the ten Gurus gave to them are due now to Guru Granth Sahib as well. This doctrine of Guru-Granth, it must be added, is more than 150 years old, and the equation of *Gurbani* with the Guru can be traced back to the early sixteenth century. Since the Gurus have spoken through the Granth, Guru Granth Sahib has been the source of Sikh ideas and ethics. As the exclusive scripture of the Sikhs, it is the only valid source now. But to this source are added the known injunctions and practices of the ten Gurus. Both the Akalis and the followers of Sant Jarnail Singh agree that the *Adi Granth* inculcates monotheism or worship of One God and rejects gods, goddesses, incarnations and idols. Sikh doctrines and Sikh worship too, therefore, are distinctive.

The Sikh institution *par excellence,* both for the Akalis and the followers of Sant Jarnail Singh, is the *gurdwara.* There was a time when the Sikh sacred space was known as *dharmsala.* It was the place where congregational worship was held, sacred food (*parshad*) was distributed, and community meal (*langar*) was prepared and eaten. This was also the place where matters of common interest to the local community could be discussed. The *dharmsala* where the Guru was personally present was regarded for that reason as the premier institution, like Kartarpur (Dera Baba Nanak), Khadur Sahib,

Goindwal, Amritsar, Kiratpur and Anandpur. Also, the idea became current that the Guru was present in the *sangat*, which added a new dimension to the sanctity of the *dharmsala*. This idea became all the more important when there was no personal Guru. This development reached its culmination with the doctrine of Guru-Granth, because the presence of the Guru-Granth in the *dharmsala* approximated its sanctity to that of the premier *dharmsalas* of the days of the Gurus. Gradually, the name *dharmsala* was dropped in favour of *gurdwara*, literally the door of the Guru, because of the presence there of both the *sangat* and the Granth.The change in the name given to Sikh sacred space was an index of its increased sanctity in the eyes of the Sikhs. This transition had become conspicuous before the end of the nineteenth century. Not only the Akalis and the followers of Sant Jarnail Singh but also the Sikhs of all other descriptions look upon the *gurdwara* as an indispensable institution. Its function is related to the socio-cultural as well as the religious life of the local communities everywhere. For the Akalis and the followers of Sant Jarnail Singh the *gurdwara* is also the place for political discourse and action. This is not a mere empirical fact. It gets related to the doctrine of *miri-piri* according to which the spiritual and temporal concerns of the Sikh Panth are one indivisible whole. In this specific form the doctrine is attributed to Guru Hargobind in the early seventeenth century.

Given the sanctity and the importance of the *gurdwara*, it is easy to appreciate the importance of the SGPC for the Akalis. As its name suggests, the Shiromani Gurdwara Prabandhak Committee was formed in 1920 for management of the *gurdwaras* which were historic in the sense of their associa-tion with the Sikh Gurus. But these *gurdwaras* were indirectly controlled by the colonial administrators and directly managed by approved individuals or committees who necessarily were not Singhs. The Sikh leaders who constituted the SGPC as a voluntary body did so on the assumption that the historic *gurdwaras* belonged to the Panth as the successor of the Gurus. The idea of Guru-Panth had come into currency in the early eighteenth century to take the tangible form of *gurmatas* by the Sarbat Khalsa, generally adopted at the Akal Takht, and of united action by the Dal Khalsa under the command of a single leader. With the establishment of Sikh rule in the late eighteenth century, this doctrine became less popular and the doctrine of Guru-Granth occupied the foreground. After the loss of political power finally in

1849, the idea of Guru-Panth began gradually to be revived. The demand that the historic *gurdwaras* should be controlled and managed by the true representatives of the Sikh Panth had begun to be aired much before we come upon the Gurdwara Reform Movement of the 1920s. 'Akali' was the epithet used for members of the *jathas* which were meant to take physical control of *gurdwaras* to be placed under the management of the SGPC. The Akalis and the SGPC in a sense were born together. The Sikh Gurdwaras Act of 1925 gave constitutional recognition to a Central Board which was given the name of Shiromani Gurdwara Prabandhak Committee by its members to identify it with the body founded in 1920. The Akalis informally became a political party after 1925. Between themselves, and each by itself, the Akalis as well as the SGPC have represented the temporal and religious concerns of the Sikh Panth for over seven decades by now. The erstwhile followers of Sant Jarnail Singh questioned the authority of the SGPC by holding meetings of the Sarbat Khalsa, invoking implicitly the doctrine of Guru-Panth. They failed because, among other things, this doctrine forms the basis of the SGPC as a statutory body. It embodies and contains the doctrine of Guru-Panth at one and the same time.

Both the Akalis and the Damdami Taksal maintain that the Sikh Panth was meant to be egalitarian. In other words, it was based on the idea of equality. Conversely, the degree of equality to be actually observed in the Sikh social order distinguishes the Sikhs from others and, thus, becomes a mark of their identity. In any case, equality among the Sikhs is most conspicuous in their *gurdwaras*. No Sikh, male or female, is debarred from participation in the worship, from contributing to the sacred food or receiving it, and from serving and eating in the *langar*. Equality among males in public life is also quite striking. In social life, equality is more visible in terms of 'inter-caste' relations than in terms of gender relations, more in terms of commensality than in connubium. The Sikh Panth is open for admission to all human beings, irrespective of their creed, nationality, or sex. The relatively egalitarian character of the Sikh Panth was far more striking in the past than it is in the contemporary context. The ideal of equality in the Sikh Panth presented a contrast to the idea of inequality built into the caste system and maintained in theory as well.

We have talked largely of the contemporary situation. The scholars who have studied the subject of Sikh identity most seriously are agreed that it is legitimate to talk of a distinct Sikh identity in the twentieth century, particularly after the Gurdwara Reform Movement. They are also agreed that the emergence of this identity was due to the work of the Singh Sabha Movement. However, there are politicians, journalists and publicists (perhaps some academic persons too) who still go on questioning this identity, particularly in relation to the Hindus. The debate about whether or not Sikhs were Hindu was actually over for the Sikhs before the First World War. The arguments generally used by those who wanted to prove that the Sikhs were Hindu can be summarized. To start with, Guru Nanak was a 'Hindu'. The social background of his followers and the followers of his successors was 'Hindu'. The Sikhs and Hindus intermarried and ate together. The Sikhs observed caste distinctions in matrimony and commensality, like the other Hindus. They believed in the Vedas, if not also in the other Hindu scriptures, in addition to their own Granths. The *Dasam Granth* composed by Guru Gobind Singh contained long compositions in praise of the Goddess and the incarnations of Vishnu and Shiva, particularly the human incarnations of Vishnu, that is Rama and Krishna. The *Adi Granth* was a popular version of Vedantic philosophy. The Khalsa, instituted by Guru Gobind Singh for protecting the Hindus, was a temporary measure. At any rate, the external appearance of the Khalsa did not mean and did not justify a separate identity. If all these arguments sound familiar, it is largely because they have often been repeated in the twentieth century and they are repeated even today in the same or in a modified form.

There is quite a general impression that the leaders of the Singh Sabha Movement started insisting all of a sudden that the Sikhs were not Hindu. The book entitled *Ham Hindu Nahin* (We are not Hindus) is often referred to in this connection.[6] This impression is erroneous. Speaking historically, it would be more correct to say that some Hindus began to claim that Sikhs were 'Hindu'. *Sikh Hindu Hain* (The Sikhs are Hindu) was the title actually of two books which appeared in the context of this debate. A relevant question to ask, therefore, is why in the late nineteenth century for the first time some people started arguing that the Sikhs were 'Hindu'. What was meant by the term 'Hindu'? There was a time when the term Hindu referred vaguely to the people of this country. This, for instance, is the usage in Alberuni's *Kitab al-Hind.* With the coming of the Turks, the term Hindu tended to be used increasingly for 'Indians' who were not Muslim. The term was used in two other senses during the medieval period: one, for the socio-religious system represented and upheld by the Brahmans; and two, for the upper caste non-Muslims. These connotations were not suddenly discarded in the nineteenth century, but the religious connotation steadily gained greater and greater currency. The presence of the Christian missionaries and the movements for socio-religious reform under colonial rule had much to do with this development. Even in the late nineteenth century several different meanings were attached to the term 'Hindu'. One question began to be posed rather sharply. 'That was whether Buddhists and Jains, Sikhs, members of different bhakti sects such as Kabirpanthis and Vallabhacharyas, and also of course the "untouchable" and "tribal" groups and castes who literally lived on the physical/geographical fringes of settled Hindu society, whether all of these groups were to be included among the Hindus or not'.[7] Some of the Hindus and Sikhs of the Punjab, already before the end of the nineteenth century, had given their answer that the Sikhs were Hindu.

Bhai Kahn Singh Nabha's *Ham Hindu Nahin*, which has turned out to be a classic statement of Sikh identity, was initially written in Hindi – indicating the audience for which it was primarily meant. He is quite explicit on the point that he wrote in response to the claims being made that Sikhs were Hindu. As a literary artifice though, he reproduces the arguments put forth by the 'Hindu' participant in the debate. This work has been analysed in some detail. Bhai Kahn Singh's arguments are quite comprehensive in scope, relating to scripture, religious doctrines, the mode of worship, the code of conduct, the rite of initiation, the rites of passage, the character of the Sikh Panth, and the consciousness of separate identity. It is interesting to note that most of the time Bhai Kahn Singh invokes Sikh writings of the pre-colonial centuries in support of his arguments, covering a wide range and a strikingly large volume of Sikh literature. What is remarkable about his book is that, though his preference for the Khalsa or Singh identity is quite clear, he regards the Sahajdharis (who did not take *pahul* and, therefore, did not necessarily keep their hair uncut and bear the epithet Singh) as an integral part of the Sikh Panth. The implication is extremely important. A distinct Sikh identity did not start with the Khalsa: it had already emerged during the sixteenth and seventeenth centuries. Anyone who looks upon Sikh identity as a product of the colonial period has to contend with Bhai Kahn Singh Nabha, and with much more.

Harjot Oberoi is one among those who maintain that the distinct Sikh identity in which the Sahajdharis were pushed out or pushed to the periphery and the *keshdharis* came to occupy the centre of the stage was created by the Tat Khalsa or the radical minority among the protagonists of the Singh Sabha Movement. But even he concedes that the early eighteenth century Khalsa background was helpful to the Tat Khalsa. There are other scholars who look upon the Khalsa of Guru Gobind Singh as clearly distinct from other Indians. In fact there is a long historiographical tradition in which the Khalsa figure as a community different and distinct from both Hindus and Muslims. In the eighteenth century Sikh literature itself the Khalsa are presented as different and distinct from Hindus and Muslims. They represent 'the third panth'. There is hardly any doubt that the Khalsa identity was the most dominant identity among the Sikhs of the early nineteenth century. The colonial rulers were quick to recognize this fact. The change introduced by the Singh Sabha leaders has to be understood in terms of differences of degree, coherence, magnitude and insistence on conformity. All this was made possible by the new means of communication, including education and the press.

The Khalsa identity was far more pronounced than the identity of the Sikhs in the earlier Sikh tradition. But in what sense were the Sikhs Hindu? If we apply the connotation of 'Hindu' as a non-Muslim Indian to the Sikhs of the sixteenth and seventeenth centuries, they were certainly Hindu. However, if we take the 'Hindus' to mean upper caste non-Muslim Indians, the Sikhs were not 'Hindu'. The Sikh Panth included not only Khatris, Brahmans and Rajputs but also Jats, Tarkhans, low caste labourers and outcastes. If we take 'Hindus' to represent the socio-religious systems upheld by the Brahmans, the Sikhs were not 'Hindu'. It is significant to note that the seventeenth-century *Janamsakhis* look at the Panth of Guru Nanak not only as a new Panth but also as a Panth which was distinct like the Panth of the Vaishnavas, the Panth of the Jogis, and the Panth of the Muslims. The Nanak-Panthis had their distinctive places and mode of worship. Even their mode of salutation was distinctive. The consciousness of distinct identity is much more pronounced in the compositions of Bhai Gurdas who wrote mostly in the early seventeenth century. The Sikh consciousness of distinct identity sprang from empirical realities: scriptures, doctrines, institutions, sacred spaces and sacred places, their own sense of brotherhood, and the recognition by outsiders that they were different. In any case, not to be different in every way from others around in the seventeenth century did not mean that one was a Hindu in the religious sense of the term. The context in the *Janamsakhis* in which Guru Nanak says that he is a 'Hindu' makes his meaning abundantly clear: he was not a Muslim. We have noticed already that the Sikhs could be regarded as Hindu in the sense of non-Muslim Indians. As such, they stood bracketed with millions of other Indians.

It is interesting to note that Bhai Kahn Singh Nabha has no objection to the Sikhs being called Hindu if the term meant simply Indian, without bringing in any religious dimension. The crucial question about the Hindu-Sikh debate is why at that particular juncture so much importance came to be attached to religious identity. A part of the answer is provided by Bhai Kahn Singh's *Ham Hindu Nahin.* He is keen to establish that the Sikhs were a distinct *qaum* (earlier, Panth), like Hindus and Muslims. To recognize this was to recognize that the Sikhs were a political community, a nationality. This recognition should lead to their worldly progress. To be an appendage of another *qaum* was to remain at a perpetual disadvantage. To say this was not unpatriotic. The Sikhs were prepared to struggle for the common interests of all Indians, shoulder to shoulder with the other 'nations' like Hindus and Muslims. Overarching all of them was the Indian Nation. In a sense, Bhai Kahn Singh subscribed to communitarian nationalism. He was not alone. By many others at the opening of the present century, and even later, 'the nation of Indians was visualized as a composite body, consisting of several communities, each with its own history and culture and its own special contribution to make to the common nationality. India, and the emerging Indian nation, was conceived as a collection of communities: Hindu + Muslim + Christian + Parsi + Sikh, and so on'. The point we wish to underline is that the issue of religious identity was closely linked with politics. If it is a problem, it is at least a century old.

IV

In retrospect, we can see that the pamphlet on Khalistan had nothing to do with the Akalis. Its idea appealed to some Sikhs who were actually opposed to them. The Azad Punjab scheme involved reorganization to ensure that no religious community was in absolute majority in this reorganized politico-administrative unit of the Indian State. The relationship of this unit with the Indian State was not spelt out, but it may not be unsafe to assume that it was something like 'provincial autonomy'. The Sikh state conditionally demanded by the Akalis was different from the Azad Punjab essentially in being sovereign, rather than autonomous. This was true of their later demand for a sovereign state irrespective of whether or not Pakistan was created. With no more than twenty per cent Sikhs within its frontiers, this sovereign state was not really 'Sikh'. The proposal was unrealistic. It was opposed by the Muslim leaders. It had no appeal for the Hindu or the Congress leaders. There was no scope of the proposal being taken up seriously by the colonial administrators and politicians, even if some of them were sympathetic to the Sikhs.

Though unrealistic in terms of the situation on the ground, the Akali demand for a Sikh state underlined their concern for the future and gave trenchant expression to their political aspirations based on their self-image. The literature published in connection with this demand gave an elaborate rationale for Sikh 'nationhood' on which the demand for self-determination was based. The demand of the Akalis for political recognition on the basis of Sikh identity was the culmination of a process which had started half a century earlier. They have never relinquished the claim to represent the Sikh Panth. The form in which this recognition was sought in 1945-46, that is a sovereign state, was never forgotten by their opponents after 1947. The ultimate design of sovereignty, and therefore of secession, was seen in every important political move or demand of the Akalis, parti-cularly by their opponents in the Punjab. Even at the national level there was a certain degree of distrust. The significance of the Akali demand for a sovereign Sikh state, which incidentally was supported by the Communist Party, was not merely negative. The idea could be revived by interested individuals or parties. Because of the changed demographic situation, the idea of a sovereign Sikh state or Khalistan acquires altogether a new significance and carries far different implications now than before 1947. That was why even the 'paper tigers' like Jagjit Singh Chauhan, the Dal Khalsa, and Ganga Singh Dhillon could create some political ripples.

Sant Jarnail Singh Bhindranwale's initial concern was with religious reform. His anti-Nirankari programmc was an important implication of this concern. To look upon his advocacy or use of violence in this connection as a political programme is to do violence to the ordinary connotation of 'the political'. But he used violence for other purposes as well, partly in reaction to violence used by others, which created a vicious circle. This circle was rapidly transformed into a spiral. It is absolutely clear that Sant Jarnail Singh Bhindranwale would not have been able to do all that he did without the support and protection of some Congress leaders who had their own political designs and purposes. The failure of negotiated settlement with the Akalis and the known links of Giani Zail Singh with the Sant added much to his prestige and influence. Several other factors have to be added to understand the influence and the 'authority' which Sant Jarnail Singh came to exercise. For our immediate purpose, however, it is more relevant to know the stage at which his activity became 'political'. Even more relevant is to know whether or not Khalistan became his political objective. If he had this objective in mind he did not make a public declaration. Quite obviously, he did not mobilize people in the name of Khalistan. In the absence of a declared objective, his statements and his activities have to be more carefully interpreted.

This does not mean, however, that there was no movement for Khalistan, or that this movement had nothing to do with Sant Jarnail Singh Bhindranwale. It is not possible to identify a single point of time for the beginning of the movement, but it is safe to suggest the relevance of Operation Blue Star, Operation Wood Rose, the anti-Sikh violence in Delhi, and the failure of the Rajiv-Longowal Accord for the emergence of a conscious objective and its pursuit by an increasing number of militant groups. They did not operate under the leadership of a single person, but they appear to have held Sant Jarnail Singh in high esteem. Nevertheless, they could work against one another. They were joined by individuals who were not politically committed. There was infiltration too. But they did have their sympathisers and supporters, not only outside the Punjab and in foreign countries but also in the Punjab itself. On the whole, it may be valid to talk of a movement for Khalistan. Individuals professing affiliation to the Damdami Taksal and the All India Sikh Students

Federation were more conspicuous in the movement than others, if there were others. That is why the movement has been and can be associated with Sant Jarnail Singh Bhindranwale. There are individuals, mostly abroad, who still subscribe to the idea of Khalistan. But there is no movement. In an unguarded moment K.P.S. Gill, the Director General of Police who is credited with successful handling of the militants, expressed his gratification by saying that there would be no such movement for thirty years. The implication is clear enough.

The Akalis have never demanded a sovereign state for the Sikhs after 1946. There has been a demand for Sikh Homeland standing in a special relationship with the Centre and having a special internal arrangement, but only by individuals or small splinter groups of the Akalis. Paradoxically, it is impossible to think of a 'Sikh Homeland' without the Indian Union within which the 'Sikh Homeland' is to have its being. What the Akalis have insisted upon is autonomy for the Punjab and for other states in the country, a truly federal system – something like the system visualized by the Constituent Assembly before it became clear that Pakistan was going to be created. The Akalis have never resorted to armed militancy or violence for attaining any political objective. Their approach has been constitutional or agitational since 1920. It is a very strong tradition. Their compromising gestures towards Sant Jarnail Singh Bhindranwale and his followers did not change either the political objective or the approach of the Akalis. At the most we can think of a partial and temporary convergence of *morchas*, and not of the two movements.

If we look at the development of Akali politics after Independence, it appears to have been marked more by agitational than constitutional approach, understandably because their smaller number and the adoption of the Indian Constitution did not leave much choice. The government on its part, in the state and at the Centre, has pursued a policy of resistance and confrontation, punctuated at times by accom-modation. We can think of two important demands of the Akalis for which they did not agitate. The first was for weightage and proportional representation which was not conceded. The second was about the recognition of Punjabi as the medium of school education, which was largely met by the Sachar Formula. The Regional Formula was a result of negotiations but it had been preceded by agitation for a Punjabi-speaking state.

The Regional Formula was not implemented. Logically, therefore, there was a second phase of agitation. This also meant a long delay in the creation of the Punjabi-speaking state. More important, however, was the difference in the form of this and the earlier linguistic states. This difference from the Akali viewpoint was discriminatory and it gave birth to new problems simultaneously with the creation of the new state. The Akali experience of government, marked by a feeling of interference in political terms and constraints in economic terms, added one more item to their agenda. Among other things, the political and economic demands of the Akalis were articulated in the Anandpur Sahib Resolution of 1973, and reiterated at Ludhiana in 1978. The Rajiv-Longowal Accord is the best example of accommodation on the part of the government. But it failed, partly because of the way in which it was formulated but largely because of the forces working against its implementation.

The Hindu-Sikh debate about identity has been a source of confusion. Some questions are bound to get inadequate if not wrong answers. Whether or not Sikhs were Hindu was one such question. We can persist in asking this question but without getting any wiser. Sikh identity, like every other identity, is a product of history. One can fruitfully go into the evolution of this identity, in all its complications. But one has to start at the beginning. To be a Sikh was to be a follower of Guru Nanak. It is necessary to fully grasp the meaning of this simple statement. Guru Nanak told his followers what to believe and what to do, not only through his sermons in prose but also through his poetic compositions. These compositions were used by his followers for worship in congregation. He told his followers that this mode of worship was the most efficacious for attaining to liberation and for them it was the only way. His successors wrote their own compositions, in the name of 'Nanak'. All these compositions were put together in the Granth compiled by Guru Arjan. The compositions of Guru Tegh Bahadur were added to it later. It is now known as the *Adi Granth*, and regarded as Guru Granth Sahib. Like the Granth, the doctrine of Guru-Granth can be logically and historically traced to Guru Nanak's theology. Similarly, the doctrine of Guru-Panth can be traced to his decision to establish a line of succession. The *dharmsala*, with the twin institutions of *sangat* and *langar*, which developed into the present-day *gurdwara*, has come down from the days of Guru Nanak. The ideal of social commitment can be traced to his ideas and practice. The adoption of new beliefs, practices and institutions made the Sikhs conscious of their identity quite early in their history, and this consciousness was reinforced by later historical developments. The institution of the Khalsa by Guru Gobind Singh appears to be a great landmark in this process precisely because it made Sikh identity externally and unambiguously conspicuous.

The real significance of *Ham Hindu Nahin* has been lost because of preoccupation with Hindu-Sikh debate. The Khalsa had established their power in the late eighteenth century through the force of arms and their political will. Bhai Kahn Singh's argument that the Sikhs should be recognized as a political community was based on reflection and on rational argument. Sikh identity was used as the basis for this recognition. This was altogether a new kind of development, which makes it relevant for the present. The Akalis and the followers of Sant Jarnail Singh Bhindranwale invoke the same identity, but they differ in their purposes. Even on the use of force there is no difference between them in theory. They subscribe to the idea that it is legitimate to use force. Their representatives often quote the Persian couplet from Guru Gobind Singh's *Zafarnama* which means that it is legitimate to take up the sword when all other means have failed. The difference lies in interpreting 'when all other means have failed'. For the Akalis, that time has not come. For the followers of Sant Jarnail Singh, as much as for him, the time for the use of physical force had come. It may be tempting to see the objective of sovereign rule as a logical and inevitable step from the objective of autonomy. Historically, however, the failure to tackle the demands of the Akalis entered as a factor in the rise of militancy, associated with the movement for Khalistan.

NOTES

1. Indu Banga, 'The Crisis of Sikh Politics (1940-47)'. *Sikh History and Religion in the Twentieth Century.* Ed. Joseph T.O'Connell & others. Toronto: Centre for South Asian Studies, University of Toronto, 1988, 233-55.

2. Sadhu Singh Hamdard. *Azad Punjab* (Urdu). Amritsar: 1943.

3. Gurbachan Singh and Lal Singh Giani. *The Idea of the Sikh State.* Lahore: Lahore Book Shop, 1946. Relevant in this context are also the following: G. Adhikari. *Sikh Homeland Through Hindu-Muslim-Sikh Unity.* Bombay: 1944. Harnam Singh. *Punjab: The Homeland of the Sikhs.* Lahore: 1945. Swarup Singh. *The Sikhs Demand Their Homeland.* London: 1946.

4. J.S. Grewal. *The Sikhs of the Punjab (The New Cambridge History of India,*

II, 3). Cambridge: Cambridge University Press, 1990. For more sources, the 'Bibliograhical Essay' in this book is useful. Mark Tully and Satish Jacob. *Amritsar. Mrs. Gandhi's Last Battle.* Calcutta: Rupa & Co, 1985.

5. J.S. Grewal. T*he Akalis: A Short History.* Chandigarh: Punjab Studies Publications, 1996. Relevant in this context are also the following: Indu Banga. 'The Emergence of Hindu Consciousness in Colonial Punjab'. *Self Images, Identity and Nationality.* Ed. P.C. Chatterjee. Shimla: Indian Institute of Advanced Study, 1989, 201-17. G.S. Bhalla and G.K. Chadha. *Green Revolution and the Small Peasant.* New Delhi: Concept Publishing Company, 1983. Paul Singh Dhillon. *Water Resources Development and Manage-ment in North-West India.* Chandigarh: Centre for Research in Rural and Industrial Development, 1988.

6. Bhai Kahn Singh Nabha. *Ham Hindu Nahin.* Amritsar: Singh Brothers, 1995 (reprint).

7. Gyanendra Pandey (ed). *Hindus and Others: The Question of Identity in India Today.* New Delhi: Viking/Penguin India, 1993, 246.

APPENDIX

Some Other Voices

Attempts have been made to give a coherent and multicausal explanation of what is variously termed as the recent crisis, the recent turmoil, or the Punjab problem. We may turn to Atul Kohli as an example.[1] He refers to the tendency in some of the recent literature to blame Indira Gandhi either because she was an indecisive leader or a Machiavellian leader, or a power-hungry leader who over-centralized the Indian polity. Kohli thinks that the last item mentioned best fits the evidence. But it remains inadequate. There has been a similar tendency to blame the Sikhs either because of the marriage of religion and politics in Sikhism, or because of factionalism within the Akali Party, or because the Sikh community is bent upon imposing its will on the Hindus. Kohli takes up the middle factor in his fuller explanation, but none of these propositions explains the intensity of the crisis. Concentration on socio-economic changes points to the growing differentiation among the Sikhs, resulting in antipathies. These changes are relevant for understanding the attempts 'to create political unity in a class-divided ethnic community'. But they are not decisive variables. The origins of Punjab's complex and tragic civil disorder can be traced to the political conflict between Indira Gandhi and the Akali Dal. A number of factors made the situation especially explosive. Two of these factors were not new but nonetheless relevant and important: the relatively even division of the population between the Sikhs and the Hindus; the close linkage of religion with politics, which made it difficult for the Akalis to search for political support outside the Sikh community. Four other factors are mentioned by Kohli as contributing to the growing turmoil. One of these was 'the weakness of the Akali Dal as a party'; another was some egregious political errors by Indira Gandhi, like her support to Bhindranwale and the military assault on the Golden Temple; the third was the political impact of wealth in the context of economic differentiation among the Sikhs; and lastly, the presence of educated but unemployed Sikh youth in large numbers.

After giving a condensed account of the events, Kohli comes to the conclusion that the driving force behind the conflict was a power struggle between Indira's Congress and the Akali Dal.[2] 'Both Sikh nationalism and the increasing militancy are better understood as products rather than the source of the power struggle'. It is equally clear to Kohli that leadership passed into the hands of Bhindranwale because of the failure to achieve a negotiated settlement during 1982-84. A settlement would have meant a political victory for the Akalis, with adverse electoral consequences for the Congress in the Punjab and Haryana, and possibly elsewhere in the country. A more self-assured or more enlightened leader could have followed a different track. Not that the Akalis were any better; they also demonstrated the same kind of unprincipled electoral opportunism. But the final responsi-bility of resolving the conflict was Indira Gandhi's. In any case, both the Congress and the Akalis lost initiative and made room for 'a theocratic fundamentalist movement' with all its consequences: the Operation Blue Star, the assassination of Indira Gandhi and the politically directed massacre of large numbers of Sikhs in New Delhi.

Atul Kohli is one of those writers who can see that the government or the national leaders can be partisan, can be mistaken, or can do something wrong. He does not represent the majority. There has been a general tendency to present the Punjab problem as a Sikh problem in terms of 'communalism' or 'fundamentalism' in opposition to nationalism and secularism. Even when sophisticated arguments are given which bring in the implications of 'modernization', economic change, imbalanced development, social differentiation and unemployment, the close connection between religion and politics is presented as the heart of the problem. Given one's commitment to nationalism and secularism, this is actually a foregone conclusion. Wittingly or unwittingly, therefore, one supports those who uphold or profess to uphold nationalism and secularism. On the ground, this turns out to be the ruling party. From the very start, therefore, the dice get loaded against the opponents of the government. There is no need to cite any examples. In nine cases out of ten we are likely to come upon explanations offered in terms of communalism and fundamentalism in opposition to nationalism and secularism.

However, there are some other voices. We may listen to some of the critics of the establishment and to those who are not happy with the concepts of communalism and secularism. The tragedy of the Punjab is not the making of the Punjab alone, says one such writer, and goes on to add that the entire nation is a party to it. He underlines certain facts which are generally unpalatable. The non-reading of the Anandpur Sahib Resolution, coupled with persuasive misinformation and disinformation spread by the Centre, created the chimeric image of the Sikh fanatic. The Congress never squarely faced the Akali demands. The Anandpur Sahib Resolution was called secessionist, the case of river waters was withdrawn from the Supreme Court, and the issue of Chandigarh was linked with Abohar and Fazilka. The Congress insisted on communalizing the demands of the Akalis by raising the bogey of Sikh separatism. At the same time, the Congress was able to place a communalizing catalyst in the shape of Sant Bhindranwale.[3] This approach is labelled by another writer as 'penetration strategy'. You stand for separation of religion and politics; encourage use of religion within a certain community for political purposes; and then take action against the community for mixing religion with politics.[4]

The concept of communalism does not appeal to some scholars any more. The dyad of communalism/nationalism is a poor formulation for understanding the Indian realities on the ground. The concept of communalism is a category arising out of a particular kind of political agenda. 'Just as the new nationalism-secular, democratic and, in time, socialist was defined largely in opposition to growing politics of communalism, so communalism - or the politics of "religious community" or "communities" which gave rise to such tension, suspicion and strife — was defined in opposition to what was now conceived of as nationalism'.[5] Furthermore, the problem of 'recognising and accommodating the necessary autonomies and rights of defined social "collectivities" or "segments", call them ethnic, regional, linguistic or religious, is one of the major items of the contemporary politics of States and international organisations'.[6]

Another scholar finds dichotomous conceptualizations analytically useless when applied to religious or ethnically heterogeneous societies. When an either-or conceptualization becomes the basis for policy analysis, the policy makers wedded to dichotomous analytical categories tend towards repressive solution. But there is no reason to believe that ethnic sub-political systems cannot exist side by side with secular systems and compete 'constructively within the same geographical area'.[7]

On the concept of secularism too, we hear dissenting voices. 'The academic debate that has gone on for some time, about whether or not secularism is an Indian concept, applicable to Indian conditions, seems to me to be somewhat misplaced. For the alternatives are clear: the struggle for a genuine pluralism, which would engender respect for divergent beliefs and the rights of individuals and minorities, on the one hand; narrowness, intolerance and murder, on the other'.[8] The conception of the modern state is seen as an obstacle in the way of 'a context sensitive' approach because it does not recognize within its jurisdiction any form of community except the single, determinate, demographically innumerable form of the nation. 'It must therefore subjugate, if necessary by the use of violence, all such aspirations of community identity. These other aspirations, in turn, can give to themselves a valid historical justification only by claiming an alternative nationhood with rights to an alternative state'. Unless the conception of the state changes, ethnic identities cannot be accommodated: they can revolt.[9]

NOTES

1. Atul Kohli. *Democracy and Discontent: India's Growing Crisis of Governability.* Cambridge: Cambridge University Press, 1991 (Indian Paperback Edition 1995-reprint), 353-55.

2. Ibid, 376-77.

3. Dipankar Gupta. 'The Communalising of Punjab 1980-1985'. *Punjab: The Fatal Miscalculation.* Eds. Patwant Singh and Harji Malik. New Delhi: 1985, 209-29.

For a more detailed discussion of the issue, Dipankar Gupta. *The Context of Ethnicity: Sikh Identity in a Comparative Perspective.* Delhi: Oxford University Press, 1996.

4. Vivek Sagar Minocha. *The Punjab Problem.* Delhi: Ajanta Publications, 1989, 5, 9, 11, 25.

5. Gyanendra Pandey. *The Construction of Communalism in Colonial North India.* Delhi: Oxford University Press, 1994 (Paperback, 2nd Impression), 21-22, 241.

6. Gyanendra Pandey (ed). *Hindus and Others*, 20.

7. Paul Wallace and Surendra Chopra (eds). *Political Dynamics of Punjab*. Amritsar: Guru Nanak Dev University, 1981, 3.

8. Rasheeduddin Khan. *Bewildered India: Identity, Pluralism, Discord*. New Delhi: Har-Anand Publications, 1995.

9. Partha Chatterjee. *The Nation and its Fragments*. Delhi: Oxford University Press, 1994, 238.

6

A Decade of Violence, 1983-1992

K. S. DHILLON

This paper seeks to explore the course of Sikh militancy in the Punjab, especially its more virulent phase from 1983 to 1992, with all its accompanying violence and counter-violence; trace its origin and growth in the context of the total Indian situation; pinpoint some significant causative factors; delineate the broad policy framework and the techniques employed to contain and purportedly to finally destroy it. It may be stated at the outset that some of the characteristic attitudes of the Sikhs are the product of a considerably long process of history: the qualities of self-assertion, cool and defiant courage, a vast reservoir of tough, unyielding sullen-ness in the face of injustice and cruelty, an innate superiority, and a belief in their inalienable right to exercise power. The British colonial state, appreciative of the massive Sikh support it received in 1857, fully exploited the in-built Sikh sensibilities to cultivate in them a firm conviction that they were a group of special people with an inherent claim on special privileges, regardless of their small numbers.

The arithmetic of numbers brought the community down to earth to face the reality and mechanics of power-sharing in a democracy in the post-Independence India. The denial of the long cherished 'special' status in the new Indian Constitution which the Sikhs had been led to believe by some Congress leaders would be given to them in an Independent India; the failure of the Indian State to concede a Punjabi language state when all other major Indian languages had been so accommodated; a systematic subversion of all efforts by the only Sikh political party, the Akali Dal, to come to power in the Punjab through democratic means, and finally, its near annihilation as the only legitimate political voice of the community – all these factors set aflame the long simmering discontent in large sections of the Sikhs, more so the younger elements. The violence and terrorism which accompanied militant politics were unparalleled in the world in their sweep and lethal effects. A conservative estimate puts the total number of killings during the period at over 25,000.

MILITANCY, TERRORISM AND INSURGENCY

Militancy, terrorism and insurgency are terms sometimes loosely and confusingly employed to denote acts of excessive violence against social or governmental targets by a group of disgruntled people or community in order to attain a stated objective which almost always would be of a political nature.[1] Obviously, not all these terms are interchangeable. Militancy is most often a state of mind, a psychological proclivity to forcibly resolve issues con-sidered vital for their honour and dignity by a social or religious group or community. Militancy may frequently express itself in terrorist violence though militant activity may not always be violent in itself. Insurgency is an aggravated form of terrorism leading further to guerrilla activity and civil war, if the conditions remain favourable and the underlying causes remain un- addressed. Terrorism is usually the weapon of a small group (small only in comparative terms) while insurgency enjoys far greater popular (or mass) support. Because the terrorists constitute small groups of operators, they do not seek to establish control (of a formal or informal nature) over territory, or run a 'government'. Insurgents on the other hand, try to replace the existing regime with one of their persuasion. Their endeavour is to enlarge and expand the base of their influence by governing in a manner that may attract the population and convert them to their cause. Terrorism is often met with counter-terrorism by the state and its instruments – a phenomenon common in autocratic and dictatorial regimes as also in most developing countries with a weak commitment to 'the due process'. The phenomenon is also known as 'state-terrorism'. State terror is actually far more sinister and deadly in the toll it takes of the life and property of mostly innocent citizens and in the damage it causes to social harmony and equilibrium. It amounts to an abuse of legitimate state power vested in it for national defence and public security. Not uncommonly, state terrorism promotes a more wide-spread response from terrorist groups as it sharpens grievances, discontent and alienation and broadens their support-base.[1]

An anatomy of militancy, terrorism and insurgency is diagrammatically represented in Appendix A.

CHARACTERISTICS OF TERRORISM

In spite of the fact that terrorism and militancy have emerged as major challenges to the authority of the Indian State and to the peace and security of its citizens, we are no closer to an acceptable definition of terrorism now than we were half a century ago, when the phenomenon first took concrete shape in Europe and West Asia. Largely because of the political sensitivities involved, it is virtually impossible to formulate a generic definition of terrorism that can gain universal acceptance. It may be easier and far more useful, therefore, to identify the salient characteristics of terrorist violence. Broadly in line with Parkinson's *Political Terrorism*, we may list the following:

1. *The use or the threat of the use of violence:* Acts of terrorism inevitably involve the use or the threat of the use of violence. Not all acts committed by terrorist groups are terroristic and not all terrorist acts are committed by terrorist groups. This distinction is important in formulating anti-terrorist policy.

2. *Psychological intimidation:* Terrorism is basically a physiological tactic. The physical damage done may in fact be not very large. The ultimate aim of terrorists is to use the fear they have generated psychologically to force governing authorities to bend to their will. Thus anti-terrorist policy must address the broader question of countering terror, not merely terrorist acts.

3. *Politically driven activity:* For the law-enforcement agency, there may be little intrinsically different between a criminal act by a criminal gang and one involving a known terrorist organisation. For the anti-terrorist policy-maker, however, the distinction is basic. The political aims of the organisation are what set their acts apart as a subject of policy interest. Underlying political unrest and motivations must be kept in mind by policy-makers. Timely means must be found to provide relief from grievances to pre-empt hardening postures.

4. *Ideologically justified activity:* Most terrorists justify their actions not only on the basis of political aims of the group, but by some higher 'universal truth'. It can be religious or secular, nationalist or ethnic, or any other combination of factors. By claiming a higher justification, they seek to secure the sympathies and support of those who share their beliefs or ideology. A close study of the ideological justifications of terrorists usually reveals more about the terrorists

themselves than about their claimed ideologies. This is particularly true in the case of major religious doctrines. Although several terrorists invoke religion to justify their acts, no major religion espouses or justifies terrorism.

5. *Non-combatant activity:* Terrorist strategy does not distinguish between military and civilian targets, and generally strikes at innocent (non-combatant) targets.

6. *Criminal activity:* Whatever the justification, virtually all forms of terrorism are criminal in nature – assault, murder, kidnapping, hijacking, arson, sabotage etc. The inherent criminal nature of terrorism distinguishes it from guerrilla warfare and insurgent operations which, while not fully sanctioned as conventional warfare, are still considered more in the context of military than criminal behaviour.

7. *Covert activity:* To say that terrorism is a covert activity is certainly stating the obvious, but it does underline the additional difficulties involved in investigations and intelligence gathering. Policy-makers must be alive to these difficulties in planning and committing resources to counter-terrorist activity.

8. *Maximized public exposure:* Important as secrecy is in planning and carrying out anti-terrorist operations, maximum public exposure is crucial afterwards. The concerned segments must be made aware of the full implications of a terrorist act or activity. Terrorist groups often seek to manipulate the news media to their advantage. Any worthwhile counter-terrorist strategy must meet such maneuvers with equal efficiency.

9. *Relative low cost:* Although some terrorist acts are very elaborate and sophisticated, the cost of terrorism, as compared to other forms of low intensity conflict, is very low. The low cost factor greatly enhances the value of terrorism as an option, particularly to small groups with limited resources.

10. *A sympathetic constituency:* Terrorist groups cannot operate for an extended period of time in a totally hostile operational environment. They need freedom of movement, safe houses, financial backing, manpower for recruitment and a secure base for operations. These needs are secured from a segment of society (both at home and abroad) that sympathizes either with the group's goals or its leadership, identifies with their statement of grievances or is opposed to the governing authority or policies against which the terrorist organisations' efforts are aimed. Combating terrorism must take

into account the domestic and foreign implications of seeking to isolate terrorist groups from their bases of popular support. Many terrorist groups also obtain crucial support from foreign powers, support that is often crucial for their very survival. Such support could be in the form of funds, weapons, training and motivation, and of course, shelter.

11. *Small-group activity:* Terrorism is basically a group activity. Terrorist groups impose very powerful constraints on their members and bestow very strong rewards. Rewards of groups identity are particularly attractive to those with a low self-esteem, a widely prevalent characteristic among terrorists. Terrorist groups are generally small in size. Larger groups have more difficulty in maintaining internal discipline and are more easily penetrated. The small size and the resulting mobility of terrorist groups (whether independent or sub-groups of larger organisations) make the job of identification, investigation and apprehension all the more difficult.

POLITICAL TERRORISM

The characteristics of terrorism listed above do not constitute a self-contained typology, or a generic definition of terrorism. They are almost always present in all cases in varying degrees of concentration. On a different plane, we may obtain some valuable insights into the nature and operational modes of terrorism by distinguishing political terrorism from the other forms of terrorism. Criminal terrorism is the systematic use of terror for obtaining material gain; psychic terrorism has religious or mystic dimensions; war terrorism aims at wearing down the enemy's resistance and diminishing his ability to wage war with the ultimate objective of destroying him. Political terrorism is the calculated use or threat of violence to secure political gains. It must be added that criminal terrorists seek to gain the relative respectability of political terrorists by masquerading as such. The turbulence created by political terrorism may provide climate conducive to many criminal terrorist gangs to pursue their vocation, be it smuggling, narcotic trafficking, boot-legging, kidnapping for ransom, or bank-robberies. On the other hand, political terrorists often indulge in criminal terrorism to raise funds to finance their campaigns. Such linkages and overlaps blur the ideological appeal of political terrorists and may hasten their liquidation. Political terrorism, whether the use of violence is justified or not, is an act of war against the state and in this respect it is qualitatively different from criminal terrorism. Initial reaction of law-enforcement agencies all over the world is to treat terrorism as a criminal act so as to deny the perpetrators of violence the status of a fighter in a political cause. This stage in the case of a truly political group lasts but a short while. Soon, through the sheer nature and volume of terrorist acts, with their spectacular configurations and the attendant media publicity which makes them appear larger than lifesize, those responsible for such acts establish their status and role of fighters for a cause where the fight is against the state itself. It is not long after that the state is compelled to induct the security forces to deal with the situation so created, not as a criminal activity to be handled by the police alone but as a far more serious problem, necessitating the employment of a broad spectrum of war- like measures.

THE DRUG CONNECTION

The close links between drugs and terrorism are well known. It is now no secret that in the so-called Iran-Contra affair, large quantities of cocaine were brought into the USA by intermediaries who were flying the arms clandestinely into Central America. The returning aircraft were not checked by the US Customs and other agencies since the operation was widely believed to enjoy the approval of the National Security Council. The infamous General Noreiga, indicted by a US court for allowing his country to become a conduit for drug-trafficking and money-laundering, was at one time himself an operator for the US intelligence. The prime US intelligence agency has, in fact, a long association with such activities dating back to the early 1950's in China, and later in Vietnam. The after-effects of a glut of modern weaponry in Afghanistan and the bordering areas of Pakistan are all too apparent in the almost total breakdown of law and order in Karachi and Hyderabad (Sind). The connection of Sikh terrorist groups with narco-terrorism and gun-running has been extensively documented by the Punjab Police and Indian Intelligence agencies. In fact, the drug-barons, the military establishments not accountable to democratic institutions, the covert intelligence operations, and the financial underworld which helps to launder black money – together form a powerful and unassailable combine. Terrorist groups justify their connections on the need for raising huge funds, required for purchase of arms to vigorously pursue their political objectives. In the bargain, they not only subvert the minds, morals and motivations of their active membership, but also lose credibility within their support base. Almost all terrorist movements tend to develop close linkages with drug lords, at one time or the other. Several Sikh militant groups in the Punjab have been strongly suspected of having forged close links with the narcotics mafias in Pakistan. What is certain is that the drug connection of Sikh militants grew from strength to strength after 1986 till it became a major factor (together with the horrendous orgy of violence, rapes, murders, kidnappings, robberies and other rapacious acts let loose by them against the local populace) in the success of the security forces in destroying the gangs one after the other in 1992-93.

SIKH MILITANCY AND TERRORISM

The Indian National Congress which continued to wield power in Delhi and all the states of the Union for almost 30 years after Independence, pursued partisan politics of the worst kind in order to prevent the Sikh political party, the Akali Dal, from coming to power in the Punjab. India was reorganised into linguistic states in 1956. The principle of linguistic states was, however, not made applicable to the Punjab, which became a sore point with the Sikhs. The Akali Party had to launch an agitation for a Punjabi-speaking state. The Akali Party formed their first ministry in the Punjab in 1967 in coalition with the urban Hindu party, the Jan Sangh. The Congress, however, was unhappy at this development and soon dislodged them from power with the help of defectors. The Akali Party enjoyed a second spell of office in 1977, with the help of the newly formed Janata Party after the General Elections of 1977 – in the wake of the infamous Emergency rule by Indira Gandhi. The Congress moved now not only to dislodge the Akalis from power but to finish them off altogether as the legitimate political voice of the Sikhs. For this purpose Sant Jarnail Singh Bhindranwale was chosen by some highly placed Congress leaders to be projected as a counterpoise to the Sikh political leadership. He was encouraged to extensively tour the countryside in order to undermine the Akali influence and gather support for himself. He was even allowed to openly violate the provisions of the Indian Arms Act not only in the Punjab but also in Delhi, Bombay and some Indian states. In the event, he assumed a larger than life image among the Sikh masses and in a period of five years reduced the entire Akali leadership to a helpless bunch. The Congress aim was of course fully achieved and the political voice of the Sikh community was effectively silenced with the Akali Party disintegrating through factionalism and fragmentation. Bhindranwale now strode the Punjab like a colossus gathering strength and overcoming all opposition, due to his rising appeal in the countryside and with the help of his growing band of heavily armed retainers. Soon myths and legends grew among the Sikh masses and, not very chary of using the bullet even at the best of times to settle arguments with those who opposed him, he soon became a law unto himself and the arbiter of all that happened in the Punjab. He became the foremost champion of what to him was the ultimate Sikh demand – creation of a separate Sikh state, to be called Khalistan. Though the Congress governments both in the Punjab and in Delhi were somewhat alarmed at the turn of events, deterrent action against the Sant was not taken. On the other hand, his occupation of the Akal Takht in 1983 as also the accumulation of a huge arsenal of sophisticated weaponry and other war-like stores went unchecked by the authorities. Not even the day-light killing of a senior Sikh police officer by the militants on the steps of the Temple in full view of the police and magistrates on duty at the place, brought forth a prompt and effective response from the government. Bhindranwale and his followers, operating now from the Golden Temple itself, let loose a reign of terror in the Punjab and some neighbouring states, killing with impunity police officials and informers, government agents, political foes and Hindus and striking freely at chosen targets. The era of terrorism and militancy in the Punjab had well and truly commenced and nothing seemed to check the illegal and violent activities of Sant Bhindranwale and his followers.

With the situation fast deteriorating into anarchy and total chaos, the Government of India finally decided to move the Indian Army on 3 June 1984, and struck with heavy armour and tanks. The operation was not a great success in as much as a large number of the followers of the Sant managed to escape, and a few hundred innocent pilgrims including women and children were killed. Bhindranwale and his close aides were of course eliminated but extensive damage was caused to the Akal Takht and other holy buildings. Valuable manuscripts were lost in arson that destroyed the highly prized library located in the Temple premises. 'Operation Blue Star' also involved'neutralising' other Sikh temples in the Punjab. 'Operation Wood Rose' was launched soon after to flush out the terrorists and their supporters from the countryside. Military operations are, by their very nature, cruel and ruthless. Acute harassment, untold atrocities, rough handling and humiliating behaviour on the part of non-Sikh troops during the action became a particularly sore point with the community. Although there is reason to believe that several cases of such nature were duly looked into by the authorities and disciplinary action taken, wounds inflicted during 'Blue Star' and, later 'Wood Rose', would not heal in a hurry. Military action was also perceived by a large segment of the intelligentsia as an electoral gimmick to impress upon the predominantly Hindu (85 per cent) population of India the resolve of the Congress Party to guard against Sikh secessionist designs. It generated serious unrest and resentment among the Sikh troops, many of whom mutinied. Young Sikh men crossed over to Pakistan in large numbers. It was this section of the Sikh youth who would later return to their homeland fully motivated and armed with sophisticated weapons to spark off probably the most lethal form of terrorism flaring up anywhere in the world. Their acts of violence included mass as well as selective killings, assassinations of important personages, sabotage, arson, blowing up of railway tracks, roads and bridges, looting of banks, bomb explosions in public places and public transport, and hijacking of aircraft and public buses.

Indira Gandhi was shot down by her two Sikh guards on 31 October 1984. Her assassination sparked off a widespread orgy of killings, plunder, rapes and arson directed against the Sikhs in Delhi and several other Indian cities. The killings were indiscriminate, unnecessarily cruel and carried out with meticulous planning and fore-thought, with the Sikh police disarmed and taken off duty. Thousands lost their lives, honour, property and means of livelihood. Some migration of Sikhs to the Punjab also took place. It was commonly believed then and later substantiated in many enquiry reports that the Congress Party and some of its senior leaders in Delhi were actively involved in incitement, instigation and planning the carnage. Predictably the government action was tardy, listless, half-hearted and negligent. Few, if any, investigations were pursued with vigour and competence. The discriminatory handling of the anti-Sikh riots of 1984 was another instance of the inept handling of the Sikh problem and a major step in the ongoing process of the alienation of the Sikhs.

In the post-Blue Star phase, specially after 1985, Sikh terrorism seemed to be invincible and soon enveloped almost the entire Punjab and parts of Haryana, Delhi, UP and Rajasthan. A detailed statement given in Appendix B, covering a period of 13 years from 1981 to 1993, will show the extent of depredations in the Punjab alone.

The violent activities of the Sikh terrorists in the Punjab continued to escalate till the middle of 1992 after which they started to decline. The seizures of weapons from terrorists in 1992 included 539 AK series rifles, 34 rocket launchers, 22 carbines, 324 rifles, 380 guns, over 1600 kilograms of explosives and large quantities of ammunition – a formidable arsenal by any means. However, a report based on the monthly intelligence summary of the Punjab government for November 1993 estimated the holdings of major types of weapons by terrorist groups in the Punjab as 1543 AK 47s, 106 rocket launchers, 112 General Purpose Machine Guns (GPMGs) and several quintals of explosives. The number of hardcore and non-hardcore terrorists operating in the Punjab and elsewhere was put at 144 and 963 respectively. There were also reports of fresh recruitment to the ranks of terrorists – Khalistan Liberation Force (KLF), Khalistan Commando Force (KCF Panjwar), and Babbar Khalsa International (BKI) as also fresh re-groupings and realignments. Despite the claims of sealing of the borders, the militants managed to smuggle over 400 AK 47s, 60 revolvers and pistols and 8 quintals of explosives. The success of the security forces in eliminating the major militant leadership, holding of elections to the Punjab Legislative Assembly in January 1992 and to the Panchayats in January 1993, brought a measure of confidence and the fear-psychosis in urban areas abated. A perceptible improvement in public morale in the villages also took place. The security forces were engaged in mopping up operations in the Punjab and other states of the country.

Practically the entire terrorist leadership was eliminated and the movement met with nearly total collapse. However, some of the groups still held adequate capacity to regroup and substantial fire power to carry out acts of violence, if not in the Punjab, in some other states of the Union. As late as February 1995, a well-connected industrialist was kidnapped from the Rajasthan state capital of Jaipur by the Khalistan Liberation Front led by Navneet Singh Khalsa (also known as Navneet Singh Qadian). Not only was the victim rescued in a short time, the leader of the front was also shot dead. Many of the important leaders took shelter in other states, notably UP, HP, Rajasthan, Haryana and Assam. The Khalistan Liberation Front of Navneet Singh Khalsa, the Khalistan Commando Force (P) of Paramjit Singh Panjwar and Babbar Khalsa International of Wadhawa Singh appeared to have survived in a sufficiently intact position to pose a viable potential threat. Reports indicated that Sikh militants recruited from abroad and extensively trained in the handling of weapons and techniques in using sophisticated explosive devices were in reserve with the Pakistani agencies for infiltration into India with plans to indulge in subversive and violent acts in important commercial and economic centres in the country. However, serious sectarian conflicts developing in Karachi and some other parts of Pakistan, as also the latter's total involvement with the Kashmir question, limited that country's active sponsorship of the Punjab terrorists.[3]

Sikh terrorism during most part of the 1980s possessed all the characteristics and well-known features of a politically oriented separatist movement. Subsequently and gradually it degenerated into a pure and simple criminal terrorism. This change not only facilitated police infiltration into the terrorist groups in a major way, it also turned the people totally against them. The flow of intelligence improved and soon it became a torrent. Toning down of material and logistical support by Pakistan under international pressure (its major attention now diverted to helping the Kashmir militants), sealing and fencing of the Punjab-Pak border and massive action against smugglers, drug-traffickers and their supporters, all contributed to the neutralisation of this major threat to India's territorial integrity. Another important factor which considerably improved the operational capabilities of the Punjab Police was its reorientation, modernisation and reorganisation on the recommendations of a high-power committee of experts of which this writer was the member-secretary. The across-the-board reforms in its working modes, reorientation of training systems and syllabi, motivational techniques and a large-scale expansion in its armed battalions and upgrading of their weaponry undertaken in the eighties started showing results soon after. The elimination of Sikh terrorism is obviously the culmination of long process of planning, polishing and perfection of strategies over a long period though the spectacular results achieved in 1993-94 may not, on the face of it, appear to be closely linked to the strategies devised in the past. The single most important factor in the succcss of the state in this unequal battle was the tremendous response from the people themselves in the form of intelligence and cooperation, at a time when militancy had lost its ideological base and degenerated into pure and simple criminal activity. Since the elections in January 1992 were boycotted by the Akali factions, Congress was elected (though on a minority vote sometimes as low as 10 per cent of the electorate) to form the government in the Punjab. In office, they also rediscovered a hitherto missing political will in sufficient measure to seriously set about eliminating terrorism in the state, to let the police act effectively, ruthlessly, even unlawfully, if necessary. Existing laws were amended, new laws enacted to plug loop holes, police given unprecedented freedom from legal and democratic accountability, if they would only show tangible results. They were free to resort to any means – within the law if possible, outside it if necessary – to eliminate the challenge of terrorism. As the people were fed up and the movement had lost its ideological appeal, not many complained. Feeble protests by some human rights and civil liberties organisations were ignored or suppressed.

The basic grievances of the community however remain unaddressed, with Rajiv-Longowal Accord of 1985 all but defunct. Obviously another political initiative is called for to consolidate the gains and purposefully utilise the return of peace to the trouble torn state after one of the most violent decades in recent Indian history. Unfortunately, though characteristically, with the restoration of normalcy all references to political solutions have ceased. This is hardly an indication of administrative maturity. Let us not forget that though violence and terrorism have been eliminated, political grievances still remain. A mature, informed and statesman-like approach is urgently called for.

It may be pertinent to reproduce at this point what a senior Pakistani General holding a key appointment said some time ago about Pakistani interest in the Punjab and Kashmir:

> It may be prudent to follow a policy of normalisation with India (while) maintaining a credible military deterrence. We should, however, exploit Indian instabilities through media and other psychological operations and covert means. Our external problems with Afghanistan; internal political, economic and psychological weaknesses have greatly curtailed our liberty of action. We only hope that we can overcome our problems, while the

Sikhs and the Kashmiris remain active. Pakistan should not lose its chance of the century. Recall our missing the opportunity in 1992.

This comes from Major General M. Tariq, Commandant National Defence College of Pakistan (published in *The Muslim* of 6 April 1990).

Stephen Segaller observes in the *Invisible Armies*:

> To call someone a terrorist dismisses his claim on human sympathy. However unpleasant the political illness may be, to diagnose it correctly must be the first step in reducing the symptoms and ultimately controlling, if not curing, the disease. The case for the terrorist, the small and desperate group is that it is the only weapon (and a potent one) available to those for whom the political process is discredited, or too slow to deliver. Using terror is a low-tech, low-cost high-result route to a world-wide audience. Governments prefer to explain terrorism back-wards taking the carnage and destruction as evidence of psychopathic tendencies. Instead, they should regard terrorist acts as a logical step, if one that inspires revulsion, towards tangible political gains, derived from legitimate political objectives and frustrations.[4]

For too long has the handling of terrorism and insurgency in India suffered from basic inadequacies, misconceptions, bloated thoughts of state power, political disagreements, lack of vision and statesmanship, electoral politics and corruption and inefficiency rampant in different organs of the government. An alternative strategy must take note of these weaknesses, transcend petty partisan interests and treat terrorism and insurgency as the most powerful threat ever to the political stability and territorial integrity of India.

APPENDIX A

Anatomy of Terrorism

CAUSATIVE FACTORS

Administrative

1. Ineffective and inefficient administration
2. Corruption and nepotism
3. Loss of faith in government machinery

Political

4. Autocratic, theocratic or dictatorial regime
5. Suppression of public aspirations
6. Minority and/or unstable government
7. Unpopular government policies
   (a) Reservation of seats
   (b) Family planning
8. National divide on government policies:
   (a) Caste/S.C./S.T. vacancies
   (b) Ethnic/minority priorities
   (c) Urban and rural divide on resources
   (d) Special laws (e.g. Muslim Personal Law) of various minorities
9. Extra-territorial interference

Economic

10. Neglect, apathy and unemployment
11. Undeveloped and economically backward areas
12. Exploitation and inequitable distribution of local resources
    Sociological
13. Ethnic, social or religious disparity
14. Illiteracy and backwardness

PUBLIC RESPONSE	APPARENT INDICATIONS
1. Whisper campaign	a. Talks at homes/offices/buses/ *chopals*
	b. Letters to editors in newspapers
	c. Cartoons in newspapers/magazines
2. Unrest and uneasiness	a. Discussions at various forums
	b. Roadside meetings
	c. Graffities on the walls

3. Appraisal	a. Representations and memoranda b. Resentment in the form of mass casual leave/absence c. Dharnas and local strikes
4. Agitations	a. Rallies and marches b. Demonstrations c. General strikes
5. Confrontation	a. Bandhs and agitations b. Rail and road roko calls c. Fueling of discontent by political leaders
6. Civil Disobedience	a. Confrontation with law and order agencies b. Mass arrests c. Destruction of government property
7. Militancy	a. Propaganda and subversion b. Civil disobedience and sabotage
8. Terrorism	a. Mass killings (arbitrary) b. Kidnappings c. Terrorising of government administrative law and order machinery d. Sabotage of vulnerable points areas
9. Insurgency	a. Regional rebellion b. Declaration of autonomy and independence c. Crippling of law and order and judicial machinery

GOVERNMENT REACTIONS	PUBLIC REACTIONS
1. a. No reaction b. Indifference	1. Resign to fate
2. Ignore/sweep under the carpet	2. Resentment
3. Under-estimation	3. Annoyance
4. Not being able to understand the gravity of the situation or non-comprehension	4. Hardening of attitudes
5. a. Over reaction	5. Defiance

b. Declaring it law and order situation	
c. Deployment of Police and other security agencies	
6. a. Declaring it anti-national /any other political overtone	6. Civil disobedience
b. Dissolution of state government by the Centre	
c. Turning it into a police state	
7. Repression by the government	7. Militancy
a. Arrest of leaders	
b. Unleashing state terrorism	
c. Excessive deployment of security forces	
d. Denial of basic rights of people	
8. a. Central Rule	8. Terrorism
b. Cosmetic piecemeal concession (not solution)	
9. Formation of a police/ military state	9. Insurgency Insurrection

SUGGESTED GOVERNMENT RESPONSE

1. Talks and parleys
2. Setting up of grievances committees
3. Time-bound action plan to resolve the issues
4. Political will to resolve
5. No egoistic stance by government
6. Give and take policy – more give than take

APPENDIX B

Killing Fields of Punjab

THE TERRORISTS ARSENAL			
AK 47	1700	Grenades	30
Self-loading rifles	50	Explosives	2600
G.P. machine guns	130	Night vision devices	3
Medium machine guns	20	Light machine guns	15
Rocket launchers	120	Dragnov sniper rifles	4
Rocket grenades	1350		
Launchers	5	Two inch mortars	1

Persons killed by Terrorists

Year	81	82	83	84	85	86	87	88	89	90	91	92	93
Persons	13	13	75	359	63	520	910	1949	1188	2467	2591	1813	67
Hindus	10	8	35	237	45	324	425	858	442	743	744	1682	74
Sikhs	3	5	40	122	17	193	478	1044	734	1694	1847	-	-
Cops killed by terrorists	2	2	20	20	8	42	95	110	152	493	496	246	
Terrorists killed	14	7	13	77	2	78	328	373	699	1321	2177	1916	(incl. 258 hardcore)
Terrorists arrested	84	178	296	1630	491	1581	3750	3882	2466	1759	1949	389	-

Training Camps in Pakistan

PAKISTAN	OPPOSITE INDIAN LOCATION
Hazura	Ferozepur
Kasur	Khem Karan (Amritsar Dist.)
Purana	Khalra (Amritsar Dist.)
Kahana	
Lahore	Amritsar
Sheikhupura	Ajnala (Amritsar Dist.)
Chungi point	Ajnala (Amritsar Dist.)
Dera Sahib	Ajnala (Amritsar Dist.)
Kartar Singh	
Gujranwala	Dera Baba Nanak (Gurdaspur dist.)
Zaffarwal	Dera Baba Nanak (Gurdaspur dist.)
Narowal	Dera Baba Nanak (Gurdaspur dist.)
Jalalabad	Gurdaspur
Sialkot	Gurdaspur

Strength of Terrorists

	No. of gangs		
	Patiala	Jalandhar	Firozpur
Hardcore terrorists	206	106	140
Non hardcore terrorists	50	20	38
Khalistan Commando Force	10	9	16
Bhindranwale Tiger Force	8	4	1
K.L.F. of Khalistan	10	2	5
Babbars	8	3	4
Other gangs	1	1	3

Source: *Sunday Times of India*, 9 February 1992 and other reports.

NOTES

1. Analysis broadly based a paper on Transnational Crime presented by David E. Long of United States Foreign Service at an International Conference in the University of Illinois in Chicago in August 1988.

2. *Figures for 1993 and 1994*

1993	PUNJAB	UP	HARYANA
	74 incidents	34 incidents	10 incidents
	67 killings	46 killings	7 killed
	DELHI		
	7 incidents, 10 killings		
1994	PUNJAB	UP	HARYANA
	6 incidents	2 incidents	Only one incident
	1 killed	6 killed	

3. This assessment is based on the situation on the ground in March 1993. Subsequent events have shown the near total elimination of the terrorist leadership.Whether the movement can be revived, if ever, in the same form, remains to be seen. Cf. P.D. Sharma. 'Terrorist Violence and Nation Building in India'. Ed. S.C. Tiwari. *Terrorism in India.* New Delhi: South Asian Publications, 1990.

4. Stephen Segaller. *Invisible Armies.* New Delhi: Jupiter Publications, 24-25.

7

Violence in Retrospect

PRAMOD KUMAR

Studies relating to violence in India have paid scant attention to structural roots of violence and their relationship with its various manifestations. Studies conducted on terrorism in the Punjab suffer from this theoretical inadequacy. These studies isolate 'terrorism' and more so 'the terrorists' from their social and political context. In this reductionist approach, violence is treated as merely a law and order problem and it is assumed that with the elimination of terrorists, the conditions responsible for the growth of terrorism are also eliminated. It is imperative to point out, therefore, that violence is a result of certain social conditions and is inseparable from the existence and functioning of social institutions. The return of peace to the Punjab does not imply that the conditions which caused violence have been moderated, subsumed or resolved.

Efforts have been made to study violence as a form of political activity. The nature and direction of change espoused by violent mode of political activity appear to demand serious attention because violence is not seen as an illegal or 'illegitimate' mode of political activity. This view is opposed to the assumption that violence used by the state apparatus is legitimate and, therefore, not 'violence' at all. Violence becomes a truncated subject when its study is confined to insurgent forms and non-state actors to the exclusion of the terror tactics of the sovereign state.[1] The argument that the use of violence by the state against the 'terrorists' is violence in self-defence and, therefore, normatively justifiable, becomes fallacious on this new. It is asserted that violence remains violence whether it is employed by the state or by individuals, or groups. This formulation has a limited explanatory value because the directional component of the violent political activity cannot be ignored. For example, the use of violence by the state to control or to prevent violence can be justified on the utilitarian basis or for reasons of governance or law and order.

Althusser has observed that 'the state Apparatus functions massively and predominantly by repression (including physical repression), while functioning secondarily by ideology. He goes on to add:

> In the same way, but inversely it is essential to say that for their part ideological State Apparatuses function massively and predominantly by ideology, but they also function secondarily by repression even if ultimately, but only ultimately, this is very attenuated and concealed, even symbolic.[2]

It may be observed that in the context of the collapse of 'Ideological State Apparatus' in the case of the Punjab, Kashmir and Assam the use of violence acquired a blatant form. Similarly, because of the collapse of political parties and dysfunctional nature of non-violent means of protest, the use of violence by the militants acquired terrorist character.

Therefore, in any serious analysis of violence the following questions may be posed:

(a) Is violence being used as a substitute of democratic mode of political strategy by the state as well as non-state individuals or groups?

(b) Is it being used only as one of the tactics in a broader strategy ranging from the ideological persuasion to violence?

(c) Is the cause which the users of violence espouse regarded as just by the majority of the people?

Another conceptual framework for studying violence is provided by the 'human rights' perspectives. In this framework, the causation of violence is seen as related to the manner in which the state is organized and functions. As Peterson remarks, the western notion of inalienable rights was antithetical to the interests of the colonial powers who, therefore, were slow to promote the notion among the colonized.[3] After independence, the spirit of the constitution made individual rights central to social justice. The post-colonial state did become the embodiment of individual rights, but the practice of politics and social interaction provided continuity to the colonial policies. Whereas the administrative-legal system concerned itself with and respon-ded to the individual rights, the politics and social discourse relied on ascriptive categories for mobilization and maintaining their support base. In a nutshell, the politics of colonial state found continuity in the post-Independence phase, particularly in the practice of politics.

This perspective excludes from its purview the violence perpetrated by the individuals or collectivities against each other and it does not give adequate recognition to socio-economic formations.

In the debate on violence it has been acknowledged that terrorism is a form of violence. Indeed, the demonstration and actual use of force, which has a multiplier effect, is central to terrorism, However, violence may not necessarily involve the actual use and demonstration of force because it can be actualized through the operation of anonymous social mechanisms to realize its aims and objectives.

Another characteristic feature of terrorism is that the use of this specific violence is considered as a substitute for democratic political action or mass mobilization. Further, the distinction between terrorist, militant and guerrilla has to be seen in terms of the ethical challenge posed by terrorism. The terrorist attacks are directed against non-combatant innocents also. The guerrillas direct their attacks mainly on combatants.

In any comprehensive study of violence, incorporating some of the above mentioned dimensions, the issues may be reformulated along the following lines:

(a) Terrorism is a form of violence. It is a political strategy which uses violence as a tactics to eliminate and destroy perceived exploiters and to create confidence in the justness of the cause. This definition, no doubt, is a narrow, stipulative definition. It does not include the mercenary or other types of terrorism which do not have any political claims.

(b) Violence must be seen as a part of historical process and as a product of certain specific social conditions. It will be wrong to take violence as an aberration.

(c) The latent character of violence requires a dispassionate analysis because most of the violence that occurs in societies remains latent. For example, the enormous psychological force available with the traditional institutions like caste prevents a large section of people turning into active dissidents, even if they do not regard some of the roles assigned to them by the caste structure as legitimate. This would be an instance of latent violence, for in this case, people are being constrained to act contrary to their convictions owing to the fear of being left out or tortured or punished. Therefore, any serious study of latent structural violence has to directly relate to the operation of what Westguard and Resler have called 'anonymous social mechanisms'. These mechanisms function both by violence and by ideology. The coercive nature of these mechanisms must be taken into consideration while analysing some of the basic issues relating to structural violence. The nature and form of overt violence used by the state for either acquisition, maintenance, exercise or expansion of power, which in a way is a manifestation of latent structural violence, must be studied in its proper historical and specific context.

(d) The violence of protest, i.e. counter violence against the latent structural violence must constitute the central theme of these studies.

(e) The relationship between the nation-state and society is an interactive relationship. The state violence should be seen as a manifestation of structural violence. The violence indulged in by the non-state actors or collectivities is a product of the structural violence.

These dimensions of violence can be understood in relation to various conflicts which have erupted in India in its contemporary history. The conflicts like anti-reservation and reservation movement, communal riots in almost every state of India, the ULFA assertions in Assam, JKLF movement in Kashmir, the Sikh and Hindu stridency in Punjab, the ripples of the ethnic imbroglio of Sri Lanka in Tamil Nadu are some of the obvious examples.

II

Historically, violence as a mode of political articulation has been considered legitimate in the Punjab. The cultural and religious practice has attributed a positive value to the use of violence to recover lost dignity and to fight evil. The Sikh religious tradition legitimises the use of violence provided it has its basis in human values. With the passage of time, however, the militancy with its basis in humanism became subordinated to martial militancy. The British colonialists used caste and religion-based martial skills as the organizing principle of fighting units. This reinforced the concept of martial militancy. There were movements which used violence as a method of articulating interest and there was good response to them from the people. The Namdhari or Kuka movement was launched in 1858 by Baba Ram Singh at Bhaini Sahib, a village of Ludhiana district; it was militant and anti-imperialist in character. The Ghadar Lehar was another militant movement launched in North America with repercussions in the Punjab. The main thrust of this movement was anti-imperialist. Most of the Ghadarites later joined the Communist Party and also the Naxalites. The Babbar

Akalis were anti-imperialist and believed in the physical elimination of British agents and infor-mers. The Red Communist Party also used violence as a mode of discourse in PEPSU before Independence. It organized a number of violent peasant struggles in the Phulkian states. This mode of political discourse persisted all through, but it could not become a dominant mode. It is only in the post-1980 phase that this mode has become dominant.

Given this background and context there is a need to view violence in its proper social context and as a part of the fermentation in the ideological state apparatus. Consequently, it will be logical to trace the relationship of both individual and state violence with the underlying social structure.

The structural conditions and their interaction with the state apparatus have given rise to structural violence. The state in its interaction with the structural conditions produced dwarfed articulations of secular Punjabi identity, antagonistic assertions of communal identities and distinct religious identities. The conflicting relationship between these identities in the context of partisan nature of politics and lopsided growth of economy provided fillip to retrogressive violent articulations.

All these competing identities co-existed. For instance, Punjab had a culture and language which transcended religious group boundaries and unified politico-administrative unit which was conducive for integration of diverse religious, caste and other ascriptive group identities. In spite of the formulation and reformulation of the composite linguistic cultural consciousness, the tendency to evolve a unified sub-nationality with a common urge for territorial integrity remained weak in the Punjab. On the contrary, politics mobilized people along communal lines resulting in Partition in 1947 and division of the Punjabi- speaking people in 1966.

In the pre-Independence phase, the religious reform movements like the Arya Samaj, the Singh Sabha, and the Ahmadiyah, with their emphasis on Shuddhi, Amrit Prachar, Tabligh and Tanzim produced differentiation amongst people. The British colonial government made consistent efforts to shape communal identities. The colonial historians reinforced the perceptions of communal monoliths. Constitutional development, such as the Morley-Minto reforms of 1909, the Montague-Chelmsford reforms of 1919, and the Act of 1935, incorporating principles of separate electorates and communal reservations, perpetuated and intensified the trends towards communal polarization.

This process could not be reversed even in the post-1947 phase. The interactions between the state and structural reality shaped communal articulations though it could not become dominant because non-communal assertions also co-existed. The politics reinforced the assumption that both Sikhs and Hindus have distinct interests and demands, the most obvious example of this was the Hindi agitation and the Punjabi Suba movement. Linguistic and regional issues were articulated within the communal frame. The communally divisive politics and exclusiveness emerged as a dominant mode of political activity.

The aggregation of groups in categories other than communal, primarily around class and language, was co-existing. Forty-seven per cent of the Punjabi Hindus, according to the 1971 census, mentioned their mother tongue to be Punjabi. This clearly showed that Punjabi as a subnationality has its own inner dynamism. The objective conditions thwarted the communal politics initiated by the mainstream parties.

In this context the multi-cultural character of society could not find corresponding expression in the practice of politics and the state structure. This adversely affected the state's claim to the allegiance of its members and the members' claim to some conception of shared purpose or sense of shared benefits with others belonging to different religious groups. In other words, the denial of access to the members to their own language, culture and other resources due to the nature of interactive relationship between the structural condition and state apparatus alienated a large section from the state. In this process of alienation, violence is concealed and even symbolic.

The interaction of the state with the path of development, and consequential denial of legitimate claims, produced conditions of structural disequilibrium. The differentiation in the economy sharpened the political assertions. The political discourse and symbolism, followed in the pre-1966 decades, found continuity, but the political programme represented the sectional interests. In other words, the danger to the Sikh Panth as a single political entity having common secular interests found expression in the political discourse of three Akali Dal factions, but the demands raised were more economic in nature. This became visible in the later part of the 1980's.

The three tendencies within the Akali Dal can be identified as the one standing for state autonomy, but without unduly disturbing the existing political arrangement, the second for self-determination within the constitutional framework, and the last, raising the slogan for Khalistan. This made it difficult for various factions of the Akalis to mobilize their support base under one banner. The political demagogy used communal and religious symbols in an extreme form to outcompete or eliminate each other and to keep their support base large enough to have a better bargain in politics. This provided an ideological cover to the use of violence to register claims.

The Green Revolution created agricultural surpluses which could not find expression in industry. The Green Revolution was not a total strategy and it could not throw up organic intersectoral linkages. The surpluses generated did provide an assured market to consumer goods, but the strategy did not provide channels for profitable investment of agricultural surpluses in industry and trade. In the absence of convergence of rich peasantry, with accumulated surpluses, into the national market, the increasing inter-strata inequalities of income and assets have provided basis for the growth of retrogressive conflicts.

The Green Revolution provided opportunities and access to education for a large population. This access created a large employable work force, but did not create conditions and opportunities of employment. Rising unemployment, growing disparities of wealth and income leading to unequal conditions for availing of opportunities, and poverty gave rise to individual and social anger. A sense of deprivation was seizing vast masses and leading them to insecurity and fear. In this atmosphere of insecurity and fear it was easier for retrogressive ideologies to flourish. In the absence of alternative progressive political and cultural mobilizations, the political parties have enhanced and maintained their power by exploiting the insecurities and fears of diverse sections of the people.

The Green Revolution reinforced the phenomenon of relative poverty. The high cost of living in the Punjab as compared to Bihar, Uttar Pradesh and Rajasthan, from where most of the migrant labour comes, has accentuated the socio-economic crises for the local landless labour. The preference of peasants for the low-paid migrant labourers has also contributed to new political alignments within the Akali Dal.

The penetration of Green Revolution has got its corresponding impact on religious practices and belief patterns. In the absence of rational and scientific explanations available to the common man for the riches for some and rags for many, the common man has responded to fatalism and superstitious beliefs. The growth of religious fundamentalism as epitomized by Sant Bhindranwale and Shiv Sena is an over-reaction to unwholesome modernization. The Green Revolution led to economic prosperity, but cultural and social development could not keep pace with the staggering prosperity.

The Green Revolution strategy provided basis for the growth of social tensions, but the economic differentiation within the peasantry and between agrarian rural interests and trading and industrial urban bourgeoisie weakened the communal based nationality assertions. In other words, the demand for an Independent Sikh State could not find a forceful expression in political discourse. Moreover, the slogan was raised by an insignificant political leadership.

The mainstream political forces did not articulate the demand for Khalistan. The slogan of Khalistan did not acquire mass support in spite of the unimaginative and ruthless political and administrative initiatives and the protagonists' brutal and sense-less killings. The Khalistan slogan could not acquire mass base firstly because the historical process has weakened the communal based nationality identity and strengthened the Punjabi nationality identity. It does not imply however that the formation of Khalistan can be over-ruled. The idea of Khalistan cannot be understood in terms merely of political and economic feasibility of a new sovereign state. At the time of formation of Pakistan, for instance, the question raised was not about the feasibility of the new state. It was more of a historical accident shaped by political and socio-economic processes. Similarly, the question of Khalistan must be addressed not to its feasibility, but to the forces inherent in the social processes and the practice of politics which may shape and nurture the idea of Khalistan.

Furthermore, the question of Khalistan is linked with the explosion of identities in the whole of South Asia. The various identities which are taking shape in South Asia provided impetus on the one hand to the slogans like Khalistan and, on the other, to provide necessary conditions for the growth of Punjabi identity transcending territorial boundaries. It is therefore, imperative to understand the issues relating to Khalistan and Punjabi identity in a broader context of South Asia. For instance, the fermentation process of identity formation in Pakistan, be it a Pakhtoon identity, Baluch identity or

Punjabi identity, is contrary to the ideological bias on which Partition took place in 1947. These identities question the religion based communal identities. Therefore, this broader process of identity formation may provide a new thrust to linguistic, cultural or regional identities.

The most visible dimension which appears to be providing support not merely to the national aspect of Khalistan, but in concrete terms to the so-called Khalistan movement is external stimulus. This external stimulus has two interrelated components. One is the problem of rootlessness of the immigrant population which brought to the surface some characteristic over-reactions to the social, cultural and political scenario of their place of origin and over-enthusiastic support to the slogan of Khalistan. This was partly the result of the social, cultural and political environment of their place of migration. The reality of racial discrimination, increasing intolerance within Europe particularly Britain and also the United States, reinforced the feeling of marginality, alienation and nostalgia amongst the immigrant population. Further, the conditions of 'structural dis-equilibrium', to use Johan Galtung's phrase, have further forced the immigrant population to look for dominant power placement in their place of origin. This population could multiply their wealth, but could not find corresponding social respectability and political power. The widespread support to the slogan of Khalistan outside India was partly the result of the unfavourable social placement of the immigrant population, the reality of racism, and an increasing intolerance of diverse cultural streams.

Hostile Indo-Pakistan relations and growing imperialist penetration in the region are influencing, to a large extent, answers to the 'Khalistan question'. The supporters of Khalistan hope that Sikhs will effectively intervene and restructure the geography of the region.

> He (Sikh) is the one who can trigger off the chain of events as of all the regional characters he is one who has been imbued with the most compelling human grounds for insurgency. The Sikh question in India today is not just a 'sectarian conflict', but a volcanic epicentre which when it gets activated could turn the political economy and the political geography of the entire region topsy-turvy once and for all.[4]

Why must the Sikhs act as a vanguard? Because there is a danger of increasing resurgence of Hinduism. The Indian state is increasingly coming under the influence of Hindu resurgents and therefore will be discriminatory against the Sikhs. 'Sikhs have sacrificed everything for this country, from feeding starving millions to defending the glory of Bharat Mata, and what they got in turn was Opcration Blue Star and November riots'.

This kind of rationale is a mixture of distortion of the Sikh defence, discrimination, humiliation and fear – all these are very subtly rubbed into the Sikh psyche. Therefore, it can be safely concluded that there is an attempt to reshape and reformulate identity on communal basis.

The imperialist interventions and Pakistan's hostility are providing sustenance to violent forms of political discourse. However, the external stimulus does not have a unified ideological political stance. This can be substantiated by referring to the legal views expressed on various questions. There is a controversy regarding the Sikhs being an ethnic or a religious group in U.K. Lord Denning in his judgement of July 1982 gave the ruling that Sikhs are not a racial but a religious group. Therefore, they cannot be protected by the Race Relations Act. Lord Denning has held:

> On all this evidence, it is plain to me that Sikhs, as a group cannot be distinguished from others in the Punjab by reference to any racial characteristic whatever. They can only be distinguished by their religion and culture. That is not ethnic difference at all.[5]

The case of the respondent was that the 1876 Act did not apply to Sikhs because they were essentially a religious group and they shared their racial characteristics with other religious groups, including Hindus and Muslims, living in the Punjab.

Lord J. Templeman of the House of Lords on the other hand gave judgement which conceded the claim that the Sikhs are a community or an ethnicity in the generally accepted sense.

> In my opinion, for the purposes of the Race Relations Act, a group of persons defined by reference to ethnic origins must possess some of the characteristics of a race, namely groups descent, a group of geographical origin and a group history. The evidence shows that the Sikhs satisfy these tests. As a race, the Sikhs share common ancestors from that part of the Punjab which is centred on Amritsar. As a nation the Sikhs defeated the Moghuls and established a kingdom in the Punjab which they lost as a result of the first and second Sikh wars. They are more than a religious sect, they are almost a race and almost a nation.[6]

These legal battles, however, are not inspired by political factors.

And how far these will provide basis for a separate political identity is a complex question to answer.

The Khalistan movement may be relatively stronger in the USA, UK and Canada, but it merely exists as a slogan within the Punjab. The dominant tendency within the Punjab is the demand for greater state autonomy. This became a central issue in politics within the Punjab. The Akali Dal raised this demand in 1973 and it took the form of a movement around 1978. The interactive relationship between state and structural realities reinforced the need for greater autonomy for the regions and sub-nationalities. But politics responded to this demand by greater centralization of powers. The concentration of power in individuals has in turn reduced their capacity to resolve or even accommodate social and economic interests. This process makes institutions irrelevant and individuals powerless to perform even minimum necessary functions. In a situation of non-fulfilment of genuine and legitimate demands, these individuals are identified as the source of people's discontent and, therefore, the target of cumulative frustration and anger. The increasing trend of assassination of political opponents rather than questioning the basic structure is a result of centralization of political power in individuals.

All these factors are still persisting. The structural reality continues to produce a dwarfed secular Punjabi identity, blocked economy finding it difficult to accommodate emerging agrarian interests and create greater employment opportunities. Politics is not representative, competitive and federal. The absence of conditions for conducive human development are instances of latent structural violence.

The manifest form of violence was shaped by the opportunistic character of politics, underground economic activities, excessive reliance on the repressive state apparatus and, above all, on the external support.

Much of the politics in the Punjab has been shaped by the conflicts in various class factions of the ruling class. The basic thrust of this politics during the last decade was to appease extremist sections, to make the democratic methods of interest articulation ineffective and moderate politics irrelevant, to negotiate with various political groups for the sharing of political power without addressing itself to the real issues, and to undermine the norms of competitive politics by dismissing popularly elected governments and not holding the elections. The elections to the state assembly were postponed on the pretext that the voting would be influenced by the gun and victorious militants would dictate terms. Incidentally, parties opposing the elections had secured more than 61 per cent of the votes in the 1989 Lok Sabha elections. But they still opposed the elections to the state legislatures. This politics was guided by the threat perception from the liberal democratic institutions and norms. With the 1991 elections to the state assembly after the boycott by the Akalis, the perception of threat from them to the legislative politics ceased to be real. This brought a qualitative shift in politics. A political consensus against terrorism became a reality.

The excessive use of physical force and frequent misuse of para military forces. to resolve political-economic crisis have provided legitimacy to the physical force at the disposal of the state. This has prevented a large number of people from turning into active dissidents using peaceful methods. It is in this situation that the terrorists in the Punjab shared grievances with the members of the wider community which gave them social recognition. Further, the (fake) encounters and non-trial of individuals by the courts made a mockery of the judiciary.

The delay in trial and the subsequent harassment caused to innocent persons amongst the arrested is an example of the reckless functioning and insensitivity of the state. The prevalence of underground economic activities and cultural similarities of the migrant population from West Punjab with the population living in the adjoining villages of Pakistan accelerated the process of criminalization of politics. Not only this, the politics so criminalized under the communal environment acquired legitimacy. In a nutshell, the perception of deprivation, criminalization of politics, lack of representation in the participatory political institutions, and above all, absence of progressive social and political mobilization gave an impetus to the growth of terrorism in this region.

The strategy adopted by the militants and the state was in correspondence with each other. The strategy was to acquire legitimacy and outcompete each other in this process. In the initial phase extremist politics derived its legitimacy from the 'Amrit Prachar' movement. A reservoir of religious fervour generated by the use of religion by politics was available to shape the new terms of political discourse. In the past the fillip to this process was given not only by the Akalis but also by the Congress. This was a dominant trend in the pre-Blue Star Operation days, but it also persisted till 1990 (Table 3).

In the second phase, the militants used force to acquire legitimacy. A number of Panthic codes – like dress code for the children, teaching code for the teachers, language, medical, industrial, water, election, gurdwara, Khalsa panchayat, electricity, banking, revenue and civil bureaucracy codes – adversely affected the popularity of the militants.

This phase was also coupled with the humiliation meted out to the members of the Sikh religious groups by a section of the militants. This alienated them from their own support base. The state, on the other hand, reinforced the need for isolating the militants. The state appeared to be more legitimate than the militants.

Another strategy adopted by the militants was to communalize the situation. The state continued to draw upon the reservoir of mistrust and suspicion existing amongst communities, but at the same time responded to the demand for 'stability' raised by the middle class.

Thirdly, the state successfully continued to build up a political consensus against terrorism. The militants on the other hand were a fragmented group, and they could not form a united front.

Fourthly, the external support from other countries to militancy was available, but there was no systematic support for 'Khalistan'.

TABLE 1
Number of Persons Killed, 1981-1993

Year	Civilians	Security Persons	Terrorists
1981	13	2	14
1982	13	2	7
1983	75	20	13
1984	359	20	77
1985	63	8	21
1986	520	42	78
1987	910	95	328
1988	1949	110	373
1989	1168	201	703
1990	2474	506	1411
1991	2591	496	2309
1992	1519	251	2109
1993	46	23	748

Source: Newspaper Reports, 1981-1993.

TABLE 2
Number of Arrests and Encounters, 1981-1993

Year	Terrorists Arrested	Encounters
1981	84	0
1982	178	5
1983	296	3
1984	1630	80
1985	491	20
1986	1581	109
1987	3750	410
1988	3882	416
1989	2466	582
1990	1759	706
1991	1949	1282
1992	1473	1389
1993	898	527

Source: Newspaper Reports, 1981-1993.

TABLE 3

Number of Persons who took 'Amrit', 1981-1990

District	Number
Amritsar	25000
Gurdaspur	2500
Hoshiarpur	8000
Kapurthala	1100
Jalandhar	3700
Ludhiana	2100
Sangrur	1300
Ropar	1500
Patiala	9500
Bathinda	8400
Firozpur	8000
Faridkot	8000
Total	79100

NOTES

1. The major weaknesses in current approaches to the study of terrorism are: (a) a truncated object of study, which reflects (b) a skewed focus of the researches, which stems from (c) a narrow policy oriented on prevention and control which yields (d) narrow conceptual framework which ignores the political dimension of terrorism and its historical and comparative aspects and to focus selectively on individual actors, their characteristics, their tactics and their stated ideologies.

R.D. Crelinsten. 'Definitional & Conceptual Aspects'. *Contemporary Research on Terrorism.* Eds. Paul Wilkinson and A.M. Stewart, OUP, 1989, 1-3.

2. L. Althusser. 'Ideology and Ideological State Apparatuses'. *Education: Structure and Society.* Ed. B.R. Gosin, Penguin, 1972, 251.

3. V. Spike Peterson. 'Whose Rights ?A Critique of the "Givens" in Human Rights Discourse'. *Alternatives,* XV, 303-04.

4. Ghani Jafar. *The Sikh Volcano.* Vanguard Books. Lahore: 1987.

5. For detailed analysis and documentation, Gurmit Singh. *History of Sikh Struggles,* 1989, 5-75.

6. Quoted, in the above.

8

The Logic of Sikh Militancy

BIRINDER PAL SINGH

The limited purpose of this essay is to look into the logic of the violence of the Sikh militants which assumed phenomenal importance during the 1980s. There is no dearth of literature condemning the militants as terrorists and criminals who indulged in violence for the sake of violence, or to get rich quick. However, at least two authors have tried to look at the 'condemned other' from a sympathetic viewpoint. One is Juergensmeyer (1988) who has tried to understand the logic of religious violence in the Punjab (based on the recorded speeches of Jarnail Singh Bhindranwale) and the other is Joyce Pettigrew (1995) who has analysed the guerrilla violence in the state (based on the interviews of eleven young militants of the Khalistan Commando Force (Zaffarwal). This group, according to her, is not the first one to be organized, but remained the largest and the most organized militant outfit. She addresses these guerrillas as 'Children of *Waheguru*' who were made terrorists by the state terror. All of them were inspired by Bhindranwale. They were deeply influenced by Sikh religious faith and Sikh history.

The present essay is a modest attempt to construct the logic of the Sikh militants' violence as reflected in their booklets, pamphlets, articles, statements and declarations made from time to time. Some of these documents were circulated surreptitiously, others distributed in public gatherings in the form of handouts, while some were posters pasted on walls. Quite a number of these were carried by the vernacular and English daily newspapers and news magazines.

I

The Indian state had a strong negative opinion about the militants right from the very beginning of the movement. They were characterised as 'terrorists' and 'separatists' with misplaced enthusiasm under the guidance of certain disgruntled Akali politicians. They were seen as criminal gangsters instigated by a hostile neighbour (Pakistan) to destroy the 'unity and integrity' of India as a part of its revengeful strategy to settle scores for the liberation of East Pakistan, now called Bangladesh. This characterisation was not only widely circulated through the government controlled and allied mass media but also echoed in the scholarly writings of social scientists, and other writers. Such scholars followed the Indian state in labelling their violence as acts of isolated terrorism as an end in itself. They refused to look into the internal connections and sequences in such seemingly individuated and isolated acts of violence. It has been explained by the author elsewhere that the violent actions and reactions of the militants seen over a period of time constitute a definite and clear language of violence.[1] The discovery of such language and unearthing of interrelations amongst violent acts will help understand not only the militant movement but the Punjab problem as well.

No movement, howsoever parochial, can be studied in isolation from other contemporary movements and socio-economic and political institutions of the society. The primacy of material conditions can be seen in the context of immediate political institutions and their milieu which get manifested in a particular way under the weight of a society's history. It is no secret that the predominantly agricultural economy of Punjab has witnessed tremendous strain from the late 1970s. Bhalla and Chadha note that in Punjab in 1974-75, 31 per cent marginal (below 2.5 acres) and 24 per cent small (upto 5.0 acres) farmers were living below the poverty line.[2] The net income per hectare from wheat, the dominant crop, declined from Rs 328 in 1971-72 to Rs 54 only in 1981-82.[3] The landholdings also declined consistently during the 1970s. Looking into the emerging material contradictions in the state, Gill concludes that they 'have provided an objective basis for the current crisis.... In the absence of this objective basis, present crisis was not possible. The role of external factors is secondary'.[4] Shiva too locates the Punjab problem in the ecological and political demands of the Green Revolution as an experiment in development and agricultural transformation. She argues: 'The Punjab crisis is in large measure the tragic outcome of resource intensive and politically and economically centralized experiment with food production. The experiment has failed'.[5] Commenting on the political and cultural costs of the Green Revolution in the contemporary Punjab, she writes:

> The most ardent followers of Bhindranwale in his first phase of rising popularity were children and women, both because they were relatively free of the new culture of degenerative consumption, and they were worst hit by the violence it generated. In the second phase of Bhindranwale's popularity, men also joined his following, replacing vulgar movies with visits to gurdwaras, and reading the 'gurbani' (teachings of the Gurus) in place of pornographic literature. The Sant's following grew as he successfully regenerated the 'good' life of purity, dedication and hard work by reviving these fundamental values of the Sikh religion.[6]

These issues direct our attention towards the nature of the Indian state and politics. The choice of liberal democracy in an under-developed economy after freedom from the colonial rule is the mother of many ailments afflicting the Indian society. The capitalist development was uneven, economic policies were lop-sided, disharmony and later hiatus between agriculture and industry, rural and urban centres, masses and elite, people and their leaders widened over the last five decades. The aspirations of the regional bourgeoisie grew overtime against the increasingly centralized politics and administration. The rise of Sikh militancy is no exception. The whole periphery of Hindi heartland raised arms against the Delhi controlled politics which was preferring a techno-cratic-management oriented view of society and politics from above rather than the democratic functioning from below. Javeed Alam is right in suggesting that 'secessionism is not easily explainable in terms of simple economic criteria. What seems to me to be crucial is the previous history of the relations of the regions or of the communities within them with the pan-Indian Nationalism'.[7] Any selective explication of the problem of militancy is bound to give rise to serious misinterpretation and misconstruction since any retrieval of historical facts is always subjective.

The role of the ruling Congress (I) party in its bearing on militancy has to be seen in a broad context. The erosion of internal democracy and the rise of authoritarian leadership which was losing grip on the socio-economic problems of the vast country led to the adoption of cheap tactics and populist strategies. Playing one community against another was one such notable ploy used by the ruling party. Gupta has rightly suggested that the Centre found no difficulty in dealing with and later coopting the nativist movements and those for linguistic states. 'But with regional and secular movements the ruling party at the Centre, more particularly the Congress (I), was for the first time faced with a political formation that was hostile to it'.[8] To deal with this new situation, 'the Centre struck back ethnically. It ethnicised secular issues in order to marginalise its opponents, one by one, from the national mainstream'.[9] This precisely was the treatment given to the Akali Dal vis-a-vis Bhindranwale and the later militants. The majority of economic and political demands of the Akalis were weighed against a few of the insignificant religious demands. Their non-violent struggle was made violent and the secular demands were turned communal by the ruling Congress (I) party. The Government of India held twenty-five meetings at Chandigarh and Delhi, both official and un-official, between October 1981 and February 1984 with the Akali Dal, but every time to backslide. Thus, the Congress could marginalise the largest regional party of the Punjab.

The plurality of relevant factors makes the social reality extremely complex. This dilemma confronts both the activists who want to transform the society, and the academics who make an attempt to analyse it for their understanding. The need of transcending partial views can be readily recognized but the desired holistic analysis may remain a distant goal.

II

The nature of violence depends on the self-perception of those who wield instruments of violence. The choice of means, techniques, strategies of action and tactics, and identification of objects as targets are governed not only by the ideology of the actors concerned but also by the nature and character of the enemy, its fire-power, and the socio-cultural milieu in which violence is executed. The significance of geo-political factors is not to be under-estimated. In the present age of scientific and technological innovations, given the nature of the globalised economy, the whole world has come much closer in certain respects. The relations of dependence (read exploitation) and interdependence take 'issues' out of their local spaces and connect them to centres of power and authority situated hierarchically from the metropolis to the periphery. Therefore, nothing remains local in the strict sense of the term. Still, the local conditions of culture and society retain their seminal significance for affecting the social phenomenon, violent or otherwise, and give it a peculiar complexion. This marks the specificity of a social phenomenon and distinguishes it from others of the type. Therein lies the importance of the local idiom.

A word about the self-perception of the Sikh militants is necessary before constructing the logic of their violence. Identities are not constructed in vacuum. There is the need of an 'other' in relation to whom one defines oneself. In this case the Indian state provided the militants with an 'other'. Contrary to their characterisation by the former as 'terrorists' or 'extremists', they called themselves 'revolutionaries' who were fighting for a cause, the liberation of the Sikhs. Their violence according to them was neither erratic nor meaningless. It was not an end in itself but a means to an end for the creation of an independent, sovereign state of Khalistan where the members of their community could live with grace and dignity. They issued a 'code of conduct' to the press and the other media that they should be referred to as 'militants' and not as 'terrorists or extremists' in the English language. In the vernacular, the equivalent was '*kharku*' and not '*attwadi*'. They claimed they were neither 'separatists' nor 'disintegrationists'. They asserted that violence was not their creed. They had been coerced to take up arms by the Indian state. Moreover, this degenerated state understood no other language but violence. They had identified their enemies in the Indian state and its personnel, capitalists, rich landlords, communal Hindus and all those who indulged in anti-*Panthic* activities. They proclaimed that the poor, the exploited, the oppressed castes and the minorities in India fighting for their rights are their inalienable allies. A perusal of their literature reveals that they were not against Hinduism per se but '*Brahmanwad*' (Brahmanism) and '*Baniawad*'.

A perusal of the militants' literature reveals a definite logic underlying their violence. It is not only a logic of violence but violence based on a distinctive logic. The former is reflected in their praxis, in a more or less consistent pattern in their violence. It makes their movement similar to other movements of the type in different parts of the world. It can be seen clearly in their programmes of action and their political agenda. Their logic of violence is derived largely from the Sikh religion and history. All their documents are heavily imbued with religious terminology and quotations from the *Adi Granth* and the *Dasam Granth.* The militants claim to realize the Gurus' vision in their actions. It is necessary to give an outline of the Sikh theory of religion, society and violence to situate the logic of the militants' violence.

It is not an accident of history that Sikh religion and Punjabi culture got blended, unlike the other protest movements of the Bhakti tradition which could not strike roots in the soil. In the words of Niharranjan Ray: 'Their aim seems to have been the individual, not the society in any significant sense... Guru Nanak succeeded in what he did because he had a clear social purpose in view and adopted ways and means to work the purpose out effectively and well'.[10] The Sikh religion was structured differently in the Punjab in its direct confrontation with the Mughal dynastic empire. It is interesting to note that the period of the Sikh Gurus from Nanak to Gobind Singh synchronized with Mughal rule from Babur to Aurangzeb. The geo-political situation of the Punjab as the gateway to India has made its people industrious and adventurous due to perpetual invasions. Hence the popular saying: *Punjab de jamian nu nitt muhiman.* Ray once again aptly sums up the ethos of this land of the five rivers: 'History therefore taught the Punjab and her people one very important lesson, namely, not to forget or be oblivious of temporal or secular situations of any given time or space, howsoever engrossed one might find oneself in matters of the mind and the spirit'.[11]

Sikhism was thus defined under such a weight of history and in its discourse with the politically powerful 'other', the Mughals, over a span of nearly two centuries. The early, apparently pacifist, Sikh tradition was gradually transformed into a manifestly militant organization with the last Guru who institutionalized the unity of *miri* (temporal power) and *piri* (spiritual power) and gave a distinctly military look to the Khalsa in both form (costumes and weapons) and content (ideology, the *Dasam Granth*). A new insignia, complete in all respects was given to the Sikhs.

In *Gurbani*, a Sikh was conceived as a complete unity (synthesis) of polar opposites like the fire (Sun) and coolness (Moon), saint and soldier, a wielder of arms and weapons yet modest and humble, combining *shakti* (power) with *bhagti* (devotion), and a *sanyasi* (renouncer) yet a *grihasthi* (family person). According to Uberoi:

The primary meaning of five symbols when they are taken together lies in the ritual conjunction of two opposed forces or aspects. The unshorn hair, the sword and the uncircumcised male organ express the first aspect. They are assertive of forceful human potentialities that are of themselves amoral, even dangerous, powers. The comb, the steel bracelet and the loin and thigh breeches express the second aspect, that of moral constraints and discrimination.... The aspect of assertion and the aspect of constraint combine to produce what we may call for want of a better word the spirit of affirmation, characteristic of Sikhism.[12]

The Khalsa thus created in 1699 had the sole mission to fight social oppression of Brahmanism and religious persecution perpetrated by the Mughal authority, incidentally located at Delhi. Both of these are condemned in strongest possible terms in *Gurbani* and the Sikh chronicles. The Khalsa is supposed to observe a strict code of conduct, *rehat maryada*, to serve as a model for other Sikhs. He/she also wields instruments of violence, which have to be used only sparingly against oppression and tyranny when 'all other modes of redressing a wrong have failed'. This is the last Guru's injunction. He further makes it clear that the warrior must recite the name of the Timeless One while harbouring the idea of war in one's heart. Puran Singh suggests that the sword is mind made intense. It is the visible sign of a sensitive soul. *Kirpan* is His, not his.[13]

This broad introduction would suffice to situate the formulations of the militants in the context of religious violence permissible in the Sikh theory. The militants always swore by the Sikh religion and the Guru to realize the litany Raj Karega Khalsa – that the Khalsa shall rule. This litany forms an integral part of the Sikh prayer, which is rhymed either individually or collectively whenever Guru Granth is recited. Sung together at a loud pitch, its effect on the participants is alchemic. *Ardas* is an open ended text which encapsulates the entire history of the sacrifices made by Sikhs for the sake of religion and the community.

Martyrdom has always been held in high esteem in the Sikh religion and history. And the inspiration comes from the *Gurbani*. The militants Sukha and Jinda wrote to the President of India: 'Our inspiration also stems from the same *Guru Granth Sahib*. With a fierce determination we have taken a position against your falsehood and trickery. To us, you are a symbol of evil, and whatever cruelty is being inflicted on us by your followers, we are bearing with great joy'. They went on to differentiate their violence from that of the enemy:

In comparison with the violence of the enemy, the violence of the Khalsa abounds in divine qualities and spiritual blessings. The Khalsa has to give such a divine form and beauty to its struggle that it may even burden the conscience of the enemy with the realization of its own sin. Such a moral miracle will be possible only if the concentration on the Guru of the Khalsa and rhythm of the *Guru Granth Sahib* remain fully connected and intact.... It is also the chief spring of our inspiration to advance towards the destination of Khalistan.

This inspiration kept them in high spirits (*chardi kala*) characteristic of Sikhism. They were optimistic of achieving the goal of Khalistan despite 'confronting a vast material state'. They observed in the same letter:

During the last decade we have overwhelmed this state of Brahmanical prejudices with martyrdom. We have been hailed in all corners. Now the matter is not restricted to the possible creation of Khalistan alone. Several oppressed nations of India have come in the open to fight for their freedom. The Dalit brothers, especially, are liberating themselves from the destructive influence of Brahmanism. The so-called hue and cry made for 'unity and integrity' does not touch them any more. They have well understood the cunning of Brahmanical rulers veiled behind this hue and cry....The guns of evil will never frighten us....Our martyrdom will radiate only integration.[14]

The Babbar Khalsa International (hereafter BKI) builds its own logic of violence on the basis of its perception of Sikh history. It remained one of the most dreaded militant outfits in the later half of the militant phase. In their undated pamphlet are recorded the heroic deeds of Sikhs and their martyrdom from the birth of Sikhism right upto 1984, the year of 'Operation Blue Star' and the so-called 'riots' in Delhi and other parts of the country. It is asserted that 'Hindu colonial rule' always betrayed the Sikhs. The Sikhs always fought for Hindus and ensured them full protection. During the freedom struggle against the British, they obtained promises from the Congress and Mahatma Gandhi, but when claimed their rights the ruling Congress not only ignored them but even Nehru remarked: 'He could tolerate civil war in the country but not the Punjabi *suba* (province)'.[15]

Later, in 1991, at a meeting in Anandpur Sahib the BKI reiterated that the 'Brahmanic culture' and the 'Brahmanic government' are their distinct enemies: We are slaves both economically and politically.... We are not the masters of our destiny in any sphere. Over the last forty four years, we had been feeling at every step that our reins are in the hands of those who are blind themselves'.[16]

The BKI's logic of violence also includes the incapacity of the then Sikh leadership and their misdeeds: 'Having seen the limits of cruelty (reference to February 1984 incidents of firing on the *Harmandir* and humiliation of the Sikhs in Haryana) the Sikh leadership did nothing except lecturing on these topics for hours together' [17] The legitimacy of leaders, both political (Akalis) and religious (*Singh Sahiban*) got further exposed in June 1984. They not only surrendered to the army but also gave 'false' statements to the media. The BKI thus admonishes the Sikhs: 'Here it must be understood that given the proof of cowardice by the Sikh leaders of the day and the *Singh Sahiban*, if we still accept their leadership then nothing worthwhile would be achieved for the *qaum* (nation community). It would be a mistake to believe... that the Sikh *qaum* would be able to break the chains of slavery'.[18]

The BKI asks, where is the hope to liberate Sikhs in these circumstances? The two incidents of 1984 have removed the veil from the faces of the 'tyrant and killer communal Hindu': 'Now it is not enough to identify the tyrants and the killers, but they should be eliminated following the Guru's command. The Khalsa has only been created to annihilate the tyrant and the tyranny for the protection of the poor and the suppression of the oppressor'.[19] Therefore. 'O'Khalsa adorn yourself with weapons following the command of the Tenth Father (*Dashmesh pita*) and bring the present (Sikh) leadership on the right track to fight against tyranny. And, if they refuse to do so then O'Khalsa remove these obstacles on your way to liberation'.[20]

The BKI is optimistic that such battles will usher Sikhs towards greener pastures. 'The sacrifices of the martyrs will not go waste.... We must make such a country nation (*desh*) where the Khalsa is supreme, which has its own constitution, flag (*nishan*) and *Nanak-shahi* currency, and where we can enforce the principle of 'welfare of all' (*sarbat da bhala*), following the principles of the Gurus. In such a country the religious people, the poor and the workers could be protected from the exploitation of the tyrant and cruel capitalists and monopolists (*ijaredar*), so that they may lead a happy life of self-respect with dignity and honour'.[21] Once again in 1991, the BKI reaffirmed its desire for the creation of a 'new society': 'A new era is about to begin on the land of Khalistan. This new milieu will have exhaustive debates on the Khalsa culture, Khalsa vision, Khalsa rule and Khalsa society which will help us construct a beautiful model for the economic, political and social structural aspects of Khalistan' [22]

The BKI and other militant organizations are quite apprehensive about the realization of their vision of a 'new society' within the frame of Indian Constitution.The BKI holds the view that it is the 'biggest hurdle in the creation of Khalistan': 'There is no space for Khalistan in this cart-load of paper'.[23] They have already waited too long since 1947. Now there is no alternative but to reject this Constitution. They caution that 'if we start any struggle without rejecting the Constitution, our struggle is bound to lose direction'. But what kind of struggle? An armed struggle which must have harmony and coordination with the people for the establishment of an independent and sovereign Khalistan. The BKI suggests that the moment is most suitable to launch the struggle. 'The international situation is in our favour and India too is a victim of serious economic and political crises'. Laying stress on its weakest points they implore the Sikhs to make full use of the situation in which 'the battle for Khalistan could be fought in a completely peaceful (non-violent) way'.[24]

The 'four militant organizations', namely Khalistan Commando Force (Panjwar), Khalistan Liberation Force (Budhsingh-wala), Bhindranwale Tiger Force of Khalistan (Chhandran), and the Sikh Students Federation (Bitu) made a fervent appeal in 1991 to reject the Indian Constitution which to them is the 'thief's mother', the root of all problems. 'This heap of garbage looks nice on the shoulders of the Brahmans only'.[25] They also laid stress on the suitability of that moment to launch a direct action as the last resort. They suggest: 'First of all we must remember that this battle is being fought on our own land. Therefore, we will exhaust all channels of the diplomatic world so that the war may be avoided. But we will not digress an inch from the path of obtaining an independent and sovereign Khalistan'.[26] They underlined the urgency of direct action: 'The international situation is so congenial, suitable and appropriate that if the Khalsa now failed to shape its diplomacy to these conditions or failed to avail of the contradictions of the world (*sansar dian virodhtaian*) in its favour, then we must understand that we have ourselves prolonged the period of our agony (*khuari di miyad*)'.[27]

They cautioned the Government of India that if the tyranny on the Sikhs continues then the country will meet the fate of Russia, one time a superpower in the world. They also issued a warning to all the countries of the world, the International Monetary Fund and other international financial institutions that 'they must sign loan agreements with India on this understanding that *the people of Khalistan will not be a party to their repayments.* Because no amount of these loans is invested on the land of Khalistan, and we do not need it either'. On the contrary: 'The brave farmers of *our country, Khalistan* are filling the empty stomachs of crores of Hindustanis. These countless Bhai Ghaniyas will maintain this tradition even after the recognition of Khalistan by the Indian government'.[28]

One of the most powerful Committees led by Doctor Sohan Singh has expressed its views against the Indian Constitution in a long rejoinder to an Akali leader, a scion of the erstwhile ruling family of Patiala. It reads: 'After all what is this Indian Constitution? What kind of a man does it envisage? Does one experience a grand flight of consciousness (*chetna di vaddi parvaz*) in it? What do we experience when it is put into practice? Listen: Under this Constitution you cannot even change the name of a village, not to think of changing the fate of a *qaum*'. Moreover, 'this Constitution has its own limits (*maryada*) which demand this surety (from the people) that if you want to live, then be a cipher. Closed from outside and empty within.... We feel suffocated in it every moment'.[29]

The anonymous author(s), Singh Khalsa, of a small booklet *Khalsa Raj* also reflect on the Constitution obliquely. They plead with the Sikhs to boycott elections, a mechanism to sustain the Congress rule. 'Both the Congress party and the Nehru family have made India their fiefdom (*riyasat*) rather than a nation. The Congress is a party of feudal lords, Brahmans and Banias'.[30] It is argued that these three classes use all kinds of means to win elections.

> Elections and the Parliament are such a fraud with which the Khalsa is oppressed. Thousands of (Sikh) youth have been killed in fake encounters. What has the Parliament done about it. It has become a mere platform to oppress the Sikhs. The poor, the exploited and the minorities are being oppressed by the majorities. Therefore, the Khalsa who is a minority must boycott the Parliament and the elections and take to an armed struggle for the creation of a separate independent country where the sovereignty of the Khalsa may be established. If this could not be achieved then the majority will swallow the Khalsa in the manner a big fish gulps down the smaller one.[31]

The socio-economic conditions prevailing in the country are also analysed by Singh Khalsa: 'This trio (feudal lords, Brahmans and the moneylenders (Banias) controls the capital, and hence the question of life and death of the people. These *manmukh* (self-oriented) forces are defeating the *gurmukh* (Guru-oriented) and Khalsa forces with their police, army and para-military'.[32] Therefore for the sake of Sikhism and the ascendancy (*chardi kala*) of Khalsa Panth, and for our rights and self-respect, the whole Sikh world is being requested to seek liberation from slavery. It is the duty of the Khalsa, wherever they may be, to over-throw the enemy and his forces from this sacred land. 'We should struggle for independence following the principle: Neither should anyone be terrorised nor should one feel terrified'.[33] In this forthcoming war only they would contribute meaningfully who love the Sikh form and the Sikh philosophy. They give the final call: 'Let us be prepared to sacrifice anything for *dharam* (the Sikh way of life). The true warrior is one who fights for *dharam* and is prepared to sacrifice oneself for it – *Sura so pehchaniye...*'.[34]

III

We have tried to construct the logic of the violence of the militants who proliferated into numerous bands after the Blue Star and dominated the political space in the Punjab for almost one decade. The discussion that follows relates to the logic of religious violence developed by Juergensmeyer especially focussing on the recorded speeches of Jarnail Singh Bhindranwale, the source of inspiration to all the militant groups. Juergensmeyer is primarily concerned with the relation of religion and violence which precisely was the core of the Punjab problem during the 1980s. He finds a definite relation between the two variables. 'Since religious language is about the tension between order and disorder, it is frequently about violence'.[35] For him disorder is inherently violent. He suggests: 'By identifying a temporal social struggle with the cosmic struggle of order and disorder, truth and evil, political actors are able to avail themselves of a way of thinking that justifies the use of violent means'.[36]

The idiom of Bhindranwale was undoubtedly rooted in the Punjab soil and Sikh history, but his formulations were no different from those of other clergies elsewhere. Juergensmeyer notes: 'Much of what Bhindranwale has to say in sermons of this period, however, might be heard in the homilies of clergies belonging to any religious tradition, anywhere on the globe. He calls for faith – faith in time of trial – and for the spiritual discipline that accompanies it'.[37] He castigated the easy-living, easy-drinking customs of Sikh villagers, especially those who clipped their beards and adopted modern ways, those who preferred government positions and pursuit of worldly affairs to faith and made compromises for the sake of personal gain (reference to Akalis in particular and Sikhs in general). Pettigrew however suggests: 'In the democratic societies of the West, these values would not be termed religious but rather would be described as civil libertarian and socialist. His (Bhindranwale) primary objective was to undercut the spread of consumerism in family life'.[38]

Bhindranwale always referred to the status of Sikhs in India as that of slaves where their dress, religion, its symbols and scriptures are not only ridiculed but disrespected. But he held the Sikhs themselves responsible for their present status, weakening the Panth too, because they have lost touch with their Guru who is the source of their empowerment. He often asked his male Sikh audience if they resembled their Father in form? Despite such grievances he never claimed Khalistan: 'We are not in favour of Khalistan nor are we against it. We wish to live in India, but would settle for a separate state if the Sikhs did not receive what they regarded as their just respect'.[39] What he often said was gullibly used by his distractors: 'I have always expressed myself in favour of mobilizing the entire Sikh world under one flag.... When they say the Sikhs are not separate we'll demand separate identity – even if it demands sacrifice'.[40]

Kapur also substantiates the above contention. According to him Bhindranwale was the strongest protagonist of Sikh unity and always inspired his Sikh audience to compel the leaders (Akalis of various factions) to come under a single *kesari* (saffron) flag. When arrested at Chowk Mehta in September 1981, he expressed his wish: 'When I reach Ludhiana Jail, I wish to hear that the whole Sikh world has come together under one *kesari* flag'.[41] He would often point to the opponents of Panthic unity in his lectures: 'Having sucked the blood of the martyrs, having beaten the drum (*dugdugi*) in Panth's name, having addressed the *narak-dharis* (Sant Nirankaris) as father, having exploited the name of the *kesari* flag, he who wants to retain his power, identify him O'Khalsa'.[42] The author concludes that driven by selfless efforts for unity, he succeeded in reuniting the Akali Dal within twenty-five months of its division.[43]

This unification strengthened the ongoing *Dharam Yudh Morcha*

(Front for holy war/religious non-violent agitation) and projected Bhindranwale into a popular mass leader to an extent that people believed him to be the *de facto* Morcha Dictator, a position formally assigned to Sant Harchand Singh Longowal, the then President of the Akali Dal. In an interview answering such a question he said: 'The Morcha is led by *Sri Guru Granth Sahib.* I am His humble servant. Otherwise there has to be a general in the war. But the Sikhs are not jumping into the Morcha for a specific personality but for the protection of their *dharam* and freedom'.[44]

Juergensmeyer suggests that in Sikh theology, including the rhetoric of Bhindranwale, the idea of cosmic struggle inside the self goes hand in hand with the conception of struggle in history. He writes:

> The key to the connection, it seems to me, is that cosmic struggle is understood to impinge upon the inner recesses of an individual person in a simultaneous conjunction with its occurrence on a worldly social plane. Neither of these notions is by itself sufficient to motivate a person to religious violence.... But when the two ideas coexist, they are a volatile concoction.
>
> Thus when Bhindranwale spoke about warfare in the soul his listeners knew that however burdensome that conflict is, they need not bear it alone. They may band together with their comrades and continue the struggle in the external arena, where the foes are more vulnerable, and victories more tangible. And their own internal struggles impel them to become involved in the worldly conflict: their identification with the overall struggle makes them morally responsible, in part, for its outcome.[45]

After discussing the Punjab violence at length, Juergensmeyer spells out five tenets of religious commitment that are found whenever acts of religious violence occur. These, however, are not the exclusive concern of the Sikh religious tradition but of other religions as well. These are: (a) the cosmic struggle is played out in history; (b) the believers identify personally with the struggle; (c) the cosmic struggle continues in the present; (d) the struggle is at a point of crisis; and (e) the acts of violence have a cosmic meaning.[46] Quite interestingly, while elaborating one of the above points (d), Juergensmeyer refers to certain pacifist movements directly engaged in conflict. Menno Simmmons and Gandhi are such leaders who at times narrowly skirted the edges of violence, propelled by a conviction that human agency is extremely important. 'In that sense Gandhi and Bhindranwale were more alike than one might suspect. Both saw the world in terms of cosmic struggle, both regarded their cause as being poised on a delicate balance between oppression and opportunity, and both believed that human action could tip the scales. The issue that divided them, of course, was violence'.[47]

Unlike the militants who laid strong emphasis on the issues of political economy affecting the development of the Punjab and the Sikhs, Bhindranwale would most of the time club them under one term 'injustices'. Juergensmeyer substantiates: 'Since the larger struggle is the more important matter, these specific difficulties are of no great concern to Bhindranwale; they change from time to time. And it is no use to win on one or two points and fail on other'.[48] In his interview to a magazine, while justifying the demands of the *Dharam Yudh* which do not concern the Sikhs alone but relate to the whole of the Punjab, Bhindranwale remarked that the Punjab and the peasant are synonyms. The former will flourish only if the latter flourishes. And only then the business of 'Hindu brother will grow, otherwise it will collapse'.[49]

The logic of violence appears to have been well internalised by Bhindranwale. He was ever ready to sacrifice his life for the Panth. He often quoted a line from the *Dasam Granth:* 'When the struggle reaches a decisive phase may I die fighting in its midst'. It is quite logical for a person with that social background – a peasant, with little formal education, inducted into a seminary, Damdami Taksal, at an early age where one remains immersed in the preaching and practice of Sikh religion, observing a strict code of conduct which even prohibits tea. Moreover his arche-types were Guru Gobind Singh and Baba Deep Singh. He would often remark about the latter. 'The first chief of the Taksal laid his life for the Harmandar Sahib and now the fourteenth (that is, himself) will do the same when need arises'. The need did arise, then came the final hour and he kept his word. The cry for Khalistan raised after his death only proved his fears: 'The day Indian army enters the Harmandar Sahib the foundation of Khalistan would be laid'.

Madan and others characterise this movement as 'fundamentalist', while Juergensmeyer hesitates to do so because fundamentalism is an imprecise, pejorative concept which does not carry any political meaning.[50] On the other hand he calls these militants 'religious nationalists', anti-modernists who attempt to establish a new society. These revolutionaries have an 'ideology of order' which is opposed to the presently dominant 'secular nationalism'. On the basis of his global study he suggests that most religious nationalist movements not only eschew a theocracy but they also envision a new political and economic order born out of religious revolution which has elements of socialism and democracy of the West.[51] These religious nationalists are modern but not modernist. They are against secular nationalism because it is not only Western but also a form of neocolonialism. Hence a useful viable alternative is a modern nation-state run on the principles of one's religion. The author has also suggested ways to come to terms with religious nationalism in secular states.[52]

The above discussion is not intended to provide legitimacy to the practice of violence by those 'killer squads' who ran a parallel government for sometime, especially in the rural Punjab. It is only a modest attempt to locate the axis which helped move the Sikh militancy for more than a decade. It is the considered view of the author that any movement, whatever be its character, cannot be sustained even for a short duration if it lacks some sort of framework for action. The logic of a movement remains even if it does not succeed which of course depends on a right combination of multiple factors. No doubt the good, the bad and the ugly formed a part of the Sikh militant movement, as is true of any movement any where in the world, it is the men of the first type who sustain the struggle. Here too there were some of this type who genuinely looked for a social transformation in favour of the oppressed castes and classes of this region. This seems well in tune with the Sikh theory of society and polity which aims at the *Khalsa Raj.* Whatever be the weaknesses in this concept, and its theory or philosophy, it is definitely a vision for a society based on freedom, liberty and justice.

Such movements, as they grow, tend to lose grip on the peripheral cadre which is a structural constraint with under-ground guerrilla movements. The holes in the boundaries of these bands meant to absorb the shocks of the state power are used by the repressive state apparatus to infiltrate such bands and explode them from within. Furthermore lumpen elements too make hay in the shining sun thus derailing the movement from its professed path. The Sikh militant movement was also afflicted with all sorts of deviations which ultimately struck down those who perpetrated violence. Probably, violence is like black magic which entraps the initiator if it does not succeed against the enemy. Moreover, there is tendency in violence, as suggested by Girard, to become the 'subject, object, instrument and purpose of action' at the height of a crisis.[53]

REFERENCES

1. For details see author's forthcoming *Violence as Political Discourse.*

2. G.S. Bhalla and G.K. Chadha. 'Green Revolution and the Small Peasant: A Study of Income Distribution in Punjab Agriculture'. *Economic and Political Weekly*, Vol. XVII, No. 21, May 22,1982, 876.

3. S.S. Gill, 'Development Crisis in Agriculture and Its Political Implications – An Enquiry into the Punjab Problem'. *Political Dynamics and Crisis in Punjab.* Eds. Paul Wallace and S. Chopra. Amritsar: Guru Nanak Dev University, 1988, 440.

4. S.S. Gill 'Socio-economic Contradictions Underlying Punjab Crisis', *Punjab: Past, Present and Future.* Ed. Gopal Singh. Delhi: Ajanta. 1994, 229.

5. Vandana Shiva. *The Violence of the Green Revolution: Third World Agriculture, Ecology and Politics.* Goa: Other India Press, 1992, 12.

6. Ibid, 185-86.

7. Javeed Alam. 'Conceptualising State Society Relations in Independent India: Some Preliminary Notes'. *Studies in Humanities and Social Sciences*, Vol II, No. 1, 1995, 64.

8. Dipankar Gupta. 'Communalising of Punjab, 1980-1985'. *Economic and Political Weekly*, Vol XX, No. 28, July 13, 1985, 1190.

9. Ibid, 1190.

10. Niharranjan Ray. *The Sikh Gurus and the Sikh Society: A Study in Social Analysis.* Delhi: Munshiram Manoharlal, 1975, 41.

11. Ibid, 105.

12. J.P.S. Uberoi. 'The Five Symbols of Sikhism'. *Sikhism.* Patiala: Punjabi University, 1969, 132.

13. Puran Singh. *The Spirit Born People.* Patiala: Punjabi University, 1976, 74.

14. S.S. Sukha and H.S. Jinda. 'Text of Sukha-Jinda's Letter to the President'. Chandigarh. *The Tribune*, 1990.

15. Sukhdev Singh Babbar, *Vangar.* Babbar Khalsa International, 7.

16. Babbar Khalsa International (BKI), 'Babbar Khalsa International Walon Sandesh'. *Paigam*, October 1991, 18.

17. Sukhdev Singh Babbar, *Vangar*, 9.

18. Ibid, 19.

19. Ibid, 17.

20. Ibid, 21.

21. Ibid, 22.

22. BKI. *Paigam*, October 1991, 19.

23. Ibid, 18.

24. Ibid, 19.

25. Paramjit Singh Panjwar et al. *Benati* (Punjabi), 1991, 3.

26. Ibid, 6.

27. Ibid, 3.

28. Ibid, 5.

29. Sohan Singh *et al.*, 'Sanu Apna Virsa Yaad Hai'. *Punjabi Tribune*, 1990.

30. Singh Khalsa. *Khalsa Raj* (Punjabi), 1985, 28.

31. Ibid, 28-29.

32. Ibid, 45.

33. Ibid, 48.

34. Ibid, 48-49.

35. Mark Juergensmeyer. 'The Logic of Religious Violence: The case of the Punjab'. *Contributions to Indian Sociology* (n.s.), 22,1, January-June 1988, 73.

36. Ibid, 77.

37. Ibid, 69.

38. Joyce Pettigrew. *The Sikhs of Punjab: Unheard Voices of State and Guerrilla Violence.* London and New Jersey: Zed Books, 1995, 55.

39. Juergensmeyer, 1988, 76.

40. Ibid, 76.

41. Satinderpal Singh Kapur. *Bhindranwale* (Punjabi). Jalandhar: Bharti Publishers, 1983, 157.

42. Ibid, 158.

43. Ibid, 159

44. 'Sant Bhindranwalian nal Interview' (Punjabi). *Qaumi Rajniti*, August 1983, 51.

45. Mark Juergensmeyer, 1988, 82-83.

46. Ibid, 80-87.

47. Ibid, 85-86.

48. Ibid, 71.

49. *Qaumi Rajniti*, 1983, 49.

50. Mark Juergensmeyer. *Religious Nationalism Confronts the Secular State.* Delhi: Oxford University Press, 1994, 4-5.

51. Ibid, 149.

52. Ibid, 195-96.

53. Rene Girard. *Violence and the Sacred.* Tr. Patrick Gregory. Baltimore: The John Hopkins University Press, 1977, 144.

9

Demographic Change

GOPAL KRISHAN

Perhaps no other state of India has undergone such stupendous population change during the last about half-a-century as Punjab has (Table 1). It has witnessed remarkable transformation in the distribution, composition and disposition of its population. This development was related initially to the partition of the Indian subcontinent in 1947 resulting in transfer of populations across the border, and subsequently to successive reorganizations of the state till it assumed its present form in 1966. No less crucial has been the role of the intensive use of land and water resources, the appropriate strategy which focused on rural development through consolidation of landholdings, land reclamation, irrigation, electrification and construction of village link roads, and above all, the progressive nature of the people who sought greener pastures within or without their home state.

On the eve of Independence, the present Punjab territory had a population of nearly ten million, a little less than one-half of its population of 20 million today. This was divided roughly equally amongst the Muslims, the Hindus, and the Sikhs. In the frame-work of the present boundaries of various districts of Punjab, the Muslims were in absolute majority only in Kapurthala, the Sikhs in Faridkot, and the Hindus in none.

In relative terms, the Muslims found greater concentration in the districts of Kapurthala, Gurdaspur, Amritsar, Firozpur and Jalandhar, especially in the riverine tracts of the Ravi, the Beas and the Satluj; the Hindus in the eastern districts of Hoshiarpur, Ropar and Patiala and in the urban centres; and the Sikhs in Faridkot, Ludhiana, Firozpur, Amritsar and Patiala districts, more particularly in the Malwa region. Thus, the Muslims and the Hindus were concentrated in the western and eastern districts respectively, while the Sikhs found a greater spread in the middle.

POPULATION REPLACEMENT

The first phase of population change in Punjab after Independence was due to a virtual replacement of the Muslims by the non-Muslims, except in a few pockets like Malerkotla. An estimated 12 million persons moved across the international border in cross-currents, and around a quarter million were killed in communal frenzy (Singh, 1972, 132). The displaced non-Muslims from Pakistan were rehabilitated on lands vacated by the Muslims leaving India. There was a geographic design underlying the process: persons displaced from particular districts were resettled in specific districts of similar nature in Punjab.

The imbalance in residential, occupational and economic status as well as the number of the departing Muslims and the incoming non-Muslims had a manifold impact on Punjab demography at the time of partition (Rai, 1986, 159-206). Though the number of Muslims who moved to Pakistan exceeded that of non-Muslims who replaced them by 10 per cent yet the cultivable land they left behind was less by about 20 per cent in terms of simple acreage and by 40 per cent in terms of standard acres of productivity. This intensified pressure on the cultivable land available in the state and thousands of displaced agriculturists, who could not be rehabilitated within Punjab, were accommodated in the neighbouring states of Rajasthan and Uttar Pradesh.

Furthermore, less than one-fifth of the departing Muslims were of urban origin. The proportion of the non-Muslims who replaced them was over one-fourth. This led to a fast increase in the state's urban population. The number of houses left behind by the Muslims was less by about 30 per cent of that left behind by the non-Muslims. This rendered the task of urban rehabilitation very difficult. To meet the situation, model townships or new residential localities on planned lines were raised in several existing cities and towns, among other measures. The number of artisans, such as weavers, blacksmiths, carpenters, leather workers, oil extractors and potters, among the departing Muslims was in excess by one-third of that of non-Muslims who took their place. This caused serious scarcity of the skilled workers. Thousands of displaced persons had to be imparted vocational training to fill the gap.

In 1951, one-fifth of the state's population was accounted for by these displaced persons (Table 2). Their proportion was over one-third in Gurdaspur district and over one-fourth in Kapurthala,

Firozpur and Jalandhar districts (Map 1). A large minority of these persons were Sikhs. The net outcome was the transformation of the present Punjab into a Sikh majority tract for the first time in the history of the region.

POPULATION REDISTRIBUTION

Before long the state moved into a phase of explosive growth and extensive redistribution of population. With a typical agricultural birth rate staying high at 40 to 45 and a quasi-industrial death rate of 15 to 20 at a level less than half of the former, Punjab was distinguished by a significantly higher rate of natural increase than India till the mid-sixties, and even afterwards (Table 3).

The intensified pressure on land found relief mainly through agricultural migration to newly reclaimed wastelands in other parts of India, notably northern Haryana, north-western Rajasthan, and the Terai in Uttar Pradesh. There was some urbanward outflow also. The number of net migrants from Punjab to other Indian areas during 1951-61 equalled that of all time surviving migrants from the state up to 1951 (Gosal, 1967, 108). The actual population growth rate of the state's population has been consistently lower than that of India since Independence (Table 4 and Fig. 1).

Similarly a greater land-people equilibrium was established within the state through a shift of population from the more crowded northern districts to the newly irrigated and faster urbanising southern districts. The percentage share of Amritsar, Gurdaspur, Jalandhar and Hoshiarpur districts in total population declined by about 6 points while that of Ludhiana, Patiala, Bathinda and Faridkot districts increased by practically the same magnitude during 1951-91 (Table 5). The population density increased from 182 persons per km^2 in 1951 to 403 in 1991 but regional disparities in population density declined (Table 6). Population growth rate was comparatively lower in high density districts and vice versa, representing a negative relationship between density and growth (Map 2). This population redistribution illustrates how a progressive population tries to attain a finer equation with the resource base partly by voting with the feet for new areas and partly by optimising the opportunities available within their own habitat.

Here it will not be out of place to highlight the migratory propensity of the Punjabis, especially of the Sikhs. In 1951, about 15 per cent of the Sikhs in India were residing outside Punjab; by the mid-sixties this percentage had risen to 22 (Krishan, 1971, 41). The main factors underlying this tendency on their part have been a long tradition in army service, an eagerness to colonise new agricultural lands, and a keen desire to avail of any economic opportunity. In recognition of their special qualities, the British gave them preference in recruitment to imperial army and settle-ment of newly developed canal colonies. The intensifying pressure of fast increasing population on cultivable land, in the context of predominantly agricultural economy of the Sikhs, accelerated the process. The out-migration of Punjabi Hindus, especially of those displaced from Pakistan, was also of high order. This flow was directed mainly to big cities, such as Delhi, Bombay, Calcutta and Kanpur, among others.

The recent data on the religious composition of population made available by the Census of India reflect a discernible demographic impact of the difficult political situation prevailing in Punjab during the eighties. During 1981-91, the Sikh population of the state grew by 25.2 per cent and the Hindu by 12.7 per cent. These figures reflect net in-migration of the Sikhs and net out-migration of the Hindus, the annual rate of natural increase of population being around 2 per cent. The percentage of the Sikhs in the state's total population increased from 60.8 to 63.0 and that of the Hindus declined from 36.9 to 34.5.

The enterprising nature of Punjabis took them not only to other parts of India but also to other countries of the world. In the early years of the present century, three channels of emigration from Punjab had been established: erstwhile Burma and Malaya states, Hong Kong and Canada; Australia and Fiji Islands; and East African countries. After Independence, United Kingdom and Canada became more popular destinations. This trend continued till the mid-sixties after which the United States became a more cherished dream. This stimulus is unabated.

POPULATION CONTAINMENT

There are definite signs that Punjab entered a phase of population containment after assuming its present form in 1966. The avenues of its agricultural colonisation in other parts of India got virtually closed and any further relief on this count was to be found within. The opportunities of migration to other countries are also getting highly restricted.

The Green Revolution beginning in the mid-sixties was a timely event. It generated additional employment and higher incomes. There was considerable inmigration from other states, such as Uttar Pradesh, Haryana, Himachal Pradesh and Jammu and Kashmir (Census of India, 1981, 166–73). Urbanward migration was largely for industrial labour and ruralward for agricultural labour.

The Punjabis, though visibly prosperous in relative terms, are finding their economic space squeezed. This situation is now being taken care of through diversification of rural economy, impetus to large and medium scale industry, and promotion of service sector. The process gained momentum as an aftermath of the Green Revolution. The non-agricultural sector of the working force grew at an annual compound rate of 3.2 per cent during 1971-91. This was two times the growth rate of agricultural sector of 1.6 per cent. The percentage of agricultural workers declined from 62.7 in 1971 to 55.3 in 1991. This reduced somewhat the direct pressure of population on agricultural land. The capacity of the state to hold larger numbers increased.

SOME DISTORTIONS

Punjab is not free from some disturbing aspects in its demo-graphic scenario. It is ahead of India by 16 years in economic time distance (nation's per capita income of Rs. 2,222 in 1992 at 1980-81 prices was achieved by the state in 1976) but only by 8 years in fertility regulation, and hardly by 6 years in literacy performance. There is a lag in Punjab's social advancement vis-a-vis its economic development.

What we observe is that, during 1971-91, Punjab's birth rate came down by 6.4 points as compared with 6.8 points in India. A better record was expected on the part of the state which is materially almost two times better off than the rest of the country. Fall in its death rate was 3.9 points as against 6.1 points in India. The net outcome is that the rate of natural increase in Punjab's population has generally been higher, though by just decimal points, than that of India as a whole (Table 3).

An exceptionally high growth rate of the state's scheduled caste population deserves a special mention. During 1961-91, this economically, socially and educationally deprived section of society recorded a compound annual growth of 2.8 per cent while the rest of the population grew by 1.8 per cent every year on the average

(Table 7). Its percentage in the total increased from 22 in 1961 to 28 in 1991. At the time of Independence, scheduled caste population had accounted for about one-fifth of the total.

In association with their traditional occupations like agricultural labour, menial services and household industry, scheduled castes have predominantly been rural by residence. As against 33.1 per cent of Punjab's non-scheduled caste population as urban, the corresponding figure for its scheduled caste population is 20.6 per cent (Table 7).This section of population is showing an increasing tendency toward migration to towns for employment in casual labour, industry, petty retailing and construction. Migration to cities is more pronounced. A significant rise has been observed in the share of scheduled castes in the total population of various cities (Table 8).

The literacy level of Punjab refuses to match its economic lead. With a literacy rate of 58.5 per cent in respect of population in the 7 plus age group, the state ranked 18th amongst different states and union territories of the country in 1991. It is placed below the much less economically developed neighbouring state of Himachal Pradesh. A redeeming feature is a continuous rise in the literacy rate and a gradual reduction in the disparity between literacy rate of its various districts.

Densification of rural settlements is another feature of Punjab demography which arouses serious concern. There were on an average about 119 households in a village in 1951; this figure rose to 190 in 1991. The resulting overcrowding is finding an outlet in construction of houses on land originally earmarked for cattle and even on land outside the settlement boundary. Most of this development is haphazard.

SOME POSITIVE FEATURES

There are some redeeming features of Punjab demography. Towns are fairly uniformly distributed and closely spaced and urban-rural linkages are strong. The average spacing of towns in Punjab is just 22 km as compared with 31 km in India. This is the lowest figure for any state, barring Goa and Kerala. The impact of agricultural development and agro-based industry on dispersal of urbanisation is evident (Gosal, 1985, 76).

Punjab indeed pre-empted the Integrated Development of Small and Medium Towns Programme launched by the Government of

India in 1979 (Krishan, 1991, 176). The state had enacted the New Mandi Township Development and Regulation Act in 1960, gone for the Crash Programme for the Rural Link Roads in 1968, and initiated the Focal Point Programme in 1977. This thrust on agricultural-rural development provided a stimulus to a sustained growth of towns.

Rural-urban transfer of population has been gaining momentum. Punjab is now 30 per cent urban as compared with about 20 per cent at the time of Independence (Table 9). Many rural-urban commuters finally turn into rural-urban migrants. Ex-servicemen, with rural background, normally prefer to settle in a town after retirement. All such persons retain a regular link with their native villages. A class of people is emerging whose economic interests are partly rural and partly urban.

As an outcome of all this, Punjab is distinguished by the narrowest urban-rural gap amongst all the states in the country (Krishan, 1992, 95; Gosal and Krishan, 1984, 143). The average assets per household in rural areas here are two times of that in urban places (Reserve Bank of India, 1986, p. 439). The incidence of rural poverty at 7.2 per cent in 1987-88 was not only the lowest for any Indian state but also without any rural-urban gap according to the officially released estimates (Government of India, 1993).The comparable figures for India are 33.4 and 20.1 per cent respectively.

Urban-rural continuum is most manifest in the corridor development along the roads connecting the big cities, such as Ludhiana, Jalandhar, and Amritsar. About one-half of the 400 odd large and medium scale industrial units in Punjab in 1992 were located in villages, mostly along the main road-rail routes. This establishes a new pattern of employment opportunities which is causing a fresh redistribution of population in the state. The urbanisation process, which was earlier dispersing in response to agricultural development, has started concentrating somewhat in the wake of rapid industrialisation during the eighties. About one-half of the larger and medium scale industrial units in the state came up during this decade.

In contrast to an almost regular fall in India's sex ratio from 946 in 1951 to 927 in 1991, a significant improvement is seen in Punjab's sex ratio from 844 to 882 during the same period (Fig. 2).This indicates that upgradation of the status of women has been of relatively higher order in its case. The evolving scene is, of course, not without some dark clouds on the horizon. A fast growing popularity of pre-birth sex tests and increasing incidence of female foeticide is likely to set the clock back.

An enhanced tendency towards universal marriage and a distinct reduction in widowhood are the other aspects of Punjab demography. In 1951, around 15 per cent of males in 35 plus age group were recorded as never married; by 1981, this proportion had been more than halved (Table 10). Likewise, one in every ten females in the 35-44 age group was widow in 1951; this proportion fell down to one in fifty by 1981. Though firm data are not available yet there are indications to a gradual break up of joint families, both in urban and rural areas.

THE NEXT PHASE

Economies usually race through urbanisation levels of 30 to 60 per cent in historically short periods of time, typically ranging from 30 to 60 years, when they become 30 per cent urban and achieve per capita incomes of 500 to 1000 US dollars (Mohan, 1990, 5-6). Punjab today is on the threshold of a phase of rapid growth in urban population.

CONCLUDING REMARKS

The main messages of this essay are obvious enough. First, in the process of its successive territorial reorganisations, Punjab has become demographically more homogeneous. It is the only Sikh majority state of India, with the ratio of 63 : 37. Eighty-five per cent of its population is Punjabi speaking. Regional disparities in population density have narrowed over time. The demographic distinction between the former British administered and princely ruled parts of the Punjab has got blurred in the process.

Secondly, the state has undergone three phases of population change since Independence: (i) population replacement of the Muslims by the non-Muslims at the time of partition of the Indian subcontinent in 1947; (ii) population redistribution during 1947-66 mainly in association with extension of irrigation and reclamation of new agricultural lands; and (iii) spatial containment of population due largely to a virtual check on agricultural out-migration since its reorganisation in 1966.

Thirdly, the population change in Punjab during the contemporary period of its history has been a mixed bag of gains and losses. The positive accomplishments of the state lie in reducing the urban-rural gap, establishing a greater harmony between land resources and population distribution, and improving the context of family life through enhanced tendency toward universal marriage and reduced widowhood. On the other hand, it has to work harder for regulating fertility, promoting literacy, and curbing the preference for sons.

Finally, the Punjab story reveals that the population change was strongly influenced by the factors of political change, especially in the form of territorial reorganisation, and of technological change, particularly by way of allowing a greater use of land and water resources. All this found a dynamic association with economic change witnessed in a higher level of agricultural productivity, agro-based industrialisation, and progressive urbanisation.

TABLE 1

Punjab: Population Data, 1951-91

		Census Year				
		1951	1961	1971	1981	1991
1.	Area (sq. km.)	50,362	50,362	50,362	50,362	50,362
2.	Number of inhabited villages	11,625	11,947	12,188	12,342	12,428
3.	Number of towns/urban agglomerations	112	109	108	134	120
4.	Total population (million)	9.2	11.1	13.5	16.8	20.3
5.	Rural population (million)	7.2	8.6	10.3	12.1	14.3
6.	Urban population (million)	2.0	2.5	3.2	4.7	6.0
7.	Population density (per km.^{2})	182 (117)	221 (142)	269 (177)	333 (216)	403 (273)
8.	Percentage of urban population	21.7 (17.3)	23.1 (18.1)	23.7 (19.9)	27.7 (23.3)	29.6 (26.1)
9.	Sex ratio (female per 1,000 males)	844 (946)	854 (941)	865 (930)	879 (934)	882 (927)
10.	Decadal population growth rate (per cent)	21.6 (21.5)	21.7 (24.8)	23.9 (24.7)	20.8(23.5)	
	Birth rate (per thousand)		*	34.1 (36.3)	30.3 (33.9)	27.7(29.5)
	Death rate (per thousand)	*	*	11.7 (15.9)	9.4 (12.5)	7.8(9.8)
11.	Percentage of agricultural population/workers	67.3	58.0 (66.6)	55.3(64.9)		
12.	Percentage of literate persons (7 plus)	48.1 (43.6)	58.5(52.2)			
13.	Percentage of					
	Hindus	42.3	–	–		34.5(82.0)
	Sikhs	55.7	–	–		63.0(1.9)
	Muslims	0.8	–	–		1.2(12.1)

Christians	1.0	–	–		1.1(2.3)
Others	0.2	–	–		0.2(1.7)
14. Percentage: Hindi speaking	–	–	–	14.6 (40.0)	*
(1981) Punjabi speaking	–	–	–	84.9 (2.8)	*

Source: Compiled from various volumes of Census of India, 1951-91, and *Sample Registration Bulletins,* June,1987 and January 1995.

Note: Figures in brackets are for India.
* data not available.
– data not used.

TABLE 2

Punjab: Percentage of Displaced Persons in Total Population of Some Select Districts, 1951

District	Percentage
Gurdaspur	35.0
Kapurthala	28.7
Firozpur	27.0
Jalandhar	25.9
Amritsar	24.3
Patiala	22.8
Ludhiana	21.0
PUNJAB	20.4

Source: Calculated from Census of India, 1951: *Punjab, Pepsu, Himachal Pradesh, Bilaspur and Delhi, Part II-A, General Population, Age and Social Tables,* 332.

TABLE 3

Punjab and India: Birth and Death Rates, 1941-50 to 1991

Year/s	Birth Rate		Death Rate		Natural Increase Rate	
	Punjab	India	Punjab	India	Punjab	India
1941-50	41.2	39.9	26.3	27.4	14.9	12.5
1951-60	44.7	41.7	18.9	22.8	25.8	18.9
1961-70*	39.5	39.2	15.2	19.4	24.3	19.8
1971-73	34.1	36.3	11.7	15.9	22.4	20.4
1981	30.3	33.9	9.4	12.5	20.9	21.4
1991	27.7	29.5	7.8	9.8	19.9	19.7

Source: S.P. Jain (1967): 'State growth rates' in Ashish Bose, ed., *Patterns of Population Change in India, 1851-61,* Allied Publishers, Bombay, 13-32; and Registrar General of India, *June 1987 and January 1995: Sample Registration Bulletins,* New Delhi.

* Interpolated from data for 1951-60 and 1971-73.

TABLE 4

Punjab: Population, Density and Growth Rate, 1951-1991

Census Year	Population	Density per km²	Growth rate during the preceding decade		
			Total	Rural	Urban
1951	9,160,500	182	–4.6 (13.3)*	–9.7	20.0
1961	11,135,069	221	21.6 (21.6)	19.5	29.1
1971	13,551,060	269	21.7 (24.8)	20.6	25.3
1981	16,788,915	333	23.9 (24.7)	17.5	44.5
1991	20,281,969	403	20.8 (23.9)	17.7	29.0

Source: Census of India, 1991: *Final Population Totals, Paper 2 of 1992*, 86-101.

* Figures in parenthesis are for India.

TABLE 5

Punjab: Change in Percentage Share of Different Districts in the State's Total Population, 1951-91

District	Percentage share in total population		Change in percentage points
	1951	1991	
Amritsar	14.9	12.3	–2.6
Jalandhar	11.5	10.0	–1.5
Hoshiarpur	8.6	7.2	–1.4
Gurdaspur	9.3	8.7	–0.6
Kapurthala	3.2	3.2	0.0
Sangrur	8.4	8.4	0.0
Ludhiana	9.6	12.2	+2.6
Patiala	7.6	9.4	+1.8
Bathinda	6.8	7.7	+0.9
Faridkot	8.2	8.5	+0.3
Rupnagar	4.2	4.5	+0.3
PUNJAB	100.0	100.0	

Source: Calculated from Census of India: *Punjab General Population Tables and Primary Census Abstracts, 1981*, 63-65 and *Punjab Final Population Totals, Paper 1 of 1992*, 9.

TABLE 6

Punjab: Population Density by Districts, 1951 and 1991 and Compound Annual Growth Rate During 1951-91

	Population density per km²		Annual growth rate
	1951	1991	1951-91
PUNJAB	182	403	2.00
Gurdaspur	239	493	1.83
Amritsar	269	492	1.53
Firozpur	120	274	2.09
Ludhiana	228	641	2.62
Jalandhar	310	596	1.65
Kapurthala	181	396	1.98
Hoshiarpur	205	375	1.52
Rupnagar	183	439	2.21
Patiala	152	414	2.53
Sangrur	150	335	2.03
Bathinda	112	281	2.34
Faridkot	131	302	2.11

Source: Calculated from Census of India, 1981: *General Population Tables, Punjab, Part-II-B;* and Census of India, 1991, *Punjab, Final Population Totals Paper 1 of 1992.*

TABLE 7

India and Punjab: A Comparative view of some Select Demographic Attributes of Scheduled Caste and Non-Scheduled Caste Populations, 1991

Demographic attribute	Scheduled caste population		Non-Scheduled caste population	
	India	Punjab	India	Punjab
Percentage in total population	16.73	28.31	83.27	71.69
Percentage in urban population	18.72	20.55	27.11	33.10
Annual growth rate (1961-91)	2.59	2.83	2.24	1.75
Sex ratio (females per thousand males)	922	873	928	885
Percentage of literate population (7+ age group)	37.41	41.09	55.06	65.10
Percentage of workers	39.25	30.71	33.71	30.23
Percentage of non-agricultural workers	25.49	35.37	37.24	48.37

Source: Calculated from Census of India, 1991: *India, Union Primary Census Abstract for Scheduled Castes and Tribes, Paper 1 of 1993,* 24-29; and Census of India, 1991: *India, Final Population Totals, Paper 2 of 1992,* 138-39, 192 and 212-13.

TABLE 8

Punjab: Percentage of Scheduled Caste Population in Cities, 1951 and 1991

City	1951	1991
Ludhiana	6.31	11.85
Amritsar	9.47	17.60
Jalandhar	16.63	27.61
Patiala	4.79	9.73
Bathinda	13.64	20.29
Pathankot	12.17	20.56
Hoshiarpur	10.33	24.25
Moga	14.49	17.31
Abohar	15.61	18.44
Batala	8.78	26.51

Source: Calculated from Census of India, 1961: *Punjab Primary Census Abstract* (compiled especially for the present Punjab), pp. 86-113; Census of India, 1991: *Punjab, Final Population Totals, Paper 1 of 1992,* 9-12.

* City is an urban centre with a population of at least 100,000. The above Table covers cities of 1991.

TABLE 9

Punjab: Urban Growth, 1951-91

Census year	Number of towns/ urban agglomerations	Urban population in million	Percentage of urban population	Decadal growth rate	Decadal change in percentage of points
1951	110	1.99	21.72	–	–
1961	106	2.57	23.06	29.06	1.34
1971	106	3.22	23.73	25.27	0.67
1981	134	4.65	27.68	44.51	3.65
1991	120	5.99	29.55	28.95	1.87

Source: Calculated from Census of India, 1981: *Punjab: General Population Tables, Parts II-A and B, 1981;* and Census of India, 1991: *Punjab, Final Population Totals, Paper 1 of 1992.* Also see the next essay.

TABLE 10

Ludhiana District: Percentage of Never Married Males and Percentage of Widowed Females among the Mature Adults and Old, 1951 and 1981

Age group	Percentage of			
	Never married males		Widowed females	
	1951	1981	1951	1981
35-44	13.1	6.7	9.9	2.0
45-54	19.0	6.7	19.9	11.6
55-64	17.5	7.4	36.8	24.8
65 and over	14.7	7.2	49.6	33.2

Source: Calculated from Census of India, 1951: *Punjab: Pepsu, Himachal Pradesh, Bilaspur and Delhi Part II-A - General Population, Age and Social Tables,* 116-19; and Census of India, 1981: *Punjab, Social and Cultural Tables.*

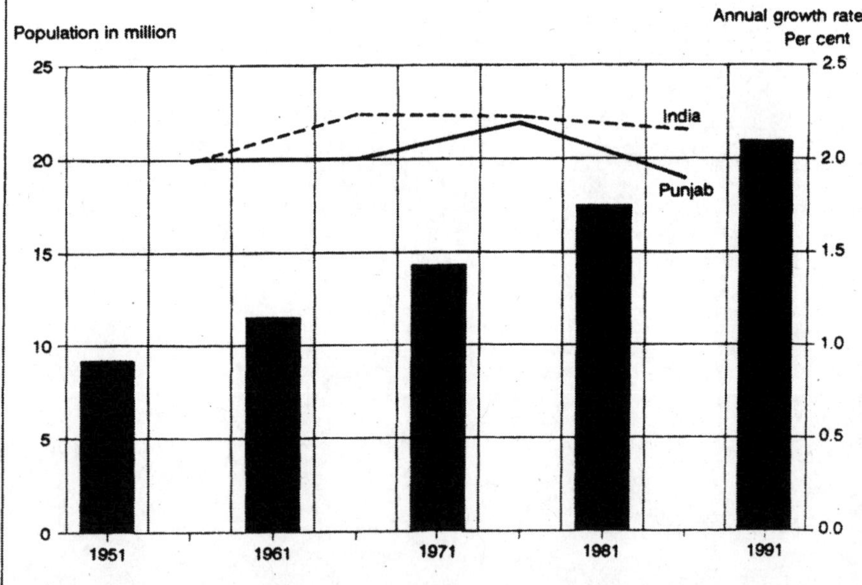

Compound Annual Growth Rate : 1951-91

India : 2.15 %
Punjab : 2.01 %

Fig. 2

Punjab : Sex Ratio, 1951-91

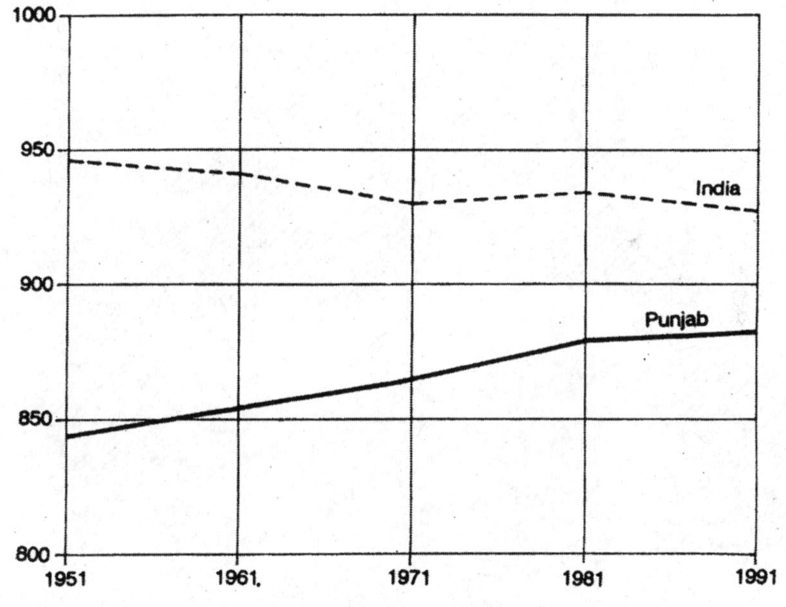

Sex Ratio Change : 1951-91

India : −17
Punjab : +38

Fig.6

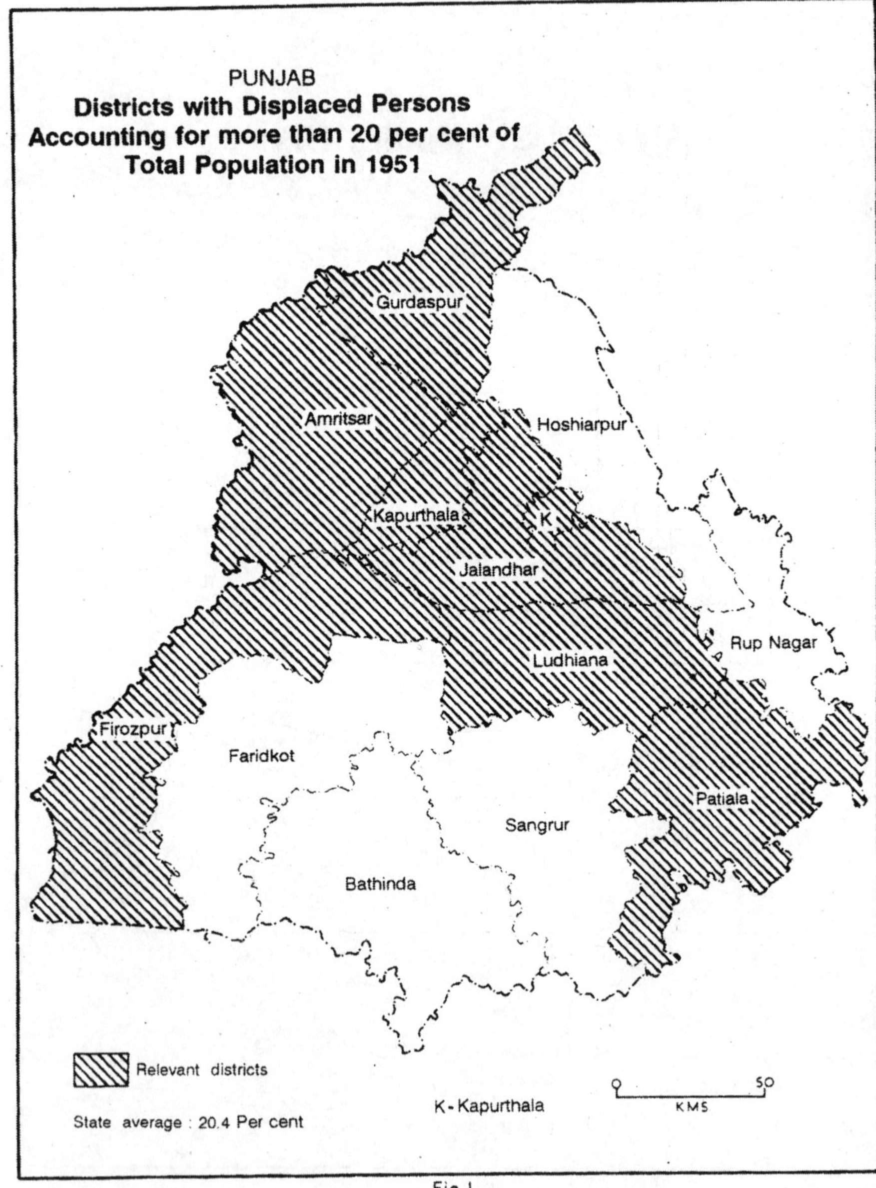
PUNJAB
Districts with Displaced Persons
Accounting for more than 20 per cent of
Total Population in 1951
Gurdaspur
Amritsar
Hoshiarpur
Kapurthala
K
Jalandhar
Rup Nagar
Ludhiana
Firozpur
Faridkot
Patiala
Sangrur
Bathinda
Relevant districts
State average : 20.4 Per cent
K-Kapurthala
0
50
KMS

Fig. 1

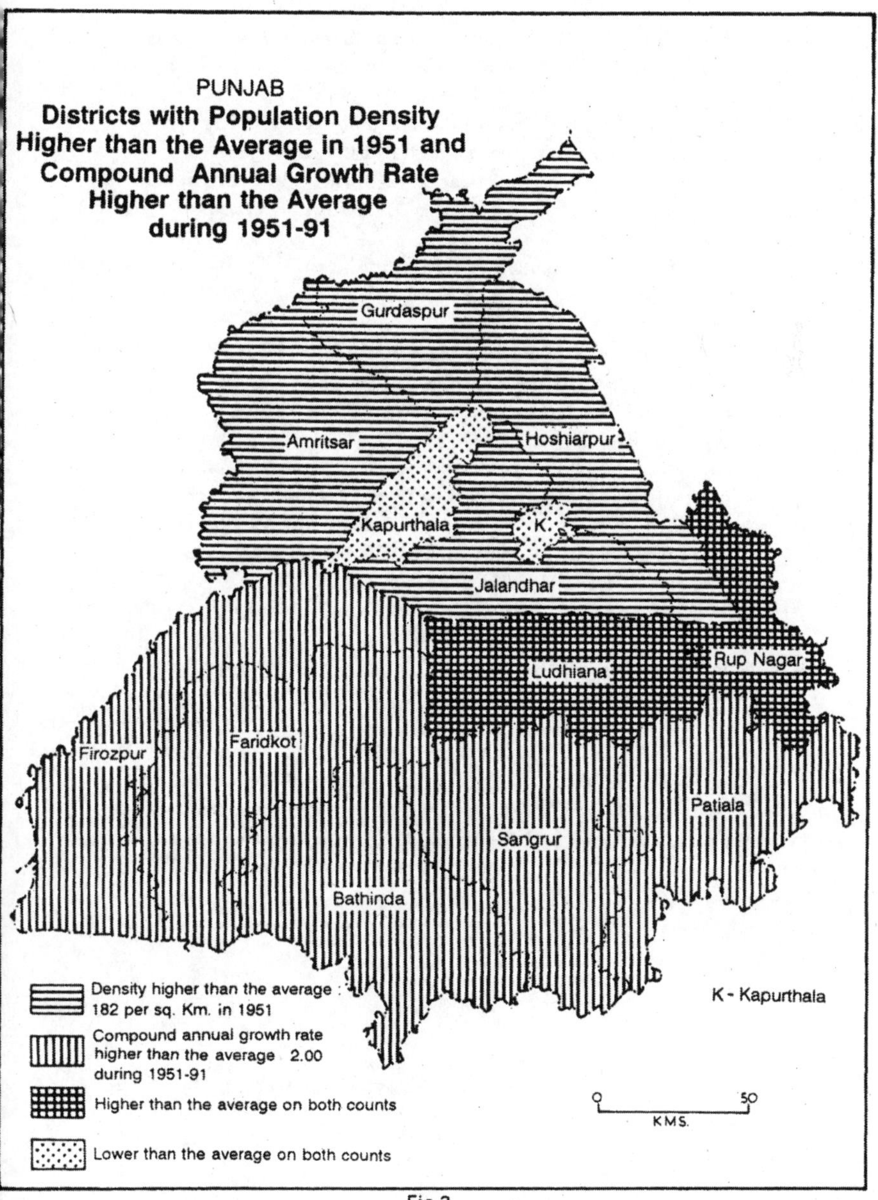
PUNJAB
Districts with Population Density Higher than the Average in 1951 and Compound Annual Growth Rate Higher than the Average during 1951-91
Gurdaspur
Amritsar
Hoshiarpur
Kapurthala
K
Jalandhar
Ludhiana
Rup Nagar
Firozpur
Faridkot
Patiala
Sangrur
Bathinda
Density higher than the average : 182 per sq. Km. in 1951
Compound annual growth rate higher than the average 2.00 during 1951-91
Higher than the average on both counts
Lower than the average on both counts
K - Kapurthala
0
50
KMS.

Fig.3

REFERENCES

Census of India (1981): *Geographic Distribution of Internal Migration in India: 1971-81.* Registrar General & Census Commissioner of India, New Delhi.

Gosal, G.S. and Gopal Krishan (1984). *Regional Disparities in the Levels of Socio-Economic Development in Punjab.* Vishal, Kurukshetra.

Gosal, G.S. (1985). 'Agricultural development and the urbanisation process with special reference to Punjab'. *Travaux et Documents de Geographic Tropicale,* Ceget, 63-76.

Gosal, G.S. (1967). 'Redistribution of population in Punjab during 1951-61'. *Patterns of Population Change in India, 1951-61.* Ed. Ashish Bose. Allied, Bombay, 105-29.

Government of India (1993). *Report on Estimation of Proportion and Number of Poor.* Planning Commission, New Delhi.

Krishan, Gopal (1971). 'Distribution of the Sikhs outside Punjab (India)' *India Geographical Journal,* 46, 35-41.

Krishan, Gopal (1991). 'Integrated development of small and medium towns programme: the Punjab experience'. *Perspectives on the Third World Development.* Ed. P.R. Sharma. Rishi Publications, Varanasi, 175-80.

Krishan, Gopal (1992). 'Urban-rural relation in India: a critique'. *Indian Association of Social Sciences Institutions Quarterly* 10, no. 1, 92-104.

Luthra, K.L. (1949). *Impact of Partition on Industries in Border Districts of East Punjab.* Ludhiana.

Mohan, Rakesh (1990). *Issues in Urban Employment Planning International Labour Organisation.* Asian Regional Team for Employment Promotion, New Delhi.

Rai, Satya M. (1986). *Punjab Since Partition.* Durga Publications, Delhi.

Reserve Bank of India (1986). *Bulletin,* June 1986, New Delhi.

Singh, Kirpal (1972). *The Partition of the Punjab.* Punjabi University, Patiala.

Singh, Tarlok (1952). *Land Settlement Manual for Displaced Persons in Punjab and Pepsu.* Controller of Printing and Stationery, Punjab, Shimla.

10

Urbanisation Since Independence

GOPAL KRISHAN

This paper is a brief narrative of Punjab urbanisation since Independence. The focus is on its evolving social scenario. This has to be inferred not only from the magnitude, pace and pattern of urbanisation but also from its composition. The change in the social scene refers to matters relating to the demographic size of urbanisation, physical lay out of towns, planning interventions by the Government and, above all, the complexion of urban population in terms of religion, caste and regional background. Our observations are based mainly on the data of the Census of India on a variety of parameters from 1951 to 1991.

DEMOGRAPHY

At the first post-Independence census in 1951, Punjab recorded an urban population of 1.99 million against the total population of 9.16 million (Table 1). With about one-fifth of its population living in urban places, as compared with one-sixth in India, Punjab was among the relatively more urbanised states of the country. It had 3 large, 19 medium and 88 small towns at that time. Urban population was divided almost equally among these three categories of towns.

In 1991 the size of Punjab's urban population was about 6 million, while its total population had grown to 20 million. Thus, whereas the rise in urban population was three times, the rise in total population was slightly more than two times of its base in 1951. The share of urban population in the total was now 30 per cent. It compared favourably with 26 per cent in India. There was only a small rise in the number of towns, from 110 in 1951 to 120 in 1991. The share of the large, medium and small towns had, however, significantly changed. Cities accounted for over one-half, medium towns for nearly one-third, and small towns for one-sixth of the urban population. Cities increased their share at the cost of the small towns while the medium towns maintained their share. The state saw the emergence of its first ever metropolitan city of Ludhiana in 1991.

DISPLACED PERSONS

Beyond this statistical data, the story of Punjab urbanisation since Independence makes an interesting reading. The first change in the social scene took place on the eve of Independence. Barring the towns of Malerkotla and Qadian, all urban places witnessed the exodus of the Muslim population. Displaced non-Muslims from Pakistan filled the vacuum created. Muslim localities or *mohallas* got transformed into concentrations of displaced persons. One-third of the urban population at that time was accounted for by these new people. This proportion was significantly higher in cities like Patiala, Jalandhar, Amritsar and Ludhiana.

The space vacated by the Muslims in urban places was far too inadequate to accommodate the entire influx of displaced persons. Some new towns, such as Chandigarh (though now outside Punjab) and Rajpura township, had to be raised to accommodate the excess. Model towns were also appended to the existing cities, as in Jalandhar, Ludhiana, Amritsar and Patiala. This set in motion the process of physical growth of towns.

THE PLANNING PROCESS

Despite the efforts of planning, much of physical growth of towns was taking place in a haphazard way. This aroused a serious concern of the government. As a response, the Town and Country Planning Department of Punjab was constituted in 1961. One of its first jobs was to prepare master plans for all the towns having a population of 20,000 and above. The concept of urban growth on planned basis took roots. Meanwhile the completely planned city of Chandigarh had assumed some visible form. Its impact was manifest on the layout and design of all newly developed localities of Punjab towns.

During the Fourth Plan (1969-74), Ludhiana, Jalandhar and Amritsar were covered under the Integrated Urban Development Programme with a view to raising the level of their infrastructure. Small and medium towns received attention somewhat later under the Sixth Plan (1980-85). This was done under the purview of the Integrated Development of Small and Medium Towns Programme.

The Environmental Improvement of Slums Programme had been initiated earlier in 1972 to take care of the proliferating slums in towns and cities. Whatever the degree of their success, all these efforts on the part of the government became an agent of change in the fabric of urban Punjab. The physical make-up of Punjab towns was changing.

AGRICULTURAL DEVELOPMENT

Meanwhile, the process of agricultural development, which picked up immediately after Independence and took the form of the Green Revolution in mid-sixties, had a multifarious influence on the urbanisation scene of Punjab. This caused a rapid growth of many a market town, promoted rural-urban linkages and stimulated rural-urban commuting. Urbanisation diffused spatially and urban hierarchy got smoothened.

The average spacing of towns in Punjab is just 22 kms as compared with 31 km in India. This is the lowest figure for any state, barring Goa and Kerala. The growth of small and medium towns was sustained through a fillip to their trade, service and agro-based industrial functions. Indeed Punjab had pre-empted the Integrated Development of Small and Medium Towns programme. It is quite clear that agricultural-rural development is likely to stimulate rather than contain rural-urban migration.

Not only cities but also the small and medium towns have expanded in their physical dimension. Changes in morphology of all types of towns became necessary for meeting the space demand of newlanduses, relocation of facility points to new sites, and coping up with the fast increasing use of motor vehicles. The response is visible in emergence of new residential colonies, resiting of old grain markets and bus stands, and construction of bypasses to divert the inter-town traffic.

REDEFINING TERRITORIAL JURISDICTION

All this made it imperative to redefine the territorial jurisdiction of towns. This has been done over time in the case of 63 towns out of 120 in all. The intention was to extend the limits of the physically expanding towns and thereby acquire additional land for residential, commercial and industrial development on planned lines.

As mentioned above, the number of towns in the state increased by only 10 during 1951-91, but the extent of urban area got more than doubled. This process was more pronounced after 1971. The aggregate area under towns in the state was 692 km2 in 1971 and 1441 km2 in 1991. The extension in the area of some of the cities was indeed phenomenal : from 20 to 135 km2 in Ludhiana, 47 to 115 km2 in Amritsar, and 44 to 80 km2 in Jalandhar (Table 2). The city and its neighbouring villages were welded together as an urban entity.

CORRIDOR DEVELOPMENT

An outcome of this tendency has been the corridor development along roads connecting big cities, such as Ludhiana, Jalandhar and Amritsar. Linear physical growth of small and medium towns was a part of this process. It may surprise many to know that about one-half of the 400 odd large and medium scale industrial units in Punjab are located in villages, mostly along such corridors. Many of these villages are potential towns. This sets in a new spatial pattern for urbanisation. The urbanisation process, which was earlier dispersing in response to agricultural development, has started concentrating in the wake of rapid industrialisation during the eighties. Regional disparities in urbanisation, which had narrowed down by 1981, have again widened by 1991.

THE DIFFICULT DECADE

The eighties, in fact, take us to a different track in respect of urbanisation. Punjab had to undergo a traumatic experience during this period. It was a time when the security considerations were paramount at all levels, social milieu was disturbed, political institutions were rather non-functional, and administrative capacity was feeble. An explosive urban growth was expected in the wake of much talked about migration from villages to towns for reasons of security. This did not happen, at least on the scale it was envisaged.

The 1991 census data revealed that the urban growth rate declined sharply from 44.5 per cent during 1971-81 to 29.1 per cent during 1981-91. Over three-fourths of the addition in urban population was on account of natural increase. Net in-migration contributed less than one-fourth. In overall terms, it seems that while there was considerable migration from villages to towns, several towns also suffered sizeable outmigration to places outside the state.

RELIGIOUS COMPOSITION

Such a growth behaviour of Punjab towns during 1981-91 was not delinked from a change in their religious composition. The Hindu population of urban Punjab increased by 21.5 per cent and the Sikh population by 42.5 during this decade. The share of the Hindus in urban population declined from 64.1 per cent in 1981 to 60.5 in 1991. There was a corresponding rise in respect of the Sikh population from 33.2 to 36.7 per cent.

A further analysis of data shows the 44-towns out of 120 experienced net outflow of the Hindus along with net-inflow of the Sikhs (Table 3). This feature was more typical of Amritsar, Patiala and Bathinda districts. Hindu population increased by 9 per cent and the Sikhs by 33 per cent in Amritsar. From 17 towns, there was net outflow of both Sikhs and Hindus. Such towns showed a greater frequency in Gurdaspur and Jalandhar districts. Many of these are small towns. Only 25 towns were noted for net in-migration of both Hindu and Sikh populations. These made a greater concentration in Ludhiana, Rupnagar and Sangrur districts. In Ludhiana city, Hindu population grew by 68 per cent and the Sikh by 78 per cent. A tendency toward parity among the Hindus and the Sikhs in urban population will go a long way in breaking the Hindu-urban and the Sikh-rural image of Punjab's population.

SCHEDULED CASTES

A gradual urbanisation of the scheduled caste population is another noticeable feature of the Punjab scene. In 1961, 12.9 per cent of urban population belonged to scheduled castes. By 1991, this figure had risen to 19.8 per cent (Table 4). The annual growth rate of scheduled caste population in urban Punjab during 1961-91 was 4.3 per cent as compared with 2.9 per cent in the case of non-scheduled castes. This can be attributed partly to a higher rate of natural increase among the scheduled castes but largely to their faster pace of urban-ward migration. This is a development of great importance. Perhaps urbanisation will ultimately prove as the most effective instrument for raising the socio-economic status of this historically disadvantaged community.

The percentage rise in the share of scheduled castes in urban population has been more impressive in Jalandhar, Hoshiarpur and Gurdaspur districts. These are the districts noted for a high concentration of scheduled castes in rural areas also. All this represents a short-run nature of the scheduled castes migration in Punjab. At the city level, a greater increase in their case was observed in Batala, Jalandhar and Hoshiarpur. These were followed by cities like Amritsar, Bathinda and Ludhiana. Their migration to cities like Abohar and Moga, which are primarily agricultural markets, is of small magnitude.

THE SLUMS

Associated with the inflow of scheduled castes to urban places has been the proliferation of slum population. Around one-fifth of the urban Punjab is estimated to be living in slums though their physical conditions may not be as bad as in most parts of India. In Ludhiana city, 48 notified slums accommodate no less than 40 per cent of the city population. About one-half of these have a population of more than 5000 each. Salem Tabri is the biggest; its population is around 100,000. In their locational pattern, slums make clusters near work places, along the drainage lines, and by the side of transport routes. More often than not, these originate on the city's skirts. Some assume a location within a city's expansion beyond them at a later stage.

THE FUTURE

One may finally ask: what next in respect of Punjab urbanisation? The state is entering into a phase of accelerated urbanisation. An analysis of available data suggests that, by 2020, around 50 per cent of Punjab's total population will be living in urban places. Where would most of this urban growth take place? This certainly is a crucial question.

Going by the prevalling trends we project as follows. First a large segment of this urban growth will get concentrated along the corridors—Amritsar-Jalandhar, Jalandhar-Ludhiana, Ludhiana-Rajpura, Ludhiana-Malerkotla, and Chandigarh-Lalru. These urban corridors are already attracting a number of large and medium scale industrial units. The process is going to accelerate in future. Secondly, cities like Ludhiana, Jalandhar and Patiala will continue growing fast with emergence of planned urban estates, within or on the periphery. Finally, urbanisation will be rapid in Punjab areas adjoining Chandigarh.

TABLE 1
Punjab: Urban Growth, 1951-91

Census year	Number of towns/ urban agglome-rations	Urban popu-lation (in millions)	Percent-age of urban popu-lation	Decadal growth rate of urban population	Decadal change in percentage
1951	110	1.99	21.72	—	—
1961	106	2.57	23.06	+29.06	+1.34
1971	106	3.22	23.73	+25.27	+0.67
1981	134	4.65	27.68	+44.51	+3.65
1991	120	5.99	29.55	+28.95	+1.87

Source: Census of India, 1991, *Punjab: General Population Tables and Primary Census Abstracts, Part II - A and Part II-B,* 14, 19 and 99.

TABLE 2
Punjab: Increase in Urban Area, 1961-91

	State/City Area in km²			
	1961	1971	1981	1991
Punjab	673	692	1199	1441
Ludhiana	20	42	110	135
Amritsar	47	47	115	115
Jalandhar	44	62	80	80
Patiala *	34	NA	NA	31
Bathinda	21	21	NA	97
Pathankot*	11	16	21	22
Hoshiarpur	10	10	21	28
Moga*	7	7	16	16
Abohar	14	14	14	23
Batala*	6	NA	NA	9

Source: Census of India, 1991, *Punjab: General Population Tables and Primary Census Abstracts, Part II - A and Part II - B,* 99-103.

* Excluding outgrowths.

TABLE 3

Punjab: Classification of Punjab Towns by Migration Behaviour of the Hindus and the Sikhs during 1981-91

State/District	Number of towns characterised by					
	Hindu-Outmigration and Sikh-Inmigration	Hindu-Inmigration and Sikh-Inmigration	HinduInmigratin and Sikh-Inmigration	Hindu-National Growth and Sikh-Inmigration	Others	Total
Punjab	44	26	16	12	22	120
Gurdaspur	4	2	4	0	2	12
Amritsar	5	0	1	0	4	10
Firozpur	4	3	1	1	1	10
Ludhiana	5	4	0	0	1	10
Jalandhar	4	2	4	2	2	14
Kapurthala	2	1	0	0	0	3
Hoshiarpur	3	1	1	1	3	9
Rupnagar	1	3	0	1	3	8
Patiala	6	3	0	2	1	12
Sangrur	4	4	2	1	1	12
Bathinda	6	1	2	1	1	11
Faridkot	0	2	1	3	3	9

Source: Census of India, 1991, *Punjab: Religion, Part IV-B* (ii), and Census of India, 1981, *Punjab: Religion, Paper 1 of 1984*.

* Out migration denotes an increase rate below the rate of natural increase and inmigration stands for an increase rate above the rate of natural increase.

** Hindu population in urban places of Punjab increased by 21.5 per cent and the Sikh population by 42.5 per cent, during 198191.

*** Rate of natural increase of Punjab's urban population, during 1981-91 was 23.7 per cent. See Census of India, 1991, *India: Provisional Population Totals, Rural-Urban Distribution, Paper 2 of 1991*, 58.

TABLE 4
Punjab District-wise Change in Percentage of Scheduled Caste Population in Urban Places, 1961-1991

State/district	Percentage of scheduled caste population in urban places		Increase in percentage points
	1961	1991	1961-1991
Punjab	12.94	19.76	6.82
District-wise change			
Gurdaspur	11.90	22.23	10.33
Amritsar	10.64	18.87	8.23
Firozpur	14.76	18.96	4.20
Ludhiana	9.44	14.62	5.18
Jalandhar	18.27	29.19	10.92
Kapurthala	13.90	23.25	9.35
Hoshiarpur	13.46	25.27	11.81
Rupnagar	12.29	16.83	4.54
Patiala	7.49	11.87	4.38
Sangrur	13.05	18.77	5.72
Bathinda*	18.45	23.78	5.33
City-wise change			
Batala	8.78	26.51	17.73
Pathankot	12.17	20.56	8.39
Amritsar	9.47	17.60	8.13
Abohar	15.61	18.44	2.83
Moga	14.49	17.31	2.82
Ludhiana	6.31	11.85	5.54
Jalandhar	16.63	27.61	10.98
Hoshiarpur	10.33	24.25	13.92
Patiala	4.79	9.73	4.94
Bathinda	13.64	20.29	6.65

Source: Census of India, 1991, *Punjab: General Population Tables and Primary Census Abstracts, Part II - A and Part II - B,* 392. and 324-389, and Census of India, 1961, *Punjab: Primary Census Abstract (Special for Reorganised Punjab)*, 86-113.

* Includes Faridkot district.

PUNJAB
Urban Places by Population Size (1991) and Compound Annual Growth Rate :1951-91
Sujanpur
Pathankot
Behrampur
Dina Nagar
The Ravi
GURDASPUR
Dera Baba Nanak
Ramdas
Fatehgarh Churian
Dhariwal
Fateh Nangal
Mukerian
Talwara
Qadian
Batala
Dasua
Rajasansi
Majitha
Garhdiwala
Amritsar Cantt
Sri Hargobindpur
AMRITSAR
Urmar Tanda
Hariana
Jandiala
Bhogpur
Rayya
Hoshiarpur
Tarn Taran
Alawalpur
Sham Churasi
Adampur
Kartarpur
Bhikhiwind
JALANDHAR
Naya Nangal
Nangal Township
KAPURTHALA
Jalandhar Cantt
Patti
PHAGWARA
Garhshankar
Anandpur Sahib
Sultanpur
Banga
Nakodar
Nawanshahr
Goraya
Nurmahal
Rahon
FIROZPUR
Kot Ise Khan
Shahkot
Phillaur
The Satluj
Zira
Dharamkot
Rup Nagar
Talwandi Bhai
Machhiwara
FIROZPUR CANTT
Mullanpur Dakha
LUDHIANA
Moga
Doraha
Samrala
Morinda
Kurali
Kharar
KHANNA
MOHALI
Guru Har Sahai
FARIDKOT
Jagraon
Badhni Kalan
Akalgarh
Payal
Bassi
Bagha Purana
Raikot
Ahmedgarh
Gobindgarh
Jalalabad
Sirhind
KOT KAPURA
Amloh
Dera Bassi
Bhadaur
MUKTSAR
MALERKOTLA
Banur
FAZILKA
Jaitu
RAJPURA
BARNALA
NABHA
Goniana
Tapa
Dhuri
MALOUT
Bathinda
Dhanaula
SANGRUR
Patiala
Sanaur
Rampura Phul
Abohar
Giddarbaha
Bhucho Mandi
Longowal
Bhawanigarh
Sangat
Kot Fatta
Samana
Maur
Sunam
MANSA
Patran
Raman
Budhlada
Lehra Gaga
Bareta
Population size class
500,000 and above (Half million cities)
100,000 - 499,999 (Small cities)
20,000 - 99,999 (Medium towns)
Below 20,000 (Small towns)
0 50
KMS.
Compound annual growth rate
2.3% and above (Net inmigration)
1.9% to 2.3% (Growth mainly by natural increase)
Below 1.9% (Net outmigration cases)
N Towns which emerged after 1951
Average : 2.1%

11

Patriarchal Structure and Violence Against Women

RAINUKA DAGAR

I

The gender system constitutes an ideology of gender differentiation based on the (mis)appropriation of the biological sex differences. It is a coercive but largely invisible force. The sex differences are biological, but the ideology of patriarchy is historical and contextual. The gender system finds continuity not only in the practice of patriarchy i.e. male ascendancy, male inheritance and gender typed roles, but also in the nature of the capitalistic development process, religious sanctions and socio-cultural placement.

A pivotal aspect in the maintenance and propagation of male descendance and male inheritance is provided by gender practices and gendered social functioning which then determine male-female access to resources, skills and placements within the systemic functioning. The rigid allocation of roles in terms of biological sex attributes systematically deprives and discriminates against the female gender. The gender system not only creates conditions for confining women to household functioning, but also provides them with opportunity to acquire skills in household management and the qualities of a good nurturer. The male is typed as the earner, the protector, the decision maker. The logical implication is the denial of access to education, health, political power and gainful employment to women, and the enhancement, opportunities for men to have maximum access to resources with greater social and financial obligations and corresponding power and superiority.

The concept of gender specified role allocations draws on normative and even utilitarian justification with wide social acceptability which lends it an invisible character. The ideology of gender system is intermeshed with 'anonymous social mechanisms' through the institutions of family, education, religion, politics, law, social norms and value patterns.[1] Since the functioning of the gender system is integrated into the normative socio-cultural, economic and political spheres, it remains largely invisible. At the same time, the gender system uses coercion to ensure the norms, values and practices to conform to the typed male and female role behaviours.

Furthermore, typed female behaviour decrees greater gender conformity. The gender system determines women's personal behaviour, dress, sexual activity, choice of partner and reproductive options, all visible aspects, therefore easier for 'coercive forces' to control. In a broad sense, the gender system, its instruments, both men and women who are propagators of its ideology, social institutions, norms and traditions are all coercive. Thus the differentiating gender system silently propagates deprivation, discrimination and even atrocities against women. They are deprived in terms of access to facilities and resources and even life. They undergo discrimination in earnings, inheritance, medical care, nutrition, and education. The normative gender system acquires visibility when fundamentalist forces appropriate these typed roles and practices.[2]

Given these dimensions, any definition of violence against gender must include both the socially sanctioned and recognized acts that inflict injury on the female gender. The following definition of gender violence suitably captures this phenomenon:

> Violence against gender may be defined as those acts and situations which either visibly or invisibly harm or injure the female gender and degrade even its own instruments by discrimination, degradation, subjugation and oppression, and derive their justification and legitimacy from patriarchal structures and norms.[3]

An important aspect of this definition is that of visible and invisible violence. The violent acts which are visible to the perpetrators, victims and the community acquire a manifest character. Latent violence refers to the socially invisible and individually unperceived components of violence against gender. The pervasiveness of visible or invisible violence is a function of perception and would vary according to the nature and level of acceptance of the gender ideology, nature of the development process, socio-cultural placements and the impact of interventionists. The definition also points to inclusion of gender discriminations, and deprivations as instances of gender violence. Based on typed roles gender differentiation in practice becomes gender discrimination, since it negates women's rights to productive resources. Gender deprivation is denial of access to resources and skills to women.

The gender system guides male-female access and quality of participation within the systemic functioning in accordance with the ideology of gender differentiation. This situation results in the cultivation of male capacities to control resources on an unequal basis, even to the extent of determining life chances. All efforts to empower women through increased access and participation within the social system are hampered. So long as empowerment of women is sought through the provision of access, participation and skills within the existing gender differentiating system, it remains ineffective because social activity is the ideological setting within which skills are used and power is exercised.[4]

II

A glance at Table 1 would show that sex ratio is more unfavourable to women in the Punjab i.e. 882 as compared to all India average i.e. 929 in 1991. A major factor responsible for this is preference for the male child in the socio-cultural milieu of the Punjab. Our study reveals that a large number of first pregnancies are predetermined male pregnancies. There is a difference of degree in the utilization of sex determination tests in rural and urban Punjab, but the overall utilization is rather high (Table 2).

This percentage does not reflect the number of abortions undertaken to beget a male child. In any case the study reveals a high degree of misappropriation of development techniques to acquire male children. By the third pregnancy even abortions are performed to avoid a third female child. Thus technology is differentially utilized to conform to the norms of the gender system. It is highly significant to note in this connection that the male child preference in the upper strata, as shown by male child determined pregnancies, is higher as compared to other strata (Table 3).

The mere availability of infrastructural resources does not ensure their utilization by women. The access to resources is more a function of individual attitude, family norms and social setting. It is mainly because of this that in spite of the relatively better health infrastructure in the Punjab, in comparison with the country as a whole, the access of women to it is low i.e. 34 per cent in the rural and 47 per cent in the urban areas (Table 4).[5] In the rural Punjab, only 18 per cent and 16 per cent of women visit the public health system and private qualified doctors respectively. Interestingly, about 66 per cent of women take treatment from quacks or village elders. This is higher as compared to male utilization of this service.

In addition to cultural neglect, there is a gender bias in terms of making provision for females in hospitals. For instance, in government hospitals allocation of beds for females is 15 per cent less than what it is for males even though women have additional gynaecological problem. It is not that the state infrastructure is itself gender discriminatory; rather it is a reflection of bias in utilization of the infrastructure.[6]

Furthermore, the health system is not equipped to cope with the effects of gender based violence, such as pelvic inflammatory diseases, third degree burns, miscarriage, post-traumatic stress disorder, mental illness etc. There is no trained staff to provide immediate psycho ogical support and to collect necessary evidence for community and legal prosecution.[7]

Many health workers, under the influence of the gender bias, are not even aware of the need for making the health system respond to these victims of systemic atrocities (Table 5). They are not sensitive to the health consequences of social neglect, domestic violence, sexual abuse etc.

The typed gender roles influence women's access to education, skills and participation in social and political processes. Since the male is perceived to be the 'worker' with financial obligations and responsibilities to the family, he is 'justifiably' the inheritor not only of material resources but also of productive education and skills. The general typed roles not only direct the extent of women's access to education but also influence to a large extent the specific fields of education and skills imbibed (Table 6).

Though female literacy rates in the Punjab have improved from 31.3 per cent in 1971 to 49.70 per cent in 1991, they remain substantially lower than the male literacy rates for the same period.[8] Moreover, in the cohort 1985-1994, female enrolment is lower than males for the primary, middle and high school levels. There is a marginal difference of one per cent in drop-outs at the primary level but becomes a substantial six per cent for the high and middle levels (Table 7).

The need for providing girls with access to education was not generally felt in view of their position in the home. Another reason mentioned for restricted female education was the incidence of sexual abuse of girl children by the teachers, particularly in the rural areas.

Besides lower utilization of educational facilities by females, the nature of education to be imparted to them also shows a gender bias. The enrolment of girls in productive areas such as science and commerce was much lower than male enrolment: in commerce, 36.4 per cent for girls and 63.5 per cent for boys; in science, 39.5 per cent for girls and 60.4 per cent for boys.

In vocational education, the pattern of enrolment is almost the same. The preponderance of girls in foodcraft, textile and garment departments is due to the assumption that these skills are specific to women. Similarly agriculture related skills are the sole domain of males. They constituted 99.74 per cent of the students in 1994. This is happening in spite of the fact that women are involved in large numbers in dairying, and agriculture. Further, in engineering courses, males constitute 89.5 per cent of the total enrolment in the state. Women do not have access to skills which are in demand in the market.

Female work participation rate in the Punjab rose from 1.18 per cent in 1971 to 6.78 per cent in 1991. However, the quality of women's participation reflects the following trends: (a) It is maximum in the non-expanding tertiary sector accounting for 50.39 per cent of the total female participation; (b) its rate in the dominant agricultural sector is low, engaging 34.2 per cent of the female workforce; (c) female participation in manufacturing activity is the lowest and is confined largely to the unorganised sector as unskilled labour; (d) female participation in the tertiary sector has been restricted to the non-productive and inferior skilled tasks. This accounts for 90.3 per cent of the services provided by them, with negligible female participation in areas of higher growth and productivity, such as transport and communication (1.35 per cent) or trade and commerce (3.7 per cent). In the primary sector 72 per cent of the women workers are agricultural labourers. In the manufacturing industry women are either unskilled workers and manual labourers as in the construction industry or they are involved in traditional crafts which bring low wages. Indirect employment of females is very large in sub-contracting of labour intensive production processes. Women are employed either in small local work units or they work in their homes and are paid piece-rate wages as a part of a 'putting out' network utilized by multinational manufacturers, traders, wholesalers and retailers (Table 8). A study of industries in the urban centres of Mohali, Ludhiana, Amritsar and Jalandhar reveals that the percentage of female wage earners to contractual female workers is as high as nine contractual workers per wage earner in the large industries but diminishes to 2.5 contractual workers in the small industries (Table 9).[9]

These facts reflect a high degree of exploitation of the contractual and unskilled workers. Wage differential decreases in the skilled workers category i.e. skill is a gender neutralizing factor which is visible in the wage differential. However, another aspect to be kept in mind is that women perceive their work role as that of income augmenters rather than wage earners. A reason given for working as contractual workers by 69 per cent of the women is that contractual work within the home allows them to perform their central role of child rearer and caretaker of household functions.

On the whole, female work participation in the Punjab, characterized by low participation, is distributed largely in sectoral categories that provide for 'secondary jobs', brings poor remuneration and offers little scope for upward mobility. Female participation is inferior in comparison with male participation and is confined mostly to marginal and contractual jobs.

Regarding political participation, women have received a boost by the enactment of the 73rd Amendment to the Constitution which provides for one-third female representation in the Panchayati Raj institutions. Women's access to political participation before the implementation of this Act remained rather poor. An analysis of the extent of access to the political structures reflects negligible utilization of these positions. A field survey found that among 300 women Panches only 10 per cent received regular notice for Panchayat meetings and 43 per cent never received any notice for any Panchayat meeting (Table 10).

Women's participation in the public sphere is not appreciated in the existing gender system. The percentage of women who regularly attend these meetings is 7 per cent. Even the occasional attendance by 26 per cent of these women is more due to some specific undertaking rather than an involvement in the Panchayat proceedings. For example, a Bishnoi woman Panch had gone to a meeting to pass a resolution regarding re-allotment of her deceased husband's land in her favour rather than in favour of her step sons. A large majority (67 per cent) of women Panches have never attended a single Panchayat meeting. In fact there are instances of women Panches who did not even know that they were standing for the Panchayat election until the results were declared. Given these trends, it is not surprising to have inferior quality of women's participation in Panchayats (Table 11).

Only 12 per cent of women members had ever proposed a resolution in the Panchayat and a negligible 3 per cent of these resolutions were passed by the Panchayats.

What we have discussed so far shows that the efforts to provide equality of opportunity to women has led to increased access and participation in education, employment and political representation. However, these opportunities are predetermined in accordance with gender specific needs, claimed by the gender system, and have resulted in further marginalization of women. Thus the practice of gender differentiation has resulted in female deprivation of even life, and discrimination in access to and control of resources, be it health, skills, employment or political power.

III

Enactment of gender differentiation not only perpetuates female deprivations at the level of conditions and discrimination at the level of opportunities, but also leads to atrocities against women. For instance, deprivation to life as in female foeticide is an act of physical violence. Similarly, superordinate and subordinate relationship between males and females advocated by the gender differentiating conditions is a vital factor in the occurrence of rape and molestation. Besides the direct impact of patriarchal norms, gender differentials, deprivations and discriminations constitute necessary conditions and increase physical brutalities against women. To illustrate, the gender typed roles and norms provide for the practice of dowry exchange. The practice of dowry exchange is condoned, which degenerates into dowry harassments and dowry deaths. Similarly, a husband's right to physically intimidate his wife, resort to religious bigotry to beget a male offspring, and the cultural belief that the female role caters not only to reproduction but also to male sexuality, acquire the extreme forms of wife-battering, female foeticide, eve-teasing, molestation and rape. However, the acceptance of the ideology of gender differentiation provides widespread invisibility to such violence. There is a clear dichotomy between the reported and unreported crime against women which lends invisibility to atrocities (Table 12).

It is necessary to emphasize that the quantum of unreported crime against women is much higher than the reported cases (Table 13).[10] Social invisibility attached to crime against women and the fear of social stigma contribute to the non-registration of crime with the police.

Crimes like rape do not get reported because the victims are fearful of the social stigma, and caste rapes are not seen as violations in a caste hierarchical society. Most of the times even molestation is not considered to be a crime to invite the attention of the community and the law enforcing agencies. The number of unreported cases of molestation (extrapolated on the basis of the sample) were found to be 11,198 as against 30 reported cases. Eve-teasing is a relatively 'new crime' with the police which had only three registered cases, whereas there were 27,530 unregistered cases. It should be noted that these unreported eve-teasing cases are those which have come to the notice of the Panchayats in the rural areas and the Municipal Commissioners and NGOs in the urban areas. The large majority of casual eve-teasing cases remain unaccounted for. Wife beating *per se* is rampant in households but reporting and visibility of incidents occurs only where wife bashing or battering occurs.

Dowry harassments have comparatively lower reporting rate as is the case with eve-teasing and wife beating. Only in extreme cases where there is either threat to life or severe psychological and mental harassment the intervening agencies are approached. As dowry harassment occurs within the family and relates to the institution of marriage, the attempt on the part of both parties is to arrive at a compromise, rather than jeopardize a marriage by undertaking legal measures. Reporting is resorted to as the last measure. Thus it is the brutality of the atrocity which has an effect on the visibility of the injustice rather than the injustice *per se.* Dowry exchange is not perceived as violence against women; only the external form of dowry death is.

The idea of dowry exchange itself is acceptable, legitimized and wholeheartedly practised; it remains widespread and recurrent, and its manifestation in dowry harassment continues to abound.

At times, a particular mode of behaviour has social sanction in one context yet perceived as an outrage in another context. The underlying principle to that behaviour remains acceptable yet its outcome is clamoured against. Take for example the range from eve-teasing to rape. Eve-teasing is legally defined as 'intent to insult the modesty of any woman by word, sound or gesture'. However, notice and appreciation of the opposite sex in the form of word, sound or gesture is widely prevalent. The exchange is not only acceptable but tacitly approved as a form of social exchange, especially among the urban young. But this normative behaviour becomes unacceptable and transcends the boundary of acceptable social conduct when the social status of the appreciators changes (whistle of a rickshaw wala) or if the appreciation is transmitted physically, as in bottom pinching or pushing, when it is viewed as molestation and thus an impingement of chastity. What is groused against is the extent and not the underlying assumption.

Similar is the case of wife beating. Physical intimidation by the husband practised by an occasional slap or physical force does not normatively constitute wife beating. It is wife bashing, involving battering with physical damage to limb or eye that is perceived to be wife beating. And in certain sections of society, wife beating of the slap variety is seen as a reflection of a husband's masculinity. In a survey conducted in the Punjab in 1994-95, thirty-four per cent of the women respondents were of the opinion that a husband had the right to beat his wife not only in cases of infidelity but also in case of inept household management. Even in the so-called civilized sections, a Professor opined that a new bride needs to be 'broken in' to her new home with a slap or two. It is only the extent of physical damage that allows visibility and judgement of undesirable behaviour and legal sanctions against it.

Another example of the 'physical' being visible is in the context of articulation of male child preference. Utilization of the sex determination test to acquire a male child at the cost of aborting a female foetus is readily denounced. The indulgence of such male child preference is termed derogatory by those who do not practise it. Yet resort to *tonas* and Hakim concoctions, pilgrimages, fasting and other rituals to evoke the Almighty for a male child blessing are regular preoccupations in many Indian homes, and never suspected of a derogatory bias. A survey of the Punjab revealed that as high as fifty-eight per cent of the married women had resorted to methods of religious superstition and quacks to beget a male child. Yet both practices emerge from the same desire to beget a male offspring. One is perceived to be socially undesirable and the other is not even visible as a discriminatory act. One is legally banned and yet the other draws no attention. Such behaviour reflects the invisibility provided by the absorption of culture context on gender ideology. The criterion of social unacceptability thus becomes only the harshness in method and conduct, while the assumption that advances it is accepted. So entrenched and innate is the desire for a male child that it is considered normal and above reproach and only the enacting of this preference through physical annihilation is condemned.

We have already noticed that the percentage of male-child determined-pregnancies is larger in the upper social strata than in the others. Similarly differences can be observed in relation to dowry death, dowry harassment, wife beating, eve-teasing, molestation and rape (Table 14). Though dowry exchange is rampant in the upper strata, dowry harassment and dowry deaths are lower in comparison with the middle strata. Only 10.7 per cent of the dowry deaths and 14.2 per cent of dowry harassment cases belonged to this strata. For both dowry demand and dowry deaths, the rural areas had marginally more cases than the urban areas. For the lower middle strata, the percentage of dowry deaths was 49.9 and for dowry demands 45.9; it declined to 35.5 per cent and 34.7 per cent respectively in the upper middle strata. Interestingly, women convicts of dowry deaths in the Ludhiana jail predominantly belong to the lower middle strata. Incidents in the upper middle strata drop to only 10 per cent of the total dowry convicts in the Ludhiana jail. An analysis of the convicts' socio-economic background reveals that a large number of dowry deaths in the rural areas (60 per cent of the total dowry deaths) occur mainly among the small and marginal peasantry.

Further, in the lower strata, dowry deaths and demands were not rampant, but other crimes of physical and sexual violence are endemic. For example, wife beating accounts for 57.8 per cent of the total wife beating, according to the field study. The crime from which the lower caste women suffer the most is rape. A phenomenal 80 per cent of the total rapes occur in this strata, mainly in the rural areas (54.5 per cent). In Jat dominated villages especially, scheduled caste women are the target of rape. Similarly 46 per cent of the molestations occur in the lower strata and 36.6 per cent in the lower middle. We can scc that violcncc against womcn is not only a function of normative adherence to gender ideology but is also influenced by socio-cultural placements such as social class, primordial identities of caste, and religion, and regional specificities.

The ideology of the gender system is so pervasive that it is reflected even in the assertions that attempt to counter violence against women. There have been agitations against dowry deaths, alcoholism related wife beating and even against male upper caste exploitation of lower caste women. Interestingly, these assertions also reflect the inability to see not only the gender determined discriminations and deprivations but even certain physical atrocities. Broadly, these assertions are of three categories: assertions to check 'aberrations' but to maintain the status quo; assertions for incremental space rather than change in role placements; and assertions against discrimination without questioning its ideology.

We may illustrate the character of these assertions with reference to some empirical situations. First of all, we may look at the upsurge against dowry deaths, especially in rural Punjab led by active women Panches and Mahila Mandal members. These women, supported by the larger community have risen against incidents of dowry deaths, demanding justice and initiating police and legal action. But in the case of dowry harassment the same Panchayats act as agents to assist the parties involved to arrive at 'compromise'. Dowry deaths are condemned, but the concept of dowry exchange is condoned and even encouraged. Resistance to alcoholism has arisen due to increased wife beating, financial burden on the households, and the general rise in the harassment of women. Fall-outs of the male norm are resisted to the extent that alcoholism is regarded as the cause. But the derivatives of the male norm i.e. moderate wife beating, female subjugation to the male are not questioned.

There is an increasingly felt need amongst women to earn an income, but largely through skills that utilize stereotyped female skills such as handicrafts, knitting, dairying etc. These skills result in the extension of the stereotyped roles. A work oriented role would maximize earnings and inculcate upward skill mobility. Women prefer to earn an income from within the protection of their homes, utilizing traditional female skills to augment the income of the family. Priority is given to their primary roles of bearing and rearing of children and performing domestic chores and thus contractual home centred employment is preferred. Middle class women in skilled jobs do demand spouse assistance but only in female typed chores rather than undertaking a revamping of the prescribed roles and attached responsibilities.

There are some trends that reflect scheduled castes, especially women, asserting against upper caste discriminations. For instance, Mahila Mandals constituted by the upper castes deny access to scheduled caste women to their activities. As a result the scheduled castes have created separate Mahila Mandals in the same village and they generate a parallel power structure. However, the main focus of their attention are the specific cases of harassment of women rather than harassment *per se*. Scheduled caste assertions are against the exploitation of their women by the upper castes and not against intra-caste exploitation.

IV

We may now sum up the main ideas of this discussion. Biological difference as the basis of gender differentiation provides wide-spread invisibility to violence against women. To focus on merely the visible aspects is to tackle the problem in a partial manner. Therefore, it is not proper to take visibility as a yardstick to provide gender justice. For the sensitization of the concept of gender functioning, it is essential to make it first visible and then tackle its manifestations.

Differentiation in its actual operation turns into deprivation, discrimination and even atrocities against women. Females are deprived of access to facilities and resources, even life through the practice of foeticide, discriminated against in earnings, inheritance, medical care and nutrition, and face atrocities such as dowry harassment and dowry deaths. In other words, the gender differentiating system controls women's access to and the quality of participation within the development process, predetermining their capacities to lower valued activities. The gendered attributes are further perpetuated by institutionalization of gender norms. This process of institutionalization provides a legitimate cover to the injustice and violence which is not manifest as physical brutality.

Consequently, only physically brutal acts of dowry related violence, rape, wife-battering and female foeticide resulting from sex determined abortions are perceived to be acts of injustice. A husband's innate capacity to browbeat and physically intimidate the wife and a resort to religious bigotry to beget a male off-spring are condoned since these practices are normative and ingrained in the social fabric. They remain beyond the jurisdiction of social consciousness, and social debate. The basis and relevance of dowry remains unchallenged. Why women are perceived to be, or remain liabilities, or the question of dowry exchange as a commodification of the involved parties – both the female and the male – remain unattended to.

If human beings are to be viewed only in the context of their biological difference, then women will be restricted to the household. Limited skills in a world of skill refinement and maximization will further restrict women's value in the society.

Any effort to create a gender just society cannot afford to depend merely on corrective justice such as closure of alcohol vends or stringent law enforcement. Until the larger questions of dowry exchange, and the restricted placement of women are dealt with and role transformations beyond the present typed male-female roles do not occur, women's condition will remain unequal to their potential, allow atrocities to continue against them, and gender injustice will be advanced.

Thus interventions for empowerment of women need to consider in totality the gender system at its levels of impact, prowess and ideology. Providing corrective justice at the level of impact or even aiming for distributive justice by providing women equal opportunities with men, though desirable, would be insufficient to challenge the present gender system. Strategies of empowerment that question the very assumption of the gender differentiating system would empower women and promote social justice.

TABLE 1

Comparison of sex ratio of India and Punjab, 1901-1991

Year	1901	1911	1921	1931	1941	1951	1961	1971	1981	1991
India	972	964	956	952	947	948	943	931	934	929
Punjab	832	780	799	815	836	844	854	865	879	882

Source: P.C. Abstract (Part II B (I) General Population Tables, Census of India (Punjab) Series 20, Provisional Population totals (Paper 2 of 1991)

TABLE 2

Utilization of sex determination tests for male determined pregnancies for PHs in rural areas and private clinics in urban areas

	Total utilization	
	Rural areas	Urban areas
1st pregnancy	25	43
2nd pregnancy	57	80
3rd pregnancy	65	92

All figures are in percentages.
Source: Field Survey 1994-95, I.D.C.

TABLE 3

Utilization of sex determination tests for male pregnancies in PCs in rural and private clinics for urban areas strata wise

	Strata					
	Lower		Middle		Upper	
	Rural	Urban	Rural	Urban	Rural	Urban
1st pregnancy	2	7	23	42	46	64
2nd pregnancy	12	14	64	68	78	90
3rd pregnancy	18	17	81	85	87	95

Source: Field Survey, 1994-95, I.D.C.

TABLE 4

Male-Female utilization of health facilities

		Treatment from		
		Private Qualified	Public Health System	Traditional Modes
Males	Urban	23	39	38
	Rural	20	33	47
Females	Urban	19	28	53
	Rural	16	18	66

All figures are in percentages.
Source: Field Survey, 1994-95, I.D.C.

TABLE 5

Perception of Health workers on Female health needs

1.	Maternal Problems	49
2.	Lack of Health Infrastructure	23
3.	Lack of awareness regarding Family Planning	38
4.	Deficient Dietary intakes	26

All figures are in percentages.
Source: Field Survey, 1994-95, I.D.C.

TABLE 6

Male-Female Literacy rates of Punjab

	Males	Females	Female Literacy as a percentage of male literacy
1977	49.90	31.30	62.70
1981	55.50	39.60	71.40
1991	63.70	49.70	78.10

Source: Census of India 1991, Series 1, Paper I.

TABLE 7
Enrolment and Drop-outs in 1985

Primary	Boys	Girls	Total
Enrolment in 1985	230710	198933	429643
Drop-outs	73895	65986	139881
Drop-out %	32.03	33.17	32.56
Middle	**Boys**	**Girls**	**Total**
Enrolment in 1985	230710	198933	429643
Drop-outs	85087	85969	171056
Drop-out %	36.88	43.22	39.81
High	**Boys**	**Girls**	**Total**
Enrolment in 1985	230710	198933	429643
Drop-outs	107402	104523	211925
Drop-out %	46.55	52.5	49.33

Source: DPI Schools, Punjab (Calculated by I.D.C. 1995).

TABLE 8
Main Worker Classification by Industry Categories and Sex in 1991

Sr. No.	Industry	Male	Female
1.	Cultivators	1974071	22149
2.	Agricultural Labourers	1155574	64670
3.	Livestock, Fishing, Hunting, Plantations, Orchards	53645	2950
4.	Mining and Quarrying	561	3
	Sub-Total (Primary Sector)	3183851 (34.21)	8972
5.	Manufacturing, Processing Services and Repair		
	(a) Household Industry	72640	8444
	(b) Other than Household Industry	650095	17957
6.	Construction	224077	17957
	Sub-Total (Secondary Sector)	94812 (13.11)	40398

7.	Trade and Commerce	593635	9846
8.	Transport, Storage and Communication	255258	3551
9.	Other Services	680518	118836
	Sub-Total (Tertiary Sector)	1529411 (50.39)	13223
Grand Total		5660074	262403

Figures in parenthesis are percentages.
Source: Punjab Census, 1991.

TABLE 9

Ratio of Women Wage Earners to Contractual Workers

	Female Wage Worker	Female Contractual Workers
Small Industry	1	2.5
Medium Industry	1	3.8
Large Industry	1	9.1

Source: I.D.C. Field Survey, 1994-95.

TABLE 10

Women Panches' access to Power /Position

	Regular	Occasional	Never
Notice received for Meeting	10	47	43
Meeting Attended	7	26	67

All figures are in percentages.
Source: Field Survey 1994-95, I.D.C.

TABLE 11

Women Panches' Quality of participation

Resolutions proposed in Panchayat	12
Resolutions Passed in Panchayat	3

TABLE 12
Reported Crime against Women in Punjab

Year	Dowry Deaths	Rape	Molestations	Eve-Teasing	Dowry Demand
1966	2	26	49		1
1971	4	22	72		1
1976	10	46	108		2
1981	32	74	120		11
1982	43	44	119		5
1983	40	60	96		9
1984	51	54	81		4
1985	45	83	114		9
1986	63	60	78		15
1987	58	44	67		17
1988	51	51	59		28
1989	6o	78	84		57
1990*	84	77	94		65
1991*	51	34	7		11
1992*	104	43	18	2	18
1993*	98	45	7	0	26
1994*	100	83	30	3	59

* Since there was data discrepancy, data taken for these years is that of the districts rather than the Punjab. District data was needed to match the unreported atrocities.
Source: Punjab Police.

TABLE 13
Unreported Crime for the Sample Survey in Punjab for the Year 1994

Wife beating	536
Dowry Death	46
Dowry Demand	312
Rape	76
Eve-Teasing	462
Molestation	167

Source: I.D.C., Field Survey.

TABLE 14

	Higher Strata			Upper Middle			Lower Middle			Lower Strata			Urban	Rural
	Urban	Rural	Total	Urban	Rural	Total	Urban	Rural	Total	Urban	Rural	Total		
Dowry Death	3.59	7.22	10.81	20.62	15.06	35.68	31.59	18.45	50.04	3.47	0.00	3.47	59.27	40.73
Dowry Harassment	6.77	7.36	14.13	21.82	14.88	36.70	25.79	20.37	46.16	2.39	0.62	3.01	56.77	43.23
Wife-Beating	1.59	5.34	6.93	1.60	8.87	10.47	8.50	16.40	24.90	20.31	37.39	57.70	32.00	68.00
Eve-Teasing	7.80	2.60	10.40	70.30	14.80	32.10	19.60	19.40	39.00	10.70	7.80	18.50	108.40	44.60
Molestation	3.00	2.29	5.29	6.72	6.48	13.20	13.90	20.10	35.00	18.31	28.20	46.51	41.93	58.07
Rape	1.84	1.84	3.68	3.60	1.87	5.47	3.67	10.87	10.87	24.75	55.23	79.98	33.86	66.14

All figures are in percentages.
Source: Field Survey, 1994-95, I.D.C.

NOTES

1. Westergaard and Resler (1975). *Class in a Capitalist Society.* Penguin Books, 143.

2. Hannah Papanek. 'The Ideal Women and the Ideal Society: Control and Autonomy in the Construction of Identity'. *Identity Politics and Women.* Ed. V. Moghadam. West View Press, 1994, 43, 45-46.

3. Pramod Kumar and R. Dagar. 'Atrocities Against Women in Punjab'. Institute of Development and Communication, Chandigarh (I.D.C.) 1995, 10.

4. V.L. Allen. 'Social Analysis: a Marxist Critique and Alternative'. Longman, 1975, 213.

5. Field data for this article is taken from the study 'Atrocities Against Women in Punjab' conducted in 1994-1995 by the Institute of Development and Communication, Chandigarh.

6. Punjab Government, Department of Health, 1994.

7. According to Vimla Dang (PIS Patron), it is the gaps in taking medical evidence in rape cases and dying declarations in dowry death cases which allow the crime to go unpunished. Interview, 4th March, 1995.

8. General population Tables Part II A, Punjab, Census of India 1971 and 1991.

9. Also R. Dagar. 'Working Conditions of Women in Industry of Punjab'. Labour Department Punjab, 1993.

10. In fact, six factors account for the non-reporting of atrocities:

(a) social invisibility of atrocities;

(b) social ostracization;

(c) patriarchal family norms demanding female acceptance of subjugation;

(d) legal remedies thought of as the last resort;

(e) lack of awareness of the laws; and

(f) financial compulsions.

12

Dalits in Punjab, Haryana and Himachal Pradesh

S. K. GUPTA

In India, contemporary history has received increasing attention in recent years. Along with the sociologist and the anthropologist, the social historian has begun to map the changes taking place both in the structure and functioning of the contemporary Indian society to examine the emerging socio-economic trends, and to study the 'New Social Movements' – a term of recent coinage used by scholars like Gail Omvedt. The contemporary social reality has diverse domains. Its study involves a wide range of scholarship. The present paper deals with only a section of the Indian society – the *dalits*, and that too only the *dalits* of the Punjab before its trifurcation in November 1966.

I

The *dalits* of the present Punjab, Haryana and the parts of Himachal Pradesh included in the Punjab before 1966 had never been placed in the degraded position of the Pariahs, the Malas and the Madigas of the South. Nor was their position ever akin to the Mahars and the Mangs of Maharashtra. There were no such groups as the ones found in the South or in certain other provinces, which polluted the caste Hindus by mere propinquity. *Chhut chhat* or *chhua chhut* in the form of physical touch demanding purificatory bath was observed by only a small section of the orthodox Hindus, and the castes that caused pollution by contact were primarily the Bhangis and those Chamar sub-castes who were engaged in removing, skinning and tanning the dead cattle.[1] The condition of most of the untouchable groups was, in fact, inseparable from those who were socially and economically backward. Many factors were responsible for the relatively alleviated condition of the untouchables in the area under study. Some of them were equally applicable to all, while others were peculiar to certain specific regions.

Of all the factors, two have played the most dominant role. Firstly, the Punjab had always been a storm centre. It served the foreign invaders as a gateway to India, and there were persistent attacks on its frontiers.[2] As such, its inhabitants have been hardier, and less servile in their disposition. Secondly, in their social tendencies and religious bent of mind the people of the Punjab, Haryana and Himachal Pradesh were cast in the mould of democratic religions and sects that emerged or penetrated and flourished in areas which encouraged equalitarian ethos.

On the eve of Independence, the population of the province was mainly composed of Muslims, Sikhs, and Hindus. The Muslims were predominant in the western Punjab, now part of Pakistan, the Sikhs in the central districts and certain princely states, which constitute the present Punjab, and the Hindus formed a fairly large majority in the southern districts, which now form Haryana, and they were found in an overwhelming number in the hilly territories of the Punjab and in the hilly princely states, which together now form a full-fledged state of Himachal Pradesh. For the present purpose the numerical position in not important. What is significant is the presence of various socio-religious orders and their bearing on the social norms and ethos. Islam as religion has been more democratic and equalitarian in its philosophy and in matters concerning worship and social organization. Sikhism was also an avowed revolt against orthodoxy and caste-based instincts.[3] Guru Nanak, the founder of Sikhism unequivocally held that there is but one Supreme Being who is the creator and sustainer of all and to whom everyone belongs irrespective of creed, sex, caste, colour or nationality.[4] God has no caste nor does He give any consideration to such ascriptive social ordering. In the *Dasam Granth*, Guru Gobind Singh has said:[5]

Chakkar chihan aru varan jati aru patti nahin jih.

The Gurus identified themselves with the lower castes, the outcastes, the untouchables and women.[6] They were sharply critical of the priest-craft, Hindu rituals, and idol worship,[7] and taught the masses strict monotheism advocating that each devotee should seek God directly and that he could do so without becoming a mendicant and abandoning his family.[8] They emphasized that deeds, not birth in a particular caste or family, are the index of high or low. *Jog* and *raj* (religious faith and social commitment); *naam japna, kirt karna wand chhakana; piri* and *miri* (love and devotion to God and resistance against tyranny); and *sangat, pangat* and *langar* became the pillars of Sikh faith, a faith designed to reform the corrupt and unjust socio-political order. The Gurus had even denounced the contemporary Muslim rule. Guru Nanak argued that the rulers were unjust; they discriminated against their non-Muslim subjects. They exacted Jizya and pilgrim tax from them and heaped uncalled for disabilities on them. Notwithstanding the presence of some non-Muslims in the administration at subordinate levels, the ruling class was fleecing the cultivator and the common people.[9] In a nutshell, the Gurus envisioned a society marked by universal justice and equality, service of humanity, and an opportunity for the pursuit of happiness, self-realization, liberation and union with eternal reality irrespective of any prejudices rooted in sex and caste. *Sarbat da bhala* became central to the daily *ardas*.[10]

'Hinduism' came under severe attack in the nineteenth and twentieth centuries. The Arya Samajis launched a frontal attack against untouchability and emphasized that not birth but one's *karma, gun, svabhav* determine caste. They worked for the upliftment of lower castes and opened the portals of education for them, and for women. Other groups like the Radhasoamis, Kabirpanthis, Ghisapanthis, Parnamis, Chet Ramis, Ramdasias and Raidasias too raised voice against caste prejudices.[11] Hinduism could not remain assertive in its orthodox practices and caste exclusiveness; nor could it afford to completely alienate about one-sixth of the population categorised as the *dalits* who were being wooed by other communities. In other words, the Hindus, especially the politically-minded caste Hindus, modified their approach towards the lower castes and women.[12] Moreover, the Brahmans in these areas, did not enjoy a status of preeminence. The Jats who constituted the most numerous and predominant agricultural tribe among the Hindus, as among the Muslims and the Sikhs, were singularly indifferent to caste prejudices and social disabilities like untouchability and pollution.[13] The presence of Islam, Sikhism, Christianity and the Arya Samaj with their reforming zeal and their ever-increasing rivalry in matters of proselytization was another factor that not only had a dissolving effect on caste rigidities and the institution of untouchability but also positively helped in improving the caste atmosphere. Above all, the *dalits* in these areas were not confined to menial occupations, but took a very important part in agricultural operations, and were in considerable demand as tenants. Thus, as an institution, caste played a far less important part in the social life of the people of these areas than in other parts of India.

Howsoever salutary might have been the impact of these progressive and equalitarian socio-religious orders and movements, all was not well with the *dalits*. Prejudices die hard. Moreover, many socio-religious movements functioned in limited pockets and with all the limitations imposed by: (a) the crab-like and snail-paced character of social mobility in a caste ridden society with strong forces of resistance; (b) the lack of vast resources needed to deal with the enormity of the problem; (c) the gap created in the 'will' by the ulterior motives of proselytization and the professed philanthropic intentions; and (d) the organizations not being exclusively devoted to their welfare. Thus, in spite of a very healthy caste climate in the society, the *dalits* suffered from a number of social disabilities.

II

In 1950, there were as many as 34 Scheduled Castes in the Punjab and Pepsu.[14] In 1956, four more caste groups (Darain; Deha, Dhaya or Dhea; Dhogri, Dhangri or Siggi; and Sansoi) were declared as Scheduled Castes, and two castes (Chamar and Ramdasi or Ravidasi), shown separately in the notification order of 1950, were clubbed together, thus raising the total number of Scheduled Castes in the State to 37.[15] The Scheduled Castes and Scheduled Tribes (Amendment) Act 1976 did not bring about any change in the Scheduled Castes so notified.[16] As regards the spread of these castes, 34 castes listed as Scheduled Castes in notification of 1950 were found throughout the State. The four new groups categorised as Scheduled Castes in 1956 were reported from only certain areas: Deha, Dhaya or Dhea inhabited the districts of Patiala, Bathinda, Sangrur, Kapurthala and Mohendragarh; the other three Scheduled Castes were found elsewhere in the State but not in these four districts.[17]

However, what is more significant to note is the numerical standing of different castes. Only four castes (Chamar, Gaiety Chamar, Rehgar, Raigar, Ramdasi or Ravidasi; Balmiki, Chura or Bhangi; Mazhabi; and Ad Dharmi) – numbering 34 lacs, constituted

82.14% of the total number of 41.39 lacs. If Dhanaks and Kabirpanthis or Julahas, are also taken into consideration, the strength of six Scheduled Castes goes up to nearly 90%. Other numerically stronger groups, whose total population was less than one lac and varied between 0.84 and 0.10 lac in the numerical order, included Dumna, Mahasha or Doom, Bazigar, Kori or Koli, Megh, Bauria or Bawaria, Sansi, Od, Batwal, and Sarera. Obviously, the remaining 22 castes constituted less than one per cent of the total population.[18]

Workers amongst the Scheduled Castes formed a little more than one-third or 35.1% of the total population of the Scheduled Castes in the State. And of the total workers, 25.27% were cultivators; 27.07% were agricultural labourers; and 1.74% were engaged in livestock, forestry, fishing, hunting, plantations, orchards, mining, quarrying, etc. Apart from 2.15% in construction, 15.29% and 3.93% Scheduled Castes were engaged in household and manufacturing industry respectively. Only 1.26% of Scheduled Castes were in trade and commerce and 1.62% in transport and communication, and those employed in other services constituted 21.66%. In other words, 54.08% Scheduled Castes were employed in the primary sector, 20.83% in the secondary and 24.54% in the tertiary sector. These figures appear to be quite impressive but they conceal more than what they reveal, as all the categories except that of agricultural labourers are neither neat nor do they reflect propertied-non propertied, or employee-employer relationship. For example, 'category I: Cultivators' covers 'both owner and tenant cultivators', and similarly, 'workers' in all other categories whether employed as mere labourers for a pittance or those belonging to propertied classes holding high positions or that of employers, etc. were also clubbed together. 'Workers' and 'non-workers' categories too have their own inherent constraints and one fails to get any idea about underemployment, disguised un-employment or seasonal or casual employment.[19] It is difficult, therefore, to draw any conclusion about their precise economic condition. Nevertheless, this baseline of 1961 would help us in our later analysis.

The more revealing and helpful data for mapping the reality relates to literacy level and inter-caste placement amongst the Scheduled Castes. Nearly 90.36% of the Scheduled Castes were illiterate in 1961.[20] Of the total 3.99 lac literate Scheduled Castes, 55.43% were literate without a level, whereas 39.54% were literate up to primary level and 5.028% were Matric and above. Even the picture of the Scheduled Castes living in urban areas was not much different.[21] Out of the total urban Scheduled Caste population of 4.80 lacs, i.e. 11.6%, only 15.44% were literate. Of those Scheduled Castes who were classified as literate, 52.61% were without any level; 40.65% were literate up to primary level; 6.22% up to Matric; 0.11% held technical diploma; 0.07%, non-technical diploma; 0.32% held university degree and 0.026% technical degree.[22]

Compared with the general population, these figures do testify to the downtrodden position of the Scheduled Castes, particularly in rural areas. In 1961, the general literacy level in the State was 24.2% and those who were Matric and above constituted 12.8% of the total literates, whereas in the case of Scheduled Castes these percentages, work out to 9. 64 and 4.93 respectively. However, there was no sharp variation in the proportions of the literate Scheduled Castes (39.54%) and the general population (42.15%) educated up to primary or junior basic level. Nor do the urban data reflect much different picture; wide gap could be noticed only in the case of total literate and those who had studied up to Matric.[23]

As regards the inter-caste placement amongst the Scheduled Castes themselves, an analysis of Scheduled Castes having population above 10,000 was carried out. It revealed that the percentage of illiterates was the highest amongst the Bazigars (97%), followed by Baurias or Bawarias (94.34%), Mazhabis (93.46%), Dhanaks (93.21%), Balmikis (92.92), Ods (92.17%), Sansis (91.20%), Koris/ Kolis (91.15%), Dumnas (90.57%) and Batwals (90.26). Ad Dharmis had the highest percentage of literates, i.e. 16.01% followed by Kabirpanthis (13.94%), Sareras (13.91%), Meghs (11.91%) and Chamars. However, the proportion of literates without any level was the highest amongst the Ods, i.e. 69.88% of the total literates, followed by Bazigars, Mazhabis, Baurias, and Kabirpanthis. Amongst those Scheduled Castes who were educated up to primary level, Sansis had the highest percentage (50.42), followed by Meghs (47.22), Ad Dharmis (44), Dumnas (41.60), and Kabirpanthis (41.24). Amongst those Scheduled Castes who were educated up to Matric, Ad Dharmis had the highest percentage (6.67%), followed by Meghs (6.21), Chamars (5.28), and Kabirpanthis. As regards higher education, of the 15 Scheduled Castes, six Scheduled Castes did not have any member educated beyond Matric, whereas the other nine cases had 379 persons who had obtained education at diploma and degree levels. Out of these, 200 persons were from amongst the Chamars, followed by Balmikis (55), Ad Dharmis (46), Mazhabis (34), Meghs (18), Kabirpanthis (13), Dhanaks (7), Sansis (4), and Koris/Kolis (2).[24]

The picture drawn on the basis of these figures does not allow vertical placement of different castes as percentage of literacy amongst different Scheduled Castes varied at different educational levels. Nevertheless, the data reveal that Meghs, Ad Dharmis, Kabirpanthis, Sareras and Chamars were comparatively better educated, whereas Bazigars, Baurias and Ods were at the lowest rung of literacy.

The data pertaining to occupations pursued by the different Scheduled Castes too do not permit vertical placement of different castes and entail similar difficulties as the picture varied from caste to caste and occupation to occupation. However, if one takes into account only three categories of occupations – two polluting and one relating to agricultural labour – the Mazhabis appear to be lowest in the scale as the highest percentage (49.10%) amongst them were engaged in agricultural labour, and 4.26% in tanning. Even in scavenging, they constituted only 2.06%. Second in the scale were Balmikis, of whom 25.38% were engaged in scavenging, 0.61% in hiding and tanning, and 28.39% as agricultural labourers, followed by Chamars.[25]

After the census operations of 1961, another independent survey of the condition of the Scheduled Castes of the Punjab was conducted in 1966.[26] In the rural Punjab, 3243 Scheduled Caste households with an average family size of 5.7 members, were surveyed in 100 selected villages and 8 cities and towns (Amritsar, Jalandhar, Ludhiana, Patiala, Yamuna Nagar, Panipat, Faridabad and Bhiwani).[27] The results of the survey reveal that in the past, 'most of the families were following hereditary professions like shoe-making, leather tanning, weaving, scavenging and so on, but had now taken up cultivation of land as regular tenants or as agricultural labourers'. However, in the mid 1960s in the rural Punjab, only 13.3% of Scheduled Caste families were engaged in cultivation and 40.3% in agricultural labour. The remaining 46% were carrying on non-agricultural occupations like non-agricultural labour (22%), government and other services (5.9%), and shoe-making (5%).[28] In order to determine their precise economic status in monetary terms, the data relating to the income of earners and earning dependents was elicited. As many as 54.5% of them were earning Rs. 50 or less per month and the overwhelming majority of them (96%) were earning Rs. 100 or less. Four per cent Scheduled Castes who were earning more than Rs. 100 per month belonged to Kabirpanthi or Julaha, Sansi, Chamar, Ramdasi or Raidasi, Balmiki or Bhangi, Mazhabi and Dhanak castes. Inter-caste analysis further reveals that the economic condition of Kabirpanthis or Julahas was better than that of others, since 25 per cent of them were earning more than 100 rupees per month. The most backward caste was Megh since only 20 per cent of them were earning more than Rs. 50 per month.[29] In terms of different occupations, the castes engaged in services and business were better placed than others from the income point of view. Weaving and spinning, basket making and sweeping were, however, the least remunerative occupations since none of the Scheduled Caste earners and earning dependents engaged in these occupations was earning more than Rs. 150 per month.[30]

The survey further reveals that during the quinquennium, there had been 2.9% increase in literacy amongst the 15 Scheduled Castes having 10,000 or more population.[31] The most backward amongst them were Batwal, Bauria or Bawaria, Balmiki or Bhangi and Dhanak castes. The advanced castes were Sarera, Sansi, and Megh, and amongst these the Sansi were the most advanced since 5.2% of them were Matriculate and above. They were mostly engaged in teaching profession.[32]

As regards indebtedness amongst the *dalits,* of the total 3242 sampled households, 1856 (57.2%) were in debt and the average debt per family was Rs. 796. The caste-wise analysis indicates that out of 1856 families in debt, 887 (47.79%) belonged to Chamars. If, however, the inter-caste data about the percentage of families in debt and the quantum of average debt per family is taken into consideration, then Dhanak caste having 98.2% families in debt with an average debt of Rs. 1602 per family could be placed at number one, followed by Chamars, who had 58.1% families in debt with Rs. 864 as average debt per family; Mazhabis, having 52.7% households under debt and Rs. 754 as average debt per family; and the Balmikis or Bhangis, having 54.3% families under debt with Rs. 695 as average debt per family.[33]

The survey team further noticed that 'a majority of the households had a tendency to inflate their debt. This was due to the wrong impression that the Government was perhaps going to provide some relief to them against indebtedness'.[34] However, the most significant fact the survey revealed was that majority of the families had taken loan for unproductive purposes. As many as 63% families had incurred debt for domestic expenditure and social ceremonies; 17% had taken loan to purchase buffaloes (5.4%), bullocks (2.8%), and land 4.2%, and for business (3.6%), and the education of children (1%); 13.5% borrowed for construction and repair of houses and for other miscellaneous purposes. Of the total loan, 60% accounted for domestic expenditure and social ceremonies.[35]

To sum up, when the Punjab got trifurcated the *dalits* had already moved on to the threshold of change. The change did reveal definite signs of politico economic upward mobility, even if it did not reflect very sharp and well delineated contours exhibiting all round progress. In fact, the sources available further indicate that whatever improvement had occurred in their politico-economic condition, its spread was not even in spatial or intercaste context. Place to place, caste to caste, and category to category variations were more marked.

A survey of Mahasa Tibba, a village then located in Nalagarh *tahsil* of Ambala district of the Punjab, now a part of Himachal Pradesh, reveals that Ramdasia Chamars, the sole inhabitants of the village, were conscious of their politico-constitutional rights in the early 1960s.

> The Chamars, particularly, those of younger generation... are gradually holding their head high by shaking off the age-old complex of servility and subordination to the clean castes. For example, whereas in the past, the meanest Govern-ment official... symbolized nothing less than terror for the poor Chamar, now he gets no more deference than is actually his due. Today a Chamar knows that practice of untouchability is a penal offence; that special status has been accorded to his community by the fundamental law of the land; that he can no more be forced to perform *begar;* that he is an equally precious citizen of the country and that the Government is implementing measures to raise his political, economic and social status.[36]

They looked to the future with hope. They showed keenness to educate their children, to acquire land, and to improve their diet and dress. Coincident to the urge to educate themselves was the desire to substitute agriculture or government service for their traditional occupation of lifting dead cattle and making shoes. The study concludes that the Chamars were definitely on the move. Two of them were members of the Panchayat, 10 were members of

Rajpura Cooperative Bank, and even the *lambardar* of the village was a Chamar for the first time in its history.[37]

In the early 1960s another survey was conducted in village Kuran, Sangrur district, Punjab. Notwithstanding the fact that the village had a mixed population consisting of clean, backward and Scheduled Castes, and of Muslims, the Scheduled Castes did show signs of upward mobility. The Scheduled Castes of the village belonged to Ramdasia, Mazhabi and Bazigar castes. Of these three castes, the Ramdasias were better placed. Out of the 27 Ramdasia households, 15 owned land, though 11 households owned less than one acre of land each, and the holdings of four ranged between one and five acres. Only three households were engaged in shoe-making as a subsidiary occupation.[38] Mazhabi Sikhs were Chuhra converts to Sikhism. They did not touch night soil. But being landless, of the total 12 households, nine subsisted on casual labour or attached agricultural labour, one on sheep-rearing and dairying, and one on cattle-grazing. One person was employed as *chowkidar.*[39] Similarly, Bazigars did not own any land and lived on agricultural and manual labour and exhibition of acrobatic feats.[40]

No doubt, all the three Scheduled Castes were placed low in the social status *vis-a-vis* other clean and backward castes, yet politico-economic upward mobility among them, in particular the Ramdasias, was well marked. The legislative measures designed to transfer ownership rights to the actual tillers of the soil greatly benefited the Ramdasias who acquired proprietary rights in the holdings they had tilled as tenants before Independence.[41] This raised their economic status and brought about a significant change in the social perception of the clean castes. The study records that the agriculturalists and members of the so-called clean castes were forced to recognize the existence of the Scheduled Castes, particularly the Ramdasias, due to the new situation evolved in the wake of social and agrarian legislation prohibiting untouchability and allotting land to the landless Ramdasias. In fact the long depressed members of the village community had acquired a distinct identity. During the recent general elections inter-caste tensions developed in the village as the members of the Scheduled Castes canvassed support for the candidate of the Congress Party while the members of the clean castes supported the candidate sponsored by the Communist Party. The fact that the cultivating and non-cultivating members of Scheduled Castes could prop up a rival political viewpoint against the wishes of the members of the land-owning classes and castes enjoying higher status in the social hierarchy is in itself very significant. Different sections of the village population were progressing towards readjustment on the basis of equality.[42]

Social mobility continued to be slow; it was still slower to progress in the rural areas. No doubt, during the early 1960s, certain changes were reported, as the occasional drawing of water from the wells of the clean castes, relaxation in the rules of rigid segregation, decreasing stress on physical untouchability and increasing comingling and commensality in the towns, buses and railways, village shops and tea-stalls, schools, Panchayats and other public institutions. In the matter of smoking and dining, the clean castes have not yet relented in their attitude. For example, it was reported that all the castes could take tea from the same tea-stall at the Saini Majra bus-stop, but a clean-caste person considered it irreligious and degrading to take meals cooked by a Chamar. The general attitude of high caste people was to avoid change, if they could help it. The Chamars seemed to be convinced of the force of their arguments and betray a realization that they cannot be at par so long as they do not give up their traditional jobs and become economically independent. Complete social emancipation was not possible.[43] What, however, appears to further sustain these social dichotomies and inferiority-superiority complexes is that they themselves have not been able to shed such notions and practices as they wish the clean castes to shun and exorcise. From the survey of Mahasa Tibba, it is revealed that,

> Ramdasia Chamars hold themselves socially superior to Chuhras, Doomnas, and Chanals all of whom are believed to have a common origin. They do not share meals or smoke with them and do not lift their dead cattle. The Doomnas and Chanals, in turn, regard the Ramdasia Chamars as inferior to themselves and would not dine or share smoke with them. The Julaha and Ramdasia Chamars are, however, of the same social status and they dine and smoke together and also enter into marital relationships.[44]

A similar situation prevailed in Kuran village: 'There is no inter-dining between the Chamars and the Mazhabi Sikhs on the one hand and the Muslims and the Harijans on the other'.[45]

There was no significant improvement in the social condition of the *dalits* in the next quinquennium. The trends pertaining to slow progress of social mobility did find an echo in the main report of the Evaluation Committee on Welfare of the Scheduled Castes,

Backward Classes and Vimukat Jatis, Punjab, 1966. Not-withstanding the fact that in the post-Independence period the Punjab was the pioneer state in the country to enact law for the eradication of untouchability known as the East Punjab (Removal of Religious and Social Disabilities) Act, 1948, the Report revealed that 'untouchability was still prevalent in some form or the other in as many as 74 per cent villages. The Scheduled Castes complained of discrimination in respect of access to water sources in 51 per cent villages, eatables in 65 per cent villages, social discrimination in 46 per cent villages and accessibility to places of worship in 20 per cent villages'.[46] However, the cases actually reported to the police under the Untouchability (Offences) Act in the Punjab had been quite negligible (one in 1961; six in 1962; and four in 1963).[47] Whatever might have been the reasons for such a low reporting, it cannot be denied that upward social mobility did occur due to political, legal and economic changes. But the pace remained slow.

Notwithstanding the pace and quantum of progress, the temporal trends are somewhat unilinear and reflect progressive improvement in the condition of the *dalits,* whereas the spatial and inter-caste scenario is divergent and multifocal. If inter- regional comparisons are made within the Punjab, which of course become *suo motto* absolutely necessary after 1966, it is revealed that in matters of social ostracism the *dalits* in the present Punjab were somewhat better placed than in certain hilly areas and Haryana. A similar trend could be witnessed in urban areas of different regions. The Evaluation Committee reported that

> Untouchability is gradually becoming non-existent. It still exists relatively in a bad form in the backward hilly areas, rural areas and in some parts of what is called Haryana Region of the State. However, it does not exist in acute form, much less in any offensive form. Spread of literacy and breaking of age old customs have been responsible for removing untouchability. It could be safely said that in urban areas this has practically disappeared. In the case where some people exercise it, they do so without the knowledge of causing any offence to Harijans.[48]

III

For the post-1966 Punjab, the literacy and occupational statistics of 1971 and 1981 indicate that during this period the *dalits* of Himachal Pradesh marched ahead of both the Punjab and Haryana. The literacy rate amongst the Scheduled Castes in Himachal Pradesh, the Punjab and Haryana in 1971 was 18.82%, 16.12% and 12.60%;

and in 1981, 31.58%, 23.86% and 20.15% respectively. When occupational statistics with regard to cultivators and agricultural labourers are compared, the *dalits* of the Punjab still roll down to a third position as indicated below:

State		% of Cultivators to total workers/ Main workers	% of Agricultural to total workers/ Main workers
Himachal	(1971)	70.39	9.34
Pradesh	(1981)	71.65	4.92
Punjab	(1971)	10.68	57.99
	(1981)	6.66	61.03
Haryana	(1971)	16.08	50.65
	(1981)	11.86	51.28

This levelling down of certain categories of *dalits* requires not only explanation but an independent enquiry. More so, because the Punjab until the mid-1970s witnessed a spectacular growth and, as a result of the Green Revolution, had moved on to a new level of socio-economic development. As is well known, the Green Revolution, proved to be a mixed blessing as it resulted in uneven development and caused not only certain inter-regional imbalances but also affected the lot of the various sections of the rural population differently. The unevenness resulted in 'growing proletarianization, immerserization and 'partial pauperization' of marginal and poor peasants, thus adding to the army of the landless.[49] The number of landless farm wage-earners and of the poor peasants had increased two to three fold within two decades.[50]

Since the process of levelling down was associated with specific developments in the rural economy, it affected the lot of only certain sections of the *dalits*. Other sections of the *dalits* did continue to move gradually upward on the socio-economic scale. Many reaped the benefits of the Constitutional safeguards, reservations in legislatures, local bodies, services, and of other levelling up schemes introduced by the government from time to time. In the Punjab State services itself, their number increased from 1.73% in class I services, 8.54% in class III, and 15.90% in class IV services in 1964[51] to 4.80%, 12% and 36% respectively in 1974-75.[52] This, however, does not mean the complete end of social cob-webs or of the economic maladies in general. Many changes continued to be illusory and remained dove-tailed with the *dalit's* ostracised past. The dove-tailing was no longer smooth and friction free. But the past as a dead-set determinant of their fate and fortunes has not become completely irrelevant. It continues to linger on in new forms. For example, caste is withering but casteism is assuming new overtones, both in political and social circles. The *dalits* have come to have two layers of consciousness – one old and the other new; one, part and parcel of fossilized caste-ridden social order, and the second, shaped by the democratic processes. These two layers create their own friction, especially when the *dalits* attempt to transcend traditional forms and notions of social precedence and hierarchy and simultaneously assert their traditional past to perpetuate their material gains. The process of their levelling up is considered by many as faulty and tends to create distortions of its own kind by throwing up what may be called the 'up-starts' in certain political and bureaucratic cadres. Minority politics, politics of backwardness and politics of numbers, with their accompanying concomitants, i.e. vote-bank-centred political one-up-manship, and populism have further contributed in their own ways to the perverse understanding of social issues, making the task of fashioning a just social order still more difficult.

NOTES

1. S.K. Gupta. *The Scheduled Castes in Modern Indian Politics: Their Emergence As a Political Power.* Delhi: Munshiram Manoharlal, 1985, 124.

2. Ibid, 121-23. *The Complete Works of Swami Vivekananda,* III, 366: Speaking at Lahore in 1897, Swami Vivekananda not only paid rich tributes to Guru Nanak and Guru Gobind Singh but also said: 'This is the land which is held to be the holiest of the holy Aryavarta.... This is the land which had first to bear on its bosom every onslaught of the outer barbarians into Aryavarta'. For a detailed discussion: Niharranjan Ray. *The Sikh Gurus and the Sikh Society: A Study in Social Analysis.* New Delhi: Munshiram Manoharlal, 1975, 1-5.

3. S.K. Gupta (1985), 121.

4. *Adi Granth,* 1349-50.

5. *Dasam Granth,* 1,80, 148. *Adi Granth,* 324, 1128 -1364.

6. *Adi Granth,* 15.

7. J.S. Grewal. *The New Cambridge History of India: The Sikhs of the Punjab.* Cambridge: CUP 1990, 30-34. In this work Grewal has very lucidly brought out the critique of Guru Nanak against 'all the major forms of contemporary religious belief and practice.... Guru Nanak's attitude towards the *ulama* and the *shaikhs* is similar to his attitude towards the *pandit* and the *jogi*'.

'The *qazi* utters lies and eats what is unclean; the *brahman* takes life and then goes off to bathe ceremoniously; the blind *jogi* does not know the way; all three are desolated'.

8. Kenneth W. Jones. *The New Cambridge History of India: Socio-Religious Reform Movements in British India.* New York: CUP 1989, 12-13. Surjit Hans goes to the extent of saying that 'Guru Nanak de-legitimized the contemporary social order'. *A Reconstruction of Sikh History From Sikh Literature.* Jalandhar: ABS Publications, 1988, 4.

9. J.S. Grewal (1990), 11, 28-29.

10. It is a supplication recited after daily prayer. *Sunder Gutka.* Amritsar: SGPC, 1986, 168.

11. S.K. Gupta (1985), 122-23.

12. Ibid, 38-40, 169-70.

13. Ibid, 123.

14. Ministry of Law Notification no. SRO 385, dated 6 September 1950.

15. Ministry of Home Notification no. SRO 2477-A, dated 29 October 1956.

16. Census of India, 1981, Series 1, India, pt. IIA (ii): *Primary Census Abstract Scheduled Castes.* Delhi: Controller of Publications, 1983, lxxi. Notification no. 108 of 1976, dated 18 September 1976.

17. Census of India, 1961, 1, pt. V-B (i) *Consolidated Statement Showing Scheduled Castes, Scheduled Tribes, Denotified Communities and Other Communities of Similar Status in Different Statutes and Census Starting From 1921.* Delhi: Manager of Publications, 1966. Census of India, paper no. 2, 1960. Delhi: Manager of Publications, 1961.

18. These figures have been computed on the basis of census data contained in SCT-1, pt A -Industrial Classification of Persons at Work and Non-Workers by Sex for Scheduled Castes - Rural and Urban Census of India, 1961, 1, pt V-B (i): *Special Tables,* 52, 56, 134, 138.

19. These figures have been computed on the basis of the data available in Table SCT-1, pt. A, Census of India, 1961,1, pt. V-B (i): *Special Tables for Scheduled Castes and Scheduled Tribes.*

20. Ibid, 348, 350,383-84.

21. These figures have been computed on the basis of data contained in Census of India, 1961 Table SCT-III, A and pt. (i): *Education in Urban and Rural Areas for Scheduled Castes.*

22. Ibid, 348-51.

23. Ibid, 351-84.

24. Ibid, 348-51.

25. Ibid, 52-58,134-41.

26. This survey was conducted by the Economic and Statistical Organization on behalf of the Evaluation Committee on Welfare of Scheduled Castes, Backward Classes and Vimukta Jatis appointed by the Government of Punjab *vide* notification no. 11079-WGI-AS0 2- 65/35291, dated 7 December 1965. The survey was completed in February-April 1966. See

Report of the Evaluation Committee on the Welfare of Scheduled Castes, Backward Classes and Vimukta Jatis. Chandigarh: Controller of Printing and Stationery, 1966, 2, 209, 211.

27. Only 27.4% families had seven to nine members; 6.5% families had ten and above, and about 50% of the families had six or seven members.

28. Ibid, 14.

29. Ibid, 15.

30. Ibid, 219.

31. Ibid, 16.

32. Ibid, 222.

33. Ibid, 236. However, the conclusion recorded by the Economic and Statistical Organization that 'the families mostly in debt belonged to Chamar, Ramdasia and Ravidasia castes' is not correct as it does not tally with Table 2.5 of the Report.

34. Ibid, 21.

35. Ibid, 236-37.

36. Census of India, 1961: *Village Monograph no. 42, Mahasa Tibba: A Village in Ambala District of Punjab,* 75.

37. Ibid, 76. At page 10, it is mentioned that the strength of Chamar members was 3. 'The present Gram Panchayat, Manjhola under whose jurisdiction Mahasa Tibba falls, consisted of six members, three of whom are Ramdasias as against one Saini, one Sikh Jat, and one Rajput. The Sarpanch of the Panchayat is also Ramdasia'.

38. *Census of India,* 1961, Vol XIII, pt. iv, no. 36: *Village Survey Monograph of Punjab, Kuran, a Village in Sangrur District of Punjab,* 6-7, 35-36.

39. Ibid, 6.

40. Ibid, 7.

41. Ibid, 31.

42. Ibid, 67.

43. Ibid, 9.

44. *Village Survey of Mahasa Tibba,* 9-10.

45. *Village Survey of Kuran,* 62.

46. *Report of Evaluation Committee on Welfare,* 21.

47. *Report of the Commissioner for Scheduled Castes and Scheduled Tribes,* 1960-61, pt. 1. Delhi: Manager of Publications, 1962, 21. Report of Commissioner for Scheduled Castes and Scheduled Tribes, 1963-64, pt. 1, Thirteenth Report. Delhi: Manager of Publications, 1963, 2-3.

48. *Report of Evaluation Committee on Welfare,* 27.

49. Gopal Singh, ed. *Punjab Today.* New Delhi: Intellectual Publishing House, 1987, 9.

50. Nirmal Singh Azad. 'Distorted Economic Development'. Ibid, 46.

51. *Report of Evaluation Committee on Welfare,* 100. The data available pertain to the period from 1955 to 1964.

52. *Report of the Commissioner for Scheduled Castes and Scheduled Tribes,* 1974-75. Delhi: Controller of Publications, 1977, 100.

13

Attached Labour in Haryana

SURINDER S. JODHKA

Along with an increase in the productivity of land, the development of capitalism or 'modernization' of agriculture is also supposed to bring about a fundamental change in the social relations of production and lead to an integration of agriculture into the broader national market. This implies a basic change in the values of obligation and loyalty that bind the subordinate classes to the dominant landowners in 'pre-capitalist' agrarian structures, thus freeing the agricultural labourers and tenants from all kinds of patronage and institutionalised dependency relationships.

THEORETICAL CONTEXT

Some scholars have argued that such a change is indeed being experienced in Indian agriculture, particularly in the regions where the green revolution has been a success. Breman, for example, reported that in south Gujarat the traditional dependency and bondage relations were undergoing a fundamental change. He called this process of 'freeing' of agricultural labourers as 'depatronization' (Breman, 1974). In a later study he again argued that the intergenerational bondages characterised by extra-economic coercion no more existed in south Gujarat and the existing system of attached labour was not similarly an unfree relation (Breman, 1985, 131, 306-13). Similarly, though Bhalla found elements of continuity, she argued that in Haryana countryside the relations between farmers and attached labourers were changing into formalised contractual arrangements (Bhalla, 1974).

Taking his cue from Bhalla's study, Bhaduri highlighted the elements of continuities in production relations in the green revolution region of Haryana and provided an opposite interpretation of her data. He argued that the presence of attached labour and debt dependencies meant that the mode of production even in the green revolution belt of Haryana was 'semi-feudal' (Bhaduri, 1984, 115).

Bardhan and Rudra, however, strongly refuted the formulation that prevalence of attached labour necessarily meant 'semi- feudal' mode of production. 'This kind of careless labelling is worse than inaccurate' (Bardhan 1984, 159). Bardhan argued that the feudal institution of bonded labour marked by hereditary and long term indebtedness, entailing continuous and exclusive work for the creditor employer and some form of extra economic coercion is very different from the present day forms of attached labour which is 'voluntaristic' rather than a coercive arrangement. 'The modernisation of agricultural technology', Bardhan reported, 'had in fact increased the demand for attached labourers as they were seen to be useful in overseeing the work of casual labourers. Farmers found the two-tiered labour system useful in keeping possibilities of the emergence of class solidarity among farm workers in check (Bardhan, 1984). Bardhan not only found attached labour functional for the modern capitalist form of agriculture but also claimed that attached labourers enjoyed superior status compared to their counterpart casual daily wagers.

Rudra too contends that working for a specific employer on continuous basis does not necessarily imply semi-feudal relations. He argues that the semi-attached workers in Bengal enjoyed much better economic conditions than daily labourers while paying no cost in terms of their freedom (Rudra, 1987, 858-59). He draws parallels between the working conditions of attached labourers with those employed in the organised sector/government jobs (Rudra, 1990, 260). Bhalla had also claimed that the attached labourers (*naukars*) in Haryana received better wages than the casual labourers and they generally came from marginalised land-owning households while the casual labourers often belonged to landless lower castes. This 'privileged' position kept the attached labourers at a distance from the casual labourers belonging to menial castes in their attempt to mobilise agricultural labour for higher wages (Bhalla, 1976, A28). Bhalla, Bardhan and Rudra seem to agree with Byers who had expected that shift towards capitalist agriculture was likely to generate a new demand for attached labour. Far from stressing the elements of unfreedom in the system, Byers had called the attached labourers a 'privileged class' who 'to a certain extent, will participate in the prosperity of the green revolution' (Byers, 1972, 105, 109).

However, Brass has contested the claims made by Breman, Bardhan and Rudra and has strongly argued against their theoretical formulations that try to provide positive conceptualizations of attached labour and consequently eliminate the elements of unfreedom in the relationship. He contests the validity of their central assumption i.e., voluntarity on the part of labourer to join the relationship. 'While the recruitment may itself be voluntary, in the sense that the labourer willingly offers himself for work, it does not follow that the production relations will be correspondingly free in terms of the worker's capacity to reenter the labour market' (Brass, 1990, 55, n. 2). In contrast, he argues that 'long or short term worker attachment is a form of unfreedom, the object of which is to discipline (not habituate), control, and cheapen labour-power by preventing or curtailing both its commodification and the growth of a specifically proletarian consciousness. At a general level the existence of attached labour cannot be understood without regard to the class decomposition/ recomposition (or restructuring) that accompanies class struggle, a process which ... amounts to the deproletarianisation of agricultural labour' (Brass, 1991, 37). Taking a rather extreme position Brass goes to the extent of suggesting that this process is not confined to the permanent labourers. Even 'casual labourers' are being deproletarianized. In fact, he argues that 'in Haryana agriculture the structure of debt and bondage has shifted from permanent to casual workers' (Brass, 1995, 698).

Based on an intensive field study of three villages of a developed district (Karnal) of Haryana,[1] this paper contends that, far from being a 'privileged class', attached labourers are perhaps the most deprived category in the agrarian society of Haryana today. Even though there was no case of intergenerational bondages or generational debt transfers and, as such, the labourers entered the contract voluntarily, the elements of unfreedom were quite obvious in the relationship. Though Brass seems to be right when he says that attached labour is an unfree relationship, it is difficult to sustain his argument that there is a process of deproletarianisation of agricultural labour along with the capitalist development in Haryana agriculture. Though many of the casual labourers were also indebted to the cultivating farmers and such loans did carry a structure of obligation and loyalty, they were much better off when compared to their counterpart permanent labourers. The number of labourers available for attached labour has been decreasing.

THE HISTORICAL CONTEXT

As in other parts of the country, the agrarian structure of Haryana was marked by dependency relations between absentee landowners and cultivating tenants and attached labourers. These unequal relations were sustained partly by the ideology of patronage and partly through the perpetual indebtedness of the landless and tenant tillers. The system of attached labour was locally known as the *sajhi* or *siri* system.[2] A *sajhi* generally worked on a plot or on the entire land of the landowner and received a share from the total farm yield.

Sajhis were generally employed by the Rajput landlords who did not touch the plough. Employment of *sajhis* became more generalised during the early twentieth century with expansion of production and growth of rich peasantry in the region (Bhattacharya, 1985, 123-25). *Sajhis* were almost always indebted to the landlords they worked with. The occupation of agricultural labour being associated with *kamins* (the untouchables), most of the attached labourers came from the menial castes.

Agrarian changes during the post-Independence period brought about significant changes in the agrarian social structure and the system of attached labour. Though attachment *per se* continues, it has undergone formal as well as substantive changes. In her study in the early 1970s, Bhalla observed a gradual shift from keeping *sajhis* on share basis to employing *naukars* on a fixed annual wage. A significant change that she observed was the institutionalisation of formalised contract system where the mode of payment, its periodicity, duration of contract and advances to be made were all entered in the landlord's account book, and the agreement was formalised in the presence of three witnesses. A practice of advance payment of wages was built into the system (1976, A 25). Bhalla had also reported that *sajhis* continued to be a significant sub-category of the permanent labour class.

In the late 1980s, there were no *sajhis* working in two of the three villages. There were two *sajhis* in the third village but both were rather peculiar cases. One of them was a migrant from a less developed district of the State and in the other case the landowner was physically disabled. What brought about the change? Perhaps the most important factor was increase in productivity of land due to the introduction of HYV seeds, chemical fertilisers and mechanisation.

The big landowners, who earlier leased out their land to tenants or employed attached labourers on share basis, were the first to adopt the green revolution technology. This led to a shift to self-cultivation. Tractors and other machines made it possible to manage a much bigger operational holding. New technology also brought in multiple cropping systems. The net impact of these changes was a manifold increase in the productivity of land. Keeping *sajhis* on share basis meant sharing benefits of the new technology with the labourers. Initially the form of the relationship remained the same but share of the *sajhis* came down from one-fifth to one-fourteenth or in some cases to one-sixteenth – depending upon the operational holding of the farmer. This arrangement, however, could not last for very long.

Furthermore, in the old system, a *sajhi* used to share expenses on the crop. Mechanisation increased inputs and overall expenses on land multiplied. Seeds, fertilisers, pesticides and diesel etc. had to be bought from the market. The accounts of these expenses were obviously kept by the farmers. Labourers often complained that farmers manipulated accounts. And in cases of crop failures, the *sajhis* were made to share the expenses but they received nothing if the farmer got any 'compensation' money from the government. Consequently, tensions mounted and labourers themselves wanted a more formalised system. Hence, the *naukar* system.

ATTACHED LABOUR IN THE STUDY VILLAGES

Out of the total seventy-five case studies of agricultural labourers, thirty were currently working as attached or permanent labourers and among the other forty-five 'casual labourers', twenty-six were those who had worked as *naukars* or *sajhis* for some time in their career. So, out of the seventy-five case studies, as many as fifty-six or nearly seventy-five per cent were either working as attached labourers or were ex-attached labourers.

The working life of an attached labourer started quite early. Most of them (48 out of 75 respondents i.e. 64 per cent) had started their regular working life before they were fifteen years of age. There were only six labourers who reported that they started working regularly after they were eighteen years of age. Many of them started their career as *palis* (herdsmen).[3]

For a deeper understanding of the phenomenon it may be

relevant to raise questions regarding the working conditions of attached labourers, their perceptions on different aspects of attached labour, such as why did a labourer choose to work as attached labourer? Was it compulsion or preference that made a labourer work as attached labourer? Was it possible for a labourer to come out of the attachment if he so desired? What was the extent of their indebtedness? What were their sources of credit and did their indebtedness lead to prolonged and compulsive attachments which can be described as conditions of 'semi-bondage'?

WHY THEY WORKED AS ATTACHED LABOURERS

It is interesting to note that only rarely did a landless labourer prefer working as an attached labourer. Among both the categories of labourers perceptions on attached labour were quite negative. Out of seventy-five labourers, only nine preferred attached labour over casual labour. As many as sixty (80 per cent) preferred working as casual labourers. Out of these sixty, twenty-two saw attached labour to be as bad as 'bondage' where labourer was left with no freedom. One of the respondents said: 'Working as *naukar* is like being a wife of the farmer over whose body the farmer has complete control'.

Working conditions of an attached labourer were much more difficult than that under casual labour. He was committed to his farmer for almost twenty-four hours of the day. On an average an attached labourer worked ten to fourteen hours in a day even during lean seasons. The burden of work further increased during peak seasons. Only in a few cases were they entitled to a few days off in a year.[4] Monetarily also a casual labourer could earn as much as an attached labourer did and in some cases even more. And most importantly, labourers were not only aware of this fact but also felt strongly about it. So, obviously, attached labourers worked only under some compulsions and the immediate compulsion in almost all the cases was a need for credit.[5]

Getting credit from the local informal credit market was quite difficult for an agricultural labourer. It was more difficult when they needed more than a few hundred rupees. They had virtually no access to the institutional sources of credit, particularly for the kinds of needs they had, and they could not get credit from informal sources without offering collateral security which they rarely possessed. Even if a labourer could manage it, the interest rates were very high, ranging from two to five per cent monthly. So, the only viable source available to the landless labourer in the rural society were the big farmers and the only way that a labourer could mobilise credit was through mortgaging his labour power by accepting to work as an attached labourer.

The most attractive element in the attached labour system was the interest free advance payment of the annual wage. In most cases the annual wage itself took care of the immediate credit needs of the labourer. And if he needed more credit he could get it from the farmer on a monthly interest of two per cent.[6] And interestingly, the farmers who had been advancing credit on regular basis also reported that they advanced to the landless mainly with the intention of tying them for attached or peak season labour.[7]

NEED FOR CREDIT

Though the landless needed credit for various purposes, critical situations arose when there was a wedding in the family, or a house needed to be renovated or when a family member had to be treated for a serious and prolonged illness. They could easily get small amounts of credit required for consumption needs or for visiting a relative in a nearby village or town from petty shop keepers or big farmers. Petty shop keepers advanced money to get regular customers or for earning interest, the farmers lent with the hope that labourers would work for them during the peak season when there was scarcity of labour in the village. However, when the need was a few thousand rupees, the only way they could mobilise cash was through mortgaging labour power, i.e., accepting to work as attached labourers. Among the fifty-six respondents who were either working or had been attached labourers at some time in their career, as many as twenty-six reported that they needed cash for their weddings and another twenty-four required money either to renovate or construct a house or to clear off the debt availed for the purpose. There was only one among those working as attached labourers, who reported that he had no such compulsion and had not borrowed anything in advance from the farmer.

INDEBTEDNESS

Attached labourers were not only the most critically indebted category in the study villages, their sources were also generally local-informal where rates of interest were much higher than in the institutional sources. Their access to institutional sources was almost negligible.

As shown in Table 1, standing average informal debt of the attached labourers was the highest. And on an average only 12.1 per cent of their total outstanding debt had been borrowed from institutional sources.[8] On the other extreme, though the middle and big or very big farmers were also indebted, more than seventy-five per cent of their standing debt was from institutional sources which also implied that they borrowed mainly for productive investments – to buy a tractor or install a tubewell on the farm.

TABLE 1
Indebtedness to Institutional and Informal Sources
(Average rupees with percentage in brackets)

Category	Institutional debt	Informal debt	Total debt
Attached labourers	797 (12.1)	5,787 (87.9)	6,584
Casual labourers	2,111 (41.1)	3,024 (58.9)	5,135
Small and marginal farmers (less than 5 acres)	2,162 (27.7)	5,649 (72.3)	7,811
Middle farmers (5 to 10 acres)	12,773 (76.2)	4,000 (23.8)	16,773
Big farmers (10 to 25 acres)	14,774 (75.2)	4,871 (24.8)	19,645
Very big farmers (more than 25 acres)	15,500 (88.1)	2,100 (11.9)	17,600
All respondents	6,745 (60.9)	4,323 (39.1)	11,068

COMPULSIONS AND CONTINUITIES

Perhaps the most contentious issue in the discussions on attached labour has been the elements of compulsions and continuities in the relationship. It is not only the extent of continuity that is important, but the ability of an attached labourer to come out of the relationship, if he so desires, is also crucial.

Though a significant proportion of casual labourers interviewed (26 out of 40) had worked as attached labourers and the fact that they were presently working as casual labourers implies that many did manage to come out of the relationship, the element of continuity was also not insignificant. Most of those who once entered attachment had to work as attached labourers for a considerable number of years. Those who had worked or were working for more than five years were as many as forty-five out of the total of fifty-six respondents in this category (80 per cent). And those who had worked or were working for more than ten years were twenty-five (45 per cent). There were ten of them who had worked or were working for more than twenty years as attached labourers.[9] This obviously reflects a significant continuity in the relationship.

Considering the fact that a large majority of labourers perceived attached labour negatively and did not prefer working as attached labourers, the continuity obviously implies compulsions. And compulsions always arose out of a need for credit to finance a wedding, house repair or illness in the family.

TABLE 2
Number of Years put in as Attached Labourers

Village	Less than 5 years	5 to 9 years	10 to 14 years	15 to 19 years	20 plus	Never	Total years
I	4	6	3	2	2	8	25
II	3	6	5	2	4	7	27
III	4	3	5	3	4	4	23
Total	11	15	13	7	10	19	75

Since the annual wage received in advance was required for a special need, the labourer had to keep borrowing from the farmer for his regular consumption and social needs throughout the contract year. By the time the contract year got over, the labourer had a substantial outstanding debt to the farmer. Since he had no alternative source of income or credit, he had no choice but to continue working as attached labourer with the same farmer or with another farmer who agreed to advance enough money to clear off the outstanding debt of the previous farmer.

CONFLICTS AND EMERGING PATTERNS

Though the picture presented above does seem to suggest that the existing attachment relations in Haryana agriculture are very close to what may be described as debt bondage, there are also counter tendencies.

Labourers have been increasingly becoming conscious of the difficult working conditions of attached labour. This is also reflected in their strong negative perceptions on attached labour. The fact that many of them reported that they chose to work as attached labourers only under compulsions, makes a lot of difference. The ideology of patronage and loyalty has largely been eroded from the minds of agricultural labourers. All this has led to mounting of tensions between labourers and the employer farmers.

Big farmers often abused their attached labourers in informal chats among themselves. During group interviews also they expressed dissatisfaction and anger against the labourers. They said they could no more trust the labourers. Some of them reported that when a labourer was left alone in the field he would often let his castemen cut fodder from the farm. Since the two came from completely different caste groups, the divisions between labourers and farmers were very sharp.

Views expressed by labourers in similar group interviews conducted in their caste *mohallas* were even more bitter. While the farmers abused labourers for not working to their satisfaction, the labourers expressed their discontent by calling them cheats and exploiters. They often got angry during the interviews and tried to tell how oppressive the farmers were. Narrating the story of a fellow labourer, one of them reported:

> All big farmers are cheats. They are extremely selfish. Dina, a big *zamindar*, had employed Joga Jhimmar as an attached labourer. He also gave five acres of land for share-cropping paddy to Joga's father. Once, while cleaning the canal, Joga by chance cut a few plants of paddy. Dina on noticing it, became furious and slapped Joga. In reaction Joga refused to continue working with the *zamindar*. Dina was so shameless that he took away the five acre land shared-out to his father without paying anything for the labour Joga's father had put in the crop.

In one village an attached labourer had temporarily left the farmer because he had been badly abused by the farmer. During a detailed interview, he expressed his anger against the big farmers. He said:

'This whole *kaum* is that of cheats. They suck our blood'. When asked, whether by *kaum* he meant caste of the farmer with whom he was working, he replied: 'No, all these *zamindars*' (implying the class of big farmers).

Cases of scuffles and physical fights, particularly between attached labourers and big farmers, were reported as becoming quite frequent. At least three such cases in one village and two each in the other two were reported to have occurred in the recent past. And there were at least five cases of the labourers either absconding with a debt outstanding to the farmers or staying in the village but refusing to repay the amount. In a fluid and changing political context, not always could the farmers compel such estranged workers to pay back the outstanding debt. They also hesitated to report such cases to the police for fear of litigation. Once the case went to the 'Labour Court' the farmers lost whatever chances they had of recovering the debt.

One of the consequences of these growing tensions was a tendency among the labourers, to some extent also desired by their employer farmers, to shift from one farmer to another after one or two years. Out of the thirty respondent attached labourers, in ten cases it was their first year and in eleven cases it was their second year with the farmer at the time of the field study. There were only three cases where the labourers were working with a specific farmer for more than five years.

When asked whether it would be possible for them to stop working with their employer farmer after the completion of the year, twenty-eight out of thirty respondents said that unless his debt was cleared, he would not be able to leave his farmer. Another reported that it would be difficult for him to arrange the amount which would have to be returned to the farmer before he could leave.

However, most of them had borrowed more than their annual wages and those who had borrowed only upto their annual wage or less than that were likely to borrow more before the end of the year. This meant that only rarely was a labourer without debt at the time of the completion of his contract year. How did they return the standing amount if they chose to stop working with the farmer? Out of twenty-eight respondents who felt that they could easily stop working with the present employer, in eighteen cases they reported that they could borrow the amount from some other farmer and shift to him. So in these cases, the attachment *per se* continued. In eight other cases, the labourers reported that they could either borrow from a petty money-lender or shopkeeper and return the amount, or felt that it would not be compulsory for them to clear their debt at once if they did not want to work with the farmer next year. They could gradually return the amount with interest. The remaining four were sure that they would not be indebted to the farmer at the end of the contract year.[10]

Though substantially the ability of changing masters did not lead to any radical change, the formalised contractual arrangement in the present day *naukar* system did seem to have opened up some new possibilities. Payment in the form of an annual cash wage made it possible to translate the annual wage into monthly or even daily wages. Such a possibility did not exist in the older *sajhi* system where a labourer received payment for his labour in the form of a share from the farm yield. Hence he had no choice of shifting over to another master until the harvesting was over. While in the present day *naukar* system, a labourer had to only find a new farmer who was willing to employ him with an advance to clear the debt of the previous employer. And in the context of the factional divisions among big farmers and a general scarcity of those willing to work as *naukars*, it was not very difficult for a labourer to find another employer. There were some cases in the study villages in which labourers had actually changed their masters before the contract year was over.

Bhalla in her study of 'New Relations of Production in Haryana Agriculture', conducted in the early seventies, had found that the attached labourers (*naukars*) came from marginalised landowning households while the casual labourers came generally from the menial castes. This also divided the labourers (Bhalla, 1976, A 28).

The present study contradicts Bhalla's findings. Except for three, all attached labourers interviewed belonged to menial castes, like the casual labourers. She also reported that when the contract was signed between the *naukar* and the farmer, the latter sought at least three witnesses who often were the ones who had positions of power and authority in the village and could evoke feelings of submission and obedience from the labourer. This, in her view, reflected 'on the relations of power in Haryana villages.... The witnesses are all presumed by the villagers to stand on the side of the hirer', and no case was found 'where a witness was included who was considered a representative for the labourer' (Bhalla, 1976, A 26).

The picture in the three study villages was again very different. Out of thirty respondent attached labourers, not in all cases was a contract signed. In nine cases, the contract was oral. In four cases, where a contract was signed, no witnesses were sought. In the rest of the cases, generally a single witness was taken who always came from the caste of the labourer, usually his relative. This also reflected an erosion in the authority of the traditionally dominant sections. The farmers preferred a witness who could put social pressure on the labourer in case of default.

CASUAL LABOUR AND UNFREEDOM

In response to this formulation presented elsewhere (Jodhka, 1994), Brass argued that a shift towards casual labour does not necessarily imply their growing freedom. On the contrary, restating his earlier position he asserted, this shift has been engineered by the capitalist farmers who continued to maintain, or even tighten, control over these labourers through the mechanism of debt. Thus substantially, not only has there been no change in the phenomenon of attachment of 'unfree labour', but there was also the opposite trend in Haryana agriculture which he described as a process of 'deproletarianisation' (Brass, 1995).

However, it is very difficult to agree with Brass. In my study villages the casual labourers were neither more indebted[11] nor did they feel the kind of unfreedom that was experienced by attached labourers. Also, compared to the permanent labourers, it was much easier for a casual labourer to get an IRDP scheme sanctioned. Out of forty-five casual labourers interviewed, thirty-one (69 per cent) had availed forty-four IRDP schemes, while out of thirty permanent labourers only twelve (40 per cent) had been able to get fourteen schemes sanctioned. Consequently, the proportion of standing informal debt on an average for an attached labourer was 89 per cent while for a casual labourer it was 59 per cent (Jodhka, 1995 b). If debt leads to growing unfreedom, casualisation of labour implies an opposite trend.

Also, unlike in some other parts of India, the system of 'beck and call' (Thorner's expression) did not exist in the Haryana villages. Though casual labourers did report that they often borrowed from the big farmers with the commitment of working for them during the peak season, this did not work as a 'system' and unlike the *naukar* or the *sajhi* system, it did not have a local name. Therefore, such debt obligations of casual labourers were of a temporary nature and describing it 'bondage', as Brass does, would be an overstatement. Peak season work is largely donc on contractual basis and most of the labourers anyway preferred working on the farm during the peak season. Apart from better wages, they looked forward to storing some grain for the household during the harvesting time. The peak season labour-tying by the big farmers worked more against the smaller farmers who also needed to employ labour during peak seasons but could not pay advance wages to tie the labour. Consequently, they had to wait till the work was over in the bigger farms.

CONCLUSIONS

Discussions on the phenomenon of attached labour in the post-green revolution agriculture have ranged from characterising attached labourers as a 'privileged class' to 'unfree slaves'. The field data and the discussion presented above makes it abundantly clear that attached labourers neither enjoyed the kind of status that made them privileged among the poor nor did they see their position as being so. Attached labour functioned more as 'a labour mortgage system' where the labourer, in some sense, had to give up his freedom in order to avail an interest-free credit. Though it is a voluntary arrangement in the sense that the labourer chooses to enter the relationship, it cannot be compared with employment in the organised sector as has been argued by Rudra. Here the labourer is compelled to choose an alternative that he not only dislikes but also finds economically less rewarding. And the source of his compulsion lies in his weak economic position. Hence, the indebtedness and consequent compulsion to continue working as an attached labourer does imply that there are elements of dependency and unfreedom in the relationship.

This, however, should not lead to the conclusion that nothing has changed as far as dependency relations are concerned. There has not only been a formal change in the system of attached labour, the relationship itself has changed considerably. Growing dislike for the relationship has made these labourers try to mobilise alternative sources of credit and come out of the relationship as soon as they could. These alternatives ranged from dependence on the wife's employment or earnings for the subsistence needs of the family, and minimising borrowing more than the annual wage from the farmers, to utilising the money received under IRDP schemes to clear off the outstanding debt and defaulting the bank loan.

Development of capitalism in agriculture has also led to a growing integration of the village into the broader national economy. This has meant opening up of possibilities of employment outside agriculture and the village. The availability of alternative sources of employment, repeated experiences of participation in the electoral process of electing representatives at local, regional and national level, growing urban exposure to mass media and above all a near complete erosion of the ideology of patronage and loyalty have led to a qualitative change in the politics of the subordinate groups. The empirical instances of this new politics range from their increasing assertiveness in every day life to the emergence of a pan-India Dalit movement.

NOTES

1. This paper is a part of a broader study of agrarian change and debt dependency in Haryana agriculture. Field work for study was conducted in three medium size villages of an agriculturally developed district (Karnal) of Haryana. The field work was carried out during 1988-89 over a period of six months. Apart from observations and interviews with various people, 185 case studies of farmers and labourers representing different categories were conducted.

2. *Sajhi/siri* literally means a partner or sharer. However, it is used only for the landless labourer and never for the farmer.

3. A *pali* is usually a child labourer between 12 to 17 or 18 years of age or an aged labourer, who is unable to work as a regular casual or attached labourer. When a labourer is 17 or 18 years old, he starts working as a regular labourer – casual or attached. A *pali* is always paid less than a *naukar.* A *naukar* received annual wage ranging between Rs. 3,500 and Rs. 5,000 plus meals or a fixed amount of wheat. A *pali* got meals and an annual wage ranging from Rs. 1,000 to Rs. 2,000 depending primarily on his age.

The number of those who started their working life as *palis* was more among the attached labourers (20 out of 30 respondents in the category) than the casual labourer respondents (14 out of 45).

4. Out of 30 attached labourer respondents only 12 reported that they could avail leave upto 12 days in a year. This was written in the contract. In the rest of the cases the labourer had to either give a replacement or had to forgo his wage for the day.

5. Out of 30 attached labourers only 7 reported that they worked as

attached labourers because it offered regular employment and better wages. The rest all reported that they needed credit for wedding (11), house repair (3), to clear off another standing debt (7), or for consumption (2).

6. Twenty-eight out of 30 respondent attached labourers reported that they could easily get advances more than the annual wage from their employers. The other two said they could get only upto the annual wage. This was the single most important attraction for a labourer to accept attached labour.

7. Among the 58 farmers out of the 110 interviewed who regularly lent out a part of their surplus in the local informal credit market, as many as 41 reported that they lent either exclusively to tie labour (23) or with the dual purpose of earning interest and also tying labour (18).

8. In most cases, the institutional loan meant the outstanding loaned amount received under an IRDP scheme. The same is true of the casual labourers' institutional debt.

9. It may be important to note that a labourer could rarely get employment after the age of 50 or 55 and he starts working at the age of 18 or 20. So the total working life of a labourer is around 30 to 35 years.

10. Two important sources used by labourers to come out of attachment were, first, the IRDP schemes where the labourer utilised the money for clearing off the debt in place of buying an asset (for a detailed discussion on this issue see Jodhka, 1995 b) and second, depending on wife's casual labour income for daily expense of the family and minimising borrowings from the farmer.

11. As reported above, the average standing debt of a casual labourer from informal sources was Rs. 3,024 while the permanent labourers had an average informal debt (largely from employer farmers) of Rs. 5,756.

REFERENCES

Bardhan, P. (1984). *Land, Labour and Rural Poverty.* Delhi, OUP.

Bhaduri, A. (1984). *The Economic Structure of Backward Agriculture.* Delhi, Macmillan.

Bhalla, S. (1976). 'New Relations of Production in Haryana Agriculture'. *Economic and Political Weekly,* Vol. XI, 93.

Brass, I. (1990). 'Class Struggle and Deproletarianization of Agricultural Labour in Haryana (India)'. *The Journal of Peasant Studies,* Vol. 18 (i), 36-87.

Brass T. (1995). 'Unfree Labour and Agrarian Change: A Different View'. *Economic and Political Weekly,* April, 1.

Breman, J. (1974). *Patronage and Exploitation – Changing Agrarian Relations in South Gujarat, India.* Berkeley, University of California Press.

——. (1985). *Of Peasants, Migrants and Paupers: Rural Labour Circulation and*

Capitalist Production in West India. Delhi, OUP.

Bhattacharya, N. (1985). 'Agricultural Labour and Production: Central and South-east Punjab – 1870-1940'. *Essays on Commercialisation of Indian Agriculture.* Eds. K.N. Raj et al. Delhi, OUP.

Byres, T.J. (1972). 'The Dialectics of India's Green Revolution'. *South Asian Review,* Vol. 5, Number 2.

Harriss, J. (1992). 'Does the Depressor Still Work? Agrarian Structure and Development in India: A Review of Evidence and Argument'. *The Journal of Peasant Studies,* Vol. 19, No. 2, 189- 227.

Jodhka S.S. (1994). 'Agrarian Changes and Attached Labour: Emerging Patterns in Haryana Agriculture'. *Economic and Political Weekly,* Vol. XXIX, No. 39.

—— (1995 a), 'Bureaucratisation, Corruption and Depoliticisation: Changing Profile of Credit Cooperatives in Rural Haryana'. *Economic and Political Weekly, January,* 7.

—— (1995 b), 'IRDP and Changing Agrarian Relations: A Study of the Unintended Consequences.' *Journal of Rural Development,* Vol.14, No. 1.

Mendelsohn, O. (1993). 'The Transformation of Authority in Rural India'. *Modern Asian Studies,* Vol. 27, No. 4, 805-42.

Ramachandran, V.K. (1990). *Wage Labour and Unfreedom in Agriculture: An Indian Case Study.* Oxford, OUP.

Rudra, A (1987). 'Land Relations in Agriculture: A Study in Contrast'. *Economic and Political Weekly,* Vol. XXII, No. 17.

Rudra, A (1990). 'Class Relations in Indian Agriculture'. *Agrarian Relations and Accumulations: Mode of Production Debate in India.* Ed. U. Patnaik. Delhi, OUP.

14

The Village Community in Punjabi Novel

J. S. RAHI & S.S. KHAHRA

The Punjabi novel came into being towards the close of the last century. Its development has spanned the twentieth century. The realistic portrayal of community life, especially of village community, began to appear in it only in the early 1960s. Gurdial Singh published his first novel, *Marhi Da Deeva* in 1964.[1] It changed the tone and tenor of the genre in Punjabi and set the pattern for Punjabi novel to outgrow the manipulative fiction of socio-political movements and to engage itself with the depiction of real life situations in depth and with insight. We propose to study this development in its historical dimensions.

Gurdial Singh's novels occupy a pivotal position in realistic Punjabi fiction but he was not the first novelist in this genre. Important among the novelists who wrote before him was Surinder Singh Narula. His *Peo Puttar* (The Father and The Son), published in 1946, is considered a landmark in realistic Punjabi fiction. Sant Singh Sekhon's *Lahu Mitti* (The Blood and the Soil), published four years later in 1950, is memorable for its hard and uncompromising realism. Another novel, *Wagdi Si Ravi* (And There Flowed The Ravi) by Gurcharan Singh, published in 1951, has been hailed belatedly as a realistic novel of some reckoning. Nevertheless the way Gurdial Singh handles the tangles of community life in the rural Punjab opens a whole new range of possibilities for portraying man in the matrix of psychological and socio-cultural forces. This kind of treatment is absent from the earlier realistic fiction.

Gurdial Singh's novels do not merely document the externals of community life in the rural Punjab; they unravel the socio-psychic mysteries operating at its core. The realistic novel before Gurdial Singh is significant mainly for its value as a document on social life in a given time and space. Its socio-psychic content is thin and not quite sustained in the fabric of the narrative. Its significance is primarily historical in the sense that in characterisation and narrative structuring, it does not transgress the possible or the probable. This was in contrast with the novel echoing the call of religious reformist or progressive movements which transgressed the possible or the probable by its very nature.[2] The early realistic novel adheres to the principle and philosophy of verisimilitude which was not considered essential for the novel propagating religion, reform or revolution. Though within narrower framework, the realistic novel followed the models of Flaubert, Balzac and Zola. Compared to the novel of our indigenous tradition of didactic fiction, this framework broadened the horizons of fictional imagination. But Gurdial Singh appeared on the scene with an essentially different perception of socio-psychic realities of community life.

The evolution of perceptions in the novel before Gurdial Singh was a continuous process, closely linked with social and political history, right from the beginning of the Punjabi novel. Its systematic delineation is possible only in the framework of literary history, which requires a different kind of critical treatment. This does not fall within the ambit of the present study which is aimed at discerning the community concerns in Gurdial Singh's novels and their impact on later novelists engaged in a dialectical combat with prevalent modes of feeling and thought that emanate from tradition but get vitiated by the absurdities of the contemporary situations.

Gurdial Singh is believed to be a fiction writer of the Malwa belt of the Punjab. The region is sometimes narrowed down to the territory around Jaito Mandi in the district of Faridkot where Gurdial Singh resides in his ancestral house. Most of his characters, including the protagonists in his novels, belong to this area. By now a large number of fiction writers have emerged from the Malwa region and produced powerful short stories and novels which bear the influence of Gurdial Singh's writings. The ferment assumed the form of a literary movement which has made Malwai, the dialect of the Malwa region, a major form of the Punjabi language. This prompted quite a few scholars to consider Gurdial Singh as a literary figure in the genre of the regional novel devoted to the depiction of a sub-culture. Consequently, it has become a fashion among young researchers to study Gurdial Singh's realism primarily in the framework of the regional novel.[3]

It may be emphasized, however, that this standpoint is only partially justified. The characterology of his novels is marked by a paradox which holds the key to the fictional world he creates. This somehow has remained ignored by critics obsessed with the idea of mimetic depiction as a critical parameter. The paradox pertains to the nature of the protagonists in his novels and their tragic destiny.

The protagonists in his novels are not heroes in the traditional sense of the heroic in moral, social or spiritual terms.[4] As such, they do not happen to be the typical representation of the heroic aspirations of any community based upon caste, creed, religion or any other social group bound by affinities of belief or way of life. They represent dissent against what they feel is debased in community life and its circumstances. But they are found to be enigmatic when it comes to articulating their dissent. In matters concerning common community interest, they are essentially loners. Their impatience with the established system often lands them in dissipating outbursts or chaos of arguments. The possibility of meaningful social action becoming a reality is clouded by their lack of perspective, introversion or tempestuous nature.

In *Aathan Uggan* (The Dusk and The Dawn 1974), we find the low-caste peasantry frittering itself away in endless variance of thought and opinion. The ironic turn of events in *Anhoe* (As If They Never Were, 1966), *Adh Chanani Raat* (The Half-Moon Night, 1972), and *Parsa* (1991) lands the protagonists in schisms leading to religious or cultural lag resulting in disorientation full of tragic portents. They are dismembered by the opposing pulls of their schisms. But in the turmoil that engulfs their lives, they throw up some pertinent questions about life, religion, culture, caste, *karma*, rebirth, *avagaman*, salvation, emancipation, God, life, death, mythology and social institutions. As individuals, they have some discomforting angularities, but as structural entities in the novel, they signify thoughtful insights into the socio-cultural physiognomy of their community environment.

The temperamental seclusion, inflexibility or anger of Gurdial Singh's protagonists are rooted in their wounded innocence and sensitivity. This fact forbids them to compromise. Intrinsically, they are persons with tender feelings with a sense of fairness unobtrusively reflected in their actions. This arouses for them sympathies bordering on the appreciation for the heroic. Their apparent flaws have a strong undercurrent of moral concerns which are crucial though amorphous in their mind-set. Their concern for just social living, preservation of self-respect, human dignity and healthy community environment redeems them despite their angularities. Jagsir and Dharam Singh in *Marhi Da Deeva,* Bishna in *Anhoe,* Modan in *Adh Chanani Raat* and Munder with some of his companions in *Athan Uggan* are all manifestations of these concerns in varied forms.

Parsa in *Parsa* strikes a slightly different note as regards the nature of his concern. His destiny, in all appearance, does not languish in futility as does the destiny of Jagsir, Bishna, Modan and Munder in the previous novels. A Brahman by caste and an agriculturist by profession, he is ardently opposed to Brahmanic ritualism and caste-stratification. He believes in a way of living akin to *karmayoga,* an action-oriented faith. He pursues it with an uncompromising vehemence reminiscent of his family tradition of the legendary Brahman Parshuram who vowed to destroy the Khatris. But his care-for-none attitude is subverted when his two elder sons, fascinated by the material culture of fame, money and authority, are alienated from him and his life. His paternal relationship with them is severed because their value-system is outrageously counterpoised against his own. His youngest son with whom he shares a temperamental affinity is lost in the hazards of a militant movement. The tragic blow of his death upsets Parsa's dream-cart. Caught in the agony of the loss, he traverses a painful period of questioning and doubt. But stubborn, like some other protagonists in Gurdial Singh's novels, he eventually persuades himself under the protection of an age-old religious argument to sire a child with a lonely widow who dies soon after. Parsa brings the child home and also another woman with a seeming determination to begin afresh for achieving *karmayoga* and fulfilment through progeny. It becomes an obsession with him that his temperamental legacy should be perpetuated even after his death.

This has been interpreted as his invincible heroic urge to live in the face of adversity. The novel thus has been seen as a refreshing departure from the tragic themes of Gurdial Singh's earlier novels.[5] However the discerning reader may detect a shrewd irony in Parsa's renewed bid. It looks cheering only in appearance. Already frustrated by the furiously changing material conditions of life, his ambition is not likely to go beyond being a morbid self-deception. The struggle for existence is likely to get grimmer with the spectre of old age engulfing him like black smoke. The eventuality makes Parsa's ambition sound unrealistic and illusory. The existential portents of this situation are essentially ironical. In no way can they be perceived as univocal as some critics erroneously believe. The scepticism finds confirmation when the old-age optimism of Parsa is contextually placed against the backdrop of his alienated life.

The structural window on the tragic irony of Parsa's inevitable destiny is not provided by the state of his passion. The passion remains intact unlike the passion of the protagonists of his earlier novels. The irony is manifested in the continuing potential of the material forces typified in the earlier subversion of his fulfilment. It is different in mode but not in stance. The mode fixes a critical focus on the dynamics of subvertive forces. Parsa's character has some redeeming features which reveal by contrast the institutional deterioration in society. But the mode also brings out the chauvinistic and obscurantist strains in his assemblage of ideas and values. His apparently glorified image is dismantled by the iconoclastic character of the irony underneath.

In all, the mode turns Parsa's out-of-the-world image into a typical representation of the hard realities of community life like that of the novelist's other protagonists. Their anger and violence in thought and action or a pathetic withdrawal into their own self or craving for perpetuation and permanence through children are symptomatic expressions of their helplessness against the ruthlessness of the institutionalized forces. The portrayals bring out the crises not only of the protagonists, but also of the community as a whole, irrespective of the entities of caste, creed, religion or other social groups which constitute it. The sub-communities are subsumed by the larger entity of socio-economic and socio-political system.

The realistic details of topography, modes of dress and conversation, peculiarities of customs and beliefs, increasing fragmentation of land holdings and their consequential tremors in family and social relationships, institutionalized lust for landed property and upsurge of a deceitful mercantile culture, all reflect the Malwa region in Gurdial Singh's novels. But the existential predicaments germinating from such changes in this relatively backward region of the Punjab are not simply a regional phenomenon. They have a bearing on the life in other regions of the Punjab.

The short stories of Waryam Sandhu, a young and perceptive fiction writer from the Majha region bordering Pakistan, lay bare shockingly varied tensions, including tensions of extra-marital relationships and collusion between the rich peasantry and the politically powerful individuals and groups. Sohan Singh Seetal's *Tootan Wala Khooh* (1963) and *Jug Badal Gaya* (1972) also depict the disturbing fissures of an agrarian society swept by the degenerating forces of politics, economy and their consequential culture.

This can be seen as an ironical commentary on the archetypal image of the Punjabis as an enterprising, dynamic, hard-working and forward-looking community. To comprehend the significance of irony one needs to know that the archetypal image tends to glorify the pragmatic thrust of a limited class and ignores the dehumanizing possibilities of more typical and powerful. The fictional mode initiated by Gurdial Singh focusses on community life from a standpoint antithetical to archetypal assumptions. It replaces the outmoded yardstick with an encompassing experience of the ground realities of community life.

The experience elevated and organized in Gurdial Singh's novels is agonizing but revealing. It is agonizing because of the grim reality of the community life it brings under scrutiny. It is revealing for the insights it provides into the contradictions of Indian society, so vividly reflected in the existential predicaments of the protagonists. As they try to pull themselves out from the pit, they appear reflective and dignified, but lose the lustre in cultural cobwebs. Since their revulsion against the quagmire is temperamental only it meets a pathetic fate, but the impact of its humanistic import lingers on in the mind. The eventual death, defeat or disintegration of the protagonists does not diminish the significance of the redeeming features of their passion. In certain ways, they signify the ever-abiding human search for what transcends the trivial, the mean, and the mundane. Their fate is tragic when it signifies the termination of the urge to live. They aspire to live not just as a vegetative organisms or manifestations of the law of the jungle where the stronger overwhelm the weaker, but as moral beings with humane concerns.

The urge to live is fictionalized in different novels in specific contexts of social divisions. In *Marhi da Deeva,* it is predominantly the low-caste landless peasant struggling for breath and dignity against a heartless neo-landlordism. And he is knitted round the plight and predicaments of artisans, craftsmen and allied labour in an upcoming market town. *Adh Chanani Raat* portrays the unscrupulous politics and cultural absurdities of the peasantry afflicted by a crisis of values precipitated by the increasing fragmentation of land holdings. *Aathan Uggan* takes up the community tensions of the landed and landless peasantry together with the miseries of farm labour. *Annhe Ghore da Daan* (Gift of The Blind Horse, 1976) is an attempt at re-interpreting the ancient Indian myth of Rahu and Ketu in relation to the low-caste landless peasantry oscillating between the village and the city and falling prey to drug abuse in the wake of rapidly expanding urbanization and industrialization breeding ruthlessly debilitating competition. In *Anhoe* have been treated the adverse effects of the dynamics of commerce upon artisans and labourers in the market towns. The existential tangle in *Parsa* is complicated by the new generation's mobility towards urban living, search for prosperity in alien lands and the violence in political life. Here also the ancient Indian myth of Parshuram determines the drives of the principal character to symbolize his conflict with the overbearing system. Seen in chronological sequence, these novels provide sociological perspectives on the discomforting change sweeping the community life in the rural Punjab.[6] The phenomenon of green revolution, enthusiastically projected by agricultural economists, does not find any underpinning in Gurdial Singh's novels. He depicts tensions bred by depleted land holdings. He also depicts how the emerging urge for better living has fuelled land disputes and criminal manipulations.

In the general impression that emerges the miseries of the poor and simple folk have been compounded more than ever before. In cruel indifference, the richer among the landed class are moving away from the traditional bonds that characterized rural life earlier. The population explosion has made the struggle for existence grimmer especially for the agricultural labourer and the landless. In *Marhi da Deeva,* the life of the people from the working class, sleeping huddled together in mud-houses, is compared to that of the dogs lying in their pot-holes.[7]

The world-view emerging from Gurdial Singh's novels is re-inforced and expanded by novelists writing under his influence in subsequent years. The better known among them are Ram Sarup Ankhi, Karamjit Singh Jussa, Inder Singh Khamosh, Jasbir Mand and Mitter Sen Meet.

Ankhi's famous novel, *Kothe Kharak Singh* (1985), portrays the socio-historical movement of community life in the rural Punjab over the last sixty years. His novels are not as finished in crafts-manship as those of Gurdial Singh. But the sociological picture that emerges from chronological linkages between Gurdial Singh's novels is encompassed by Ankhi in the body of a single narrative in this novel. Ankhi is not interested in the propagation of the standpoint of the State regarding the green revolution or other developmental activities. He is primarily interested in humanistic concerns which prompt him to focus attention on the deepening crisis of community relations. The village as a cohesive social institution is seen to be crumbling in the emerging economic scenario. The physical needs of the unmarried brother are met by the wife of the married brother under an ironic game of sexual politics merely to stall depletion of land holdings. This is sometimes stretched to the point of murder to obviate the remote possibility of subversion of the objective at some later stage. The consequences of the murder are handled by alignment with the political mafia spreading its deadly tentacles among the rural folk under the influence of and as a part of the vicious State politics. The well-meaning and the committed youth seek to counter it through political activity which is chaotic.

Ankhi's *Partapi* (1993) brings out the nexus between money, religion, and politics with its bearing upon gender-relations in a society which treats the sham as the real shine, drowning the tender in the whirlpool.

Kussa's novels too omit any sympathetic reference to the green revolution. On the contrary, in his first novel, *Burke Wale Lutere* (1975), he portrays situations explicitly demythifying the green revolution from the standpoint of the unprivileged peasantry. The thematic canvas in his later novels is more akin to that of Gurdial Singh than of Ankhi. He too takes up limited themes in his narratives, though his protagonists, unlike Gurdial Singh's protagonists, are more naturalistic and less paradoxical. His *Raat de Rahi* (The Wayfarers of the Night, 1979) deals with the maladies of extra-marital relations afflicting the rural society with cracks in the institution of marriage vitiated by marginal land holding. His *Rohi Biabaan* (The Wasteland, 1983) articulates the crisis of the land-owning peasantry gradually reduced to the plight of landless peasantry, low-caste farm-labour and servants, but not prepared to be de-classed in accordance with its real position. The novel touches upon the theme of its frustrations arising out of the turmoil it is pitted against. Further down the line, his *Agg da Geet* (The Song of Fire, 1985), depicts the tragedy of physical and mental paralysis of the working class traditionally known for its vitality and vibrancy. His *Zakhmi Darya*

(The Wounded River, 1991) is an attempt at seeing the Punjab problem as a convergence of various strands of the crisis.

The two volumes of Jasbir Mand's *Aud de Beej* (The Seeds of Drought, 1986, 1989) capture the attention of the critics for a similar probing into the crisis in a style that is peculiar to him. The novel shows how the mechanization of farming, an essential means of the green revolution, becomes a costly proposition for the peasants with small holdings. Politics based on religion becomes obscurantist and retrogressive in its moorings. Politics opposed to these moorings ignores even the legitimate claims of tradition and ethnicity. The fascination of the unemployed youth for the heroic is exploited by the privileged few to underpin their egotistical sense of importance in the echelons of authority against the position of even genuine leadership.

Two novels of Inder Singh Khamosh, *Rishtian de Rang* (The Complexions of Relations, 1978), and *Bukkal da Rishta* (*The Illicit Relationship*, 1991), are marked by similar anxieties about the family life and joint family system crumbling under the weight of disruptions in the value structure of the agrarian society. Two of Mitter Sen Meet's latest novels, *Tafteesh* (The Investigation, 1990) and *Katehra* (The Witness Box, 1993) enlarge the canvas and underline the degeneration of the State machinery, especially in the context of politics, bureaucracy and judiciary with a more sophisticated and innovative sense of craft.

The aesthetic pleasure provided by all these novels is not confined to mere narrative interest. It lies more in the insights provided by the narrative. The insights so provided do not concern only the students of literature. They are equally valuable for scholars interested in agrarian economy, political developments and social history, who generally tend to ignore the evidence of creative literature.

NOTES

1. The title is untranslatable as the equivalent of *marhi* is not available in the Western ethos or in other Indian languages. Broadly speaking, it signifies a structure erected on the spot where an unmarried young man is cremated after death. It is in essence erected for a person whose desire to perpetuate himself through male progeny remains unfulfilled. The spirit of such a person is believed to turn into a *prait*, a ghostly existence from

which it may re-enter a human body for the fulfilment of its unfulfilled desires. It can achieve *gati, i.e.* release, only after such fulfilment. 'Deeva' is an earthen lamp ritually lit every evening on the *marhi* to keep the disturbed spirit in peace and to ward off its evil effects on living humans. Anthropologically, the belief could be a folkloristic survival of the primitive urge for continuance and security through male progeny.

2. Bhai Vir Singh, the first original novelist in Punjabi, is the most representative novelist of the Singh Sabha movement. He, along with the other novelists of his creed, expressed the anxieties related to the survival of the Sikhs as a community. The challenges thrown up before the Sikhs by the fall of Sikh rule, advent of the British and the Western civilization, breaking up of the joint family system and reformist propaganda and social welfare activities of the Christian missionaries are met by the novelists of Bhai Vir Singh's creed by invoking archetypal images from Sikh history or by creating normative protagonists of the Sikh way of life. The realistic portrayal of contemporary Sikh community did not fascinate them as it implied the danger of unwittingly confirming the criticism by the Christian missionaries of the discomforting realities of Indian life and culture. They, therefore, used what Sant Singh Sakhon calls 'historical romances' as counterpoise to Christian realism to ensure survival of their desired way of life. Bhai Vir Singh's *Baba Naudh Singh,* a novel in two parts published in 1917 and 1921, is a typical example of the mind-set which seeks to portray Sikh way of life at its normative best. The crisis posed by the great economic recession of the late twenties has been tackled in the novels of the reformist movement, as in Meeran Baksh Minhas's *Nawab Khan* (1930) and Nanak Singh's *Chitta Lahu* (1932), on the basis of moral values. The narrative structure of the novels under the progressive movement, typified by Jaswant Singh Kanwal's novels, is determined by the contrived portrayal of the ideals of social progress enshrined in the manifesto of the Progressive movement launched from Lucknow in 1936. All these narratives provide only inadequate portrayal of the complexities of community life.

3. Sukhbir Kaur (1985).
4. Attar Singh (1976), 20.
5. Vinod (1992), 401-02.
6. Raghbir Singh (1986), 83-84.
7. Ibid, 63-66.

BIBLIOGRAPHY

Ankhi, Ram Sarup. *Kothe Kharak Singh.* Delhi: Aarsi Publishers, 1985.

——. *Partapi.* Delhi: Aarsi Publishers, 1993.

Attar Singh. 'Novel *Anhoe*'. Gurdial Singh Samman Samaroh. Kot-Kapura Sahitak Sath, 1976.

Dusanjh, Surinder Singh. *Panjabi Itihasak Novel.* Ludhiana: Sirjna Press, 1969.

Gurcharan Singh. *Wagdi Si Ravi.* 2nd edition. Ludhiana: Lahore Book Shop,

1972.
Gurdial Singh. *Marhi da Deeva.* 4th edition. Delhi: Navyug Publishers, 1974.
——. *Anhoe.* Delhi: Navyug Publishers, 1966.
——. *Adh Chanani Rat.* Delhi: Navyug Publishers, 1972.
——. *Aathan Uggan.* Delhi: Navyug Publishers, 1974.
——. *Annhe Ghore da Dan.* Delhi: Navyug Publishers, 1976.
——. *Parsa.* Jaito (Faridkot): Sukhreet Parkashan, 1991.
Hardarshan Singh. *Punjabi Novel Vich Vaaik Da Vighathan.* Ludhiana: Panjabi Writers' Co-operative Society, 1987.
Khahra, Sukhdev Singh. *Punjabi Novel Vich Sanskritik Chetna.* Amritsar: Guru Nanak Dev University, 1988.
Khamosh, Inder Singh. *Rishtian de Rang.* Barnala: Mitter Mandal, 1978.
——. *Bukkal da Rishta.* Delhi: Aarsi Publishers, 1991.
——. *Burke Wale Lutere.* Ludhiana: Lahore Book Shop, 1994.
Kussa Karamjit Singh. *Rat de Rahi.* Delhi: Aarsi Publishers, 1979.
——. *Rohi Beaban.* Ludhiana: Lahore Book Shop, 1983.
——. *Agg da Geet.* Ludhiana: Lahore Book Shop, 1985.
——. *Zakhmi Darya.* Ludhiana: Lahore Book Shop, 1991.
Meet, Mittar Sen. *Tafteesh.* Amritsar: Mukta Sahit Parkashan, 1990.
Meet, Mitter Sen. *Katehra.* Ludhiana: Lahore Book Shop, 1993.
Mehal Singh. *Mudhla Punjabi Novel: Itihasak Adhyan.*Amritsar: Pankaj Parkashan, 1988.
Minhas, Meeran Baksh. *Nawab Khan.* Lahore: Attar Chand Kapur and Sons, 1930.
Nanak Singh. *Chitta Lahu.* Amritsar: Punjab Khalsa Book Depot, 1932.
Narula, Surinder Singh. *Peo Puttar.* Lahore: Sikh Publishers, 1946.
Nehru, Joginder Singh. *Pragtivad Ate Punjabi Novel.* Chandigarh: Punjab Parkshan, 1986.
Raghbir Singh. *Yatharthi.* Amritsar: Ravi Sahit Parkashan, 1986.
Rahi, Joginder Singh. *Punjabi Novel.* Amritsar: Nanak Singh Pustakmala, 1978.
——. *Masle Galap De.* Amritsar: Nanak Singh Pustakmala, 1992.
Seetal, Sohan Singh. *Tootan Wala Khooh.* Ludhiana: Seetal Pustak Bhandar, 1963.
——. *Jug Badal Gaya.* Ludhiana: Seetal Pustak Bhandar, 1972.
Sekhon, Sant Singh. *Lahu Mitti.* Ludhiana: Lahore Book Shop, 1950.
——. *Bhai Vir Singh ate Ohnan da Yug.* Ludhiana: Lahore Book Shop, 1962.
Sukhbir Kaur. *Gurdial Singh de Navelan Vich Anchlikta.* Amritsar: Nanak Singh Pustakmala, 1985.
Vinod, T.R. '*Parsa*'. *Khoj Patrika.* no. 35, 1992.
——. *Punjabi Novel Da Sanskritik Adhyan.* Sarhind: Lokgeet Parkashan, 1989.
Vir Singh, Bhai. *Baba Naudh Singh.* Amritsar: Khalsa Samachar, 1917-21.

Contributors

GOPAL KRISHAN, Formerly Professor Emeritus in Geography, Panjab University, Chandigarh.

SURYA KANT, Formerly Professor of Geography, Panjab University, Chandigarh.

P.H. VAISHNAVA, Former Chief Secretary, Punjab.

TEJWANT S. GILL, Formerly Professor of English, Guru Nanak Dev University, Amritsar.

P.S. VERMA, Formerly Professor of Political Science, Panjab University, Chandigarh.

J.S. GREWAL, Formerly Professor of History and Vice-Chancellor, Guru Nanak Dev University, Amritsar.

K.S. DHILLON, Former Director General Police, Punjab.

PRAMOD KUMAR, Chairman, Institute of Development and Communication, Chandigarh.

BIRINDERPAL SINGH, Formerly Professor of Sociology, Punjabi University, Patiala.

RAINUKA DAGAR, Former Director, Institute of Development and Communication, Chandigarh.

S.K. GUPTA, Formerly Professor of History and Vice-Chancellor, Himachal Pradesh University, Shimla.

SURINDER S. JODHKA, Professor of Sociology, Centre for the Study of Social Systems, Jawaharlal Nehru University, New Delhi.

J.S. RAHI, Formerly Professor of Punjabi Literature, Guru Nanak Dev University, Amritsar.

S.S. KHAHRA, Formerly Professor of Punjabi Literature, Guru Nanak Dev University, Amritsar.